Chaucer Studies I

MUSIC IN THE AGE OF CHAUCER

CHAUCER STUDIES
ISSN 0261–9822

Music in the Age of Chaucer

SECOND EDITION, WITH *CHAUCER SONGS*

Nigel Wilkins

D. S. BREWER

First published 1979
D. S. Brewer, Cambridge

Second edition, with *Chaucer Songs*, 1995
Reprinted in paperback 1999

ISBN 0 85991 461 5 hardback
ISBN 0 85991 565 4 paperback

D. S. Brewer is an imprint of Boydell & Brewer Ltd
PO Box 9, Woodbridge, Suffolk IP12 3DF, UK
and of Boydell & Brewer Inc.
PO Box 41026, Rochester, NY 14604–4126, USA
web site: http://www.boydell.co.uk

A catalogue record for this book is available
from the British Library

Library of Congress Catalog Card Number: 95–2220

This publication is printed on acid-free paper

Printed in Great Britain by
St Edmundsbury Press Ltd, Bury St Edmunds, Suffolk

To my Mother

Contents

Acknowledgements

Permission to reproduce illustrations has kindly been granted by the following bodies:
The Dean and Chapter of Beverley Minster (48, 52, 53)
Cambridge, University Library (25, 29, 30, 31)
Cambridge, The Master & Fellows of Corpus Christi College (27)
Cambridge, The Master & Fellows of King's College (26)
Cambridge, The Master & Fellows of Magdalene College (7)
London, British Library (1, 10, 20, 22, 23, 24, 32, 33, 39, 41, 42, 46, 49, 51, 54)
London, National Gallery (14, 43)
Oxford, Bodleian Library (21, 34, 36, 37, 44, 45, 50)
Paris, Bibliothèque nationale (2, 3, 4, 5, 6, 12, 16, 19, 30, 35)
Chantilly, Musée Condeé (8)
Paris, Musée des arts décoratifs (11)
Florence, Biblioteca Laurentiana (15, 18)
Naples, Biblioteca Nazionale (13)
Padova, Biblioteca Universitaria (17)
Brussels, Bibliothèque royale (28)
Vienna, Austrian National Library (47)
Valencia, National Library (40)
New York, Metropolitan Museum (9)

Illustrations

1. *Round Dance.* London, British Library, Royal 20.A. d. XVII, f.9r.
2. *L'Histoire de Fauvain* by Raoul le Petit – *The Author; Fauvel crowned by the Pope; Fauvel Hypocrite; Fauvel drinks from the same cup as Guile and Deceit.* Paris, Bibliothèque Nationale, f.fr.571, f.146r.
3. *A Motet brought up to date to celebrate the coronation of Louis X (1314): 'Ludowice prelustris Francorum/ Servant regem misericordia/ REX REGUM'. In Fauvel the Motet commences 'O Philippe', that is Philippe IV (1285–1314).* Paris, Bibliothèque Nationale, f.fr. 571, f.144r.
4. *Guillaume de Machaut at Work.* Paris, Bibliothèque Nationale, f.fr.1587, f.lr.
5. *Machaut: Kyrie from the Messe de Nostre Dame.* Paris, Bibliothèque Nationale, f.fr.9221, f.164v.
6. *Machaut: Gais et jolis.* Paris, Bibliothèque Nationale, f.fr.1584, f.472v.
7. *Machaut: En amer a douce vie, from Le Remède de Fortune.* Cambridge, Magdalene College, Pepysian Library, MS 1594, f.23v/24r.
8. *J. Galiot: Le sault perilieux, with drawing of 'La doulce compaygnie'.* Chantilly, Musée Condé, MS 564 (*olim* 1047), f.37r.
9. *Julius Caesar with Courtiers, from 'The Nine Heroes Tapestries'*, c.1385. New York, Metropolitan Museum of Art, Cloisters Collection, Gift of John D. Rockefeller, Jr., 1947.
10. *P. de Molins: De ce que fol pensé.* British Library, Add. 41667 I.
11. *Le Concert (P. de Molins: De ce que fol pensé),* Arras c.1420. Paris, Musée des Arts décoratifs, Tapestry No.Pe 602.
12. *Anon.:Or sus, vous dormés trop.* Paris, Bibliothèque Nationale, f.fr., n.a. 6771, f.78v/ 79r.
13. *Music and her Attendants (from Boethius; De arithmetica).* Naples, Biblioteca Nazionale, MS V A 14.
14. *Fra Angelico: Christ glorified in the Court of Heaven (centre of three panels).* London, National Gallery.
15. *Francesco Landini.* Florence, Bibl. Laurentiana, Palat. 87 (Codex Squarcialupi).
16. *Jacopo da Bologna: Di novo è giunt'.* Paris, Bibliothèque Nationale, ital. 568, f.10v.
17. *Francesco Landini: Gram' piant' agli ochi,* and *S'i' te so stato.* Padova, Biblioteca Universitaria, MS 684, f.51v.
18. *Francesco Landini: Questa fanciulla.* Florence, Bibl. Laurentiana, Palat, 87 (Codex Squarcialupi), f.138r.
19. *Francesco Landini: Questa fanciulla (Keyboard version).* Paris, Bibliothèque Nationale, f.fr., n.a. 6771, f.85r.
20. *Lamento di Tristano.* London, British Library, Add. 29987, f.64r.

Preface

This book is intended as a general guide and introduction for those who wish to be better acquainted with fourteenth-century music, an essentially colourful ingredient in a flamboyant and colourful age.

Chaucer, though no musician, wrote lyric texts, some of which were certainly intended to be sung; a reconstruction of certain of these songs with music borrowed from his great French contemporary Guillaume de Machaut, to whom Chaucer owed so much, and from other French sources, appears at the end of this volume. The influence of French lyric forms and constant cross-channel exchange is a vital feature of the period. The French language was still used by many at court: Henry of Lancaster, the Black Prince, the Chandos Herald, Froissart, for instance. Although Chaucer was the prime mover in the renewed use of the English language, he was heavily indebted to France both linguistically and literarily. French music dominated Europe up to and including most of the fourteenth century. Trecento Italy produced its own styles but enjoyed the French repertory at the same time. Cyprus and Spain were French dominated. England owed very much to French *Ars Nova* style, as is witnessed above all by the Old Hall manuscript, despite the presence of some native styles which were to lead to the fifteenth-century 'contenance angloise' and the positive contribution of the Englishman Dunstable to early Renaissance song types on the Continent. Chaucer constantly rubbed shoulders with France and the French and this cultural influence was strong throughout the period despite the terrible struggles of the Hundred Years War which underlie it all. Thus French music naturally looms large and takes pride of place.

Chaucer also owed much to Italy, especially to Boccaccio, and travelled there. Although he shows no influence of Italian forms on his own lyrics, he must have been well acquainted with Trecento styles, which form a rich repertory in their own right.

Music in Britain in the fourteenth century was doubtless as thriving as it was on the Continent. Different patterns of manuscript transmission seem to have resulted in much being lost, though, and the picture appears sadly fragmentary. The surviving repertory shows the scope and high standard of British ecclesiastical music. The English lyric has to be recognized more from texts than from complete songs, since in most cases words were recopied when music was not. Copious records of minstrel activity show how very busy humble performers were, especially on festive and State occasions, whether in Britain or on the Continent.

The fourteenth century was a very exciting age marked above all by the introduction of polyphony into secular music and the more subtle exploitation of polyphonic writing due to improved notation systems codified by numerous theorists.

Nowhere is the musical spirit of the age and the rôle of music at that time better conveyed than in the passages devoted to music in the anonymous allegory of the *Echecs amoureux*, c.1370–80. Music, through the sweetness of its melody, brings pleasure and comfort to the soul; even the beasts and birds are sensible to its powers. The function of music is threefold: to bring peace and recreation to the hearer and sooth the savage breast; to provide intellectual food for thought, with a demonstration of perfection in numerical proportion; to inspire virtue and good deeds, and uplift the spirit.

As Guillaume de Machaut, undoubtedly the greatest musician of the age, expressed it in the *Prologue* to his collected works, music is the supreme way in which to worship God, but perhaps above all is the means to achieving earthly happiness and the banishment of distress:

> *Et Musique est une science*
> *Qui vuet qu'on rie et chante et dance.*
> *Cure n'a de melencolie.*

1.   France

Plus ne put Musique son secret taire,
Car tant a fait tris plours, suspirs et plains
Que d'Orpheüs a fait son secretaire,
Qui de sciencie est gomier plains.

(Anon.)

Or sont vivant biaus dis faisant,
Qui ne s'en vont mie taisant,
C'est de Machau le boin Willame,
Si fait redolent, si que bausme.
Philippes de Vitri et ses freres
Font choses bielles et moult cleres
Et là mettent leur estudie.
Or y rest Jehans de le Mote
Qui bien le lettre et le notte
Troeve, et fait de moult biaus dis,
Dont maint seigneur a resbaudis,
Si k'a honneur en est venus
Et des milleurs faiseurs tenus . . .

[Among the fine and prolific writers alive today are the good Guillaume de Machaut, whose works are full of balmy fragrance; Philippe de Vitry and his colleagues, who write excellent works full of clarity and put all their efforts into studying the art; and also Jehan de la Mote who cleverly devises both words and music and writes much of excellence, thereby delighting many a lord, so that much honour is bestowed on him and he is considered to be among the best authors . . .]

When Abbot Gilles li Muisis wrote these lines of his *Meditations*[1] in 1350, probably in Tournai, there was no doubt in his mind as to who were the most important musicians of the day. Philippe de Vitry and Guillaume de Machaut are still acknowledged as the dominant musical forces of the French *Ars Nova*; Jehan de la Mote, on the other hand, is known today only as a poet, though every bit as skillful as Machaut in both lyric and narrative forms. Other attestations of Jehan de la Mote's musicianship exist, but his music is lost to us. This is a common situation in medieval times applicable to all countries, and it is worth remembering that those works which have survived the ravages of time, on manuscript pages often of great frailty, represent only part of the originally rich and prolific artistic creativity of the age. Two famous 'Musician Motets' written in the North of France in the earlier part of the fourteenth century list altogether over twenty names of chapel singers and composers including again Vitry and Machaut.[2] In *Musicalis sciencia/ Sciencie laudabili*[3] Music addresses her subjects and begs them to respect the laws of Rhetoric and of Grammar. *Appollonis eclipsatur/Zodiacum signis lustrantibus*[4] names twelve members of a *musicorum collegio*. Identifications have been made for many of these shadowy figures who may be traced through archives as they receive payments or benefices. In the main, however, very few of them can be linked with any music now remaining. The same is true for most of the twenty members of an Avignon choir under the papacy of Clement VII (1378–94) listed in *Alma polis religio/Axe poli cum arctica*[5] and the English Chapel Royal contemporaries of John Aleyn given in *Sub Arturo/Fons citharizantium*.[6]

It is clear that, despite all that has been lost, there was great musical industry in France even in the early part of the fourteenth century where sources are less numerous, though both France and Italy are richly provided in comparison with the few remaining British fragments. Music of many different kinds pervaded all walks of life for every man from youth to old age. Gilles li Muisis tells us, in his *Lamentations*,[7] that he was at school for ten years and learned to read and sing:

> *Or fui a l'escole dix ans*
> *Aprendans, cantans et lisans.*

The ever-chivalrous Froissart echoes this with his childhood recollections in *L'Espinette amoureuse*:

> *Tres que n'avoie que .xii. ans,*
> *Estoie forment goulousans*
> *De veoir danses et caroles,*
> *D'oïr menestrels et paroles.*[8]

[Even before I was twelve, I was greedy to see dances and carols, to hear minstrels and stories.]

Students, as always, made music. Gilles li Muisis describes them dancing and playing citoles in the streets of Paris, all innocent amusement:

> *Je vic en men enfanche festyer de chistolles*
> *Les clers parisiens revenant des escolles.*
> *Et que privéement on faisoit des karolles.*
> *C'est trestout reviaus, en riens n'estoient folles.*[9]

A 'bon compagnon' of his acquaintance readily abandoned care when instruments or songs were to be heard:

> *Mais il a courtois coer, tout set abandonner*
> *Instruments et canchons ot volentiers sonner.*[10]

Jehan de la Mote, even though he seems to have left us no music, almost makes up for this by his description, in his Alexander romance *Le Parfait du Paon*[11] (c.1340), of a sophisticated song contest in a royal *Puy* utterly in the tradition of the twelfth and thirteenth-century Troubadours and Trouvères and of the German Meistersinger. For the prize of a ruby and emerald-studded crown, Alexander and courtiers devise and sing eight Ballades 'de desir et d'Espoir', each fashioned differently and with great skill. A Ballade with no music is seen as inferior, and must be completed:

. . . N'est pas ordenée,
Balade vault trop peu quant elle n'est chantée.
(11. 1210–11)

Later, when the contest is over, the newly composed songs are sung again, their notes are named (*solefient*) and Alexander the King has them written down because they are worthy of being preserved. Wine and spices are brought; many instruments play; some sit and some dance:

En la chambre amoureuse s'en voisent les pucellez.
Li roys et si Grigois, Yndois et demoysellez
Chantent et solefient leur balades nouvelles.
Li rois em prist copie car bonnez sont et bellez.
Puis demandent le vin et espices isnellez;
Le vin leur apportent escuier en cotellez.
Après boire, oïssiez pipes et chalemelz,
Orgues, harpes, guiternez, douchainnez, et fretellez,
Estivez, cor a dois, trompez, tabours, viellez;
Ainssi que li un danssent, li autre sont sur sellez.
(11. 1515–24)

In this colourful century poetic and musical achievement came to rival chivalric prowess at the joust or in battle. The two co-exist: *Armes, Amours, Dames, Chevalerie*. Nearly the entire period is overshadowed by the Anglo-French struggles of the Hundred Years War and it almost seems as if it was through the very need to shut out grim realities that the French nobility in particular came eventually to indulge in excessive luxury of banquets, clothes and furnishings and to foster and encourage ever more intricate and exclusive music in their halls and chapels.

Of course, there were technical reasons also for the increasing complexity of fourteenth-century music, a complexity which forced a division between the traditionally allied poetic and musical arts, so that after Machaut no major poet was able to set his or her lyrics to music: Deschamps, Froissart, Christine de Pisan, Alain Chartier, Charles d'Orléans, François Villon. The determining factor was above all an improvement in the system of musical notation, allowing escape from the limiting modal rhythms of *ars antiqua*. As early as 1324 a Bull of the Avignon Pope John XXII criticizes excesses in a style of church music created by a *novella schola discipuli* with particular disapproval of the broken effect caused by hocketing technique. By c.1330 Jacobus of Liège, a man of the old school and still disapproving, had nevertheless to recognize that a younger generation with novel ideas had won the day. Motet writing, the sole form of secular polyphonic writing in the thirteenth century, now had to share its honours with the shorter lyric forms: *moderni quasi solis utuntur motetis et cantilenis*. It was these forms, the Ballade, Rondeau and Virelai in particular, which were so to dominate French music in the fourteenth century and poetry in both France and England long thereafter.

Adam de la Hale and Jehan de Lescurel

Two figures in particular play an important transitional rôle at the turn of the thirteenth and fourteenth centuries.

Adam de la Hale,[12] well-known for his plays, especially the dramatized pastourelle with music *Le Jeu de Robin et de Marion*, was born in Arras in mid thirteenth century, studied in Paris and worked in the French Court in Naples. His nickname *Adam le Bossu*, probably given him on account of his twisted wit rather than any physical deformity, occurs unexpectedly in the list of minstrels performing at a Feast in 1306 in Westminster.[13]

Round Dance

This is a surprise, it is true, but the conventionally accepted account of his death in Naples in 1288 and burial there within a splendid tomb derives from taking seriously his facetious joke in the short *Jeu du Pelerin*. It is just possible that he did live to see the dawn of the fourteenth century.[14] He wrote monodic *Chansons* and *Jeux-Partis* in the trouvère tradition and a few Motets according to standard thirteenth-century practice. His great importance in the present context lies in his adaptation of simple three-voice polyphonic technique for the first time to the popular dance-song form of the Rondeau; of these he left fourteen examples. Typical is *A jointes mains*,[15] no advance at all on the past in rhythm, which is firmly in the traditional 'first mode' (long-short), nor in the setting of syllables to notes, but a very significant advance in that the melody itself (the centre voice) is harmonized:

(Adam de la Hale: A jointes mains — refrain)

Two further examples, *Dieus soit en cheste maison* and *Fines amourettes,* although included with Rondeaux in the manuscript, relate formally more to the *Ballette,* an intermediary stage between the emerging Ballade and Virelai which is particularly well represented in a late thirteenth-century collection of verse sadly divorced from its music in Oxford, Bodleian Library, Douce 308.[16]

Jehan de Lescurel[17] was a student cleric at Notre Dame in Paris, but was hung for 'rape and other misdemeanours' in 1304. He left over thirty song settings, important in the first place because at this early date they provide perfect examples of the favourite forms to be: Ballade, Rondeau, Virelai.[18] With one exception they are all monodic, conforming in this with earlier tradition, but by using new possibilities offered by improved, less ambiguous notation, Lescurel begins to escape from strict modal patterns and note-against-note writing. He may set longish runs of notes to a single syllable:

(Jehan de Lescurel: Bietris est mes delis — refrain)

Elsewhere he may play with new types of rhythmic figuration, some in duple time:

(Jehan de Lescurel: Amour, trop vous doi cherir — bars 1 - 7)

Small beginnings, perhaps, but symptomatic of features which were to undergo very considerable development from Machaut onwards.

Le Roman de Fauvel and Philippe de Vitry

The *Roman de Fauvel*[19] contains a number of further songs very similar to those of Lescurel, whose works are indeed contained within the same manuscript, B.N. f.fr.146. The text of this satirical anti-Establishment romance, the central character of which is the wicked donkey-like creature Fauvel, was originally written in two parts in 1310 and 1314 by Gervais de Bus, one of a circle of notaries in Paris. In 1316 Chaillou de Pesstain extended the work and also interpolated into it about one hundred and sixty pieces of music composed between about 1189 and his own day. There are many new Motets, but also many *Conducti* from the Notre Dame School; there is a fair selection of secular songs, *lais* and Gregorian Chant. There could be no better work for observing the transition from *ars antiqua* to *ars nova* and the multi-layered nature of early fourteenth-century taste.

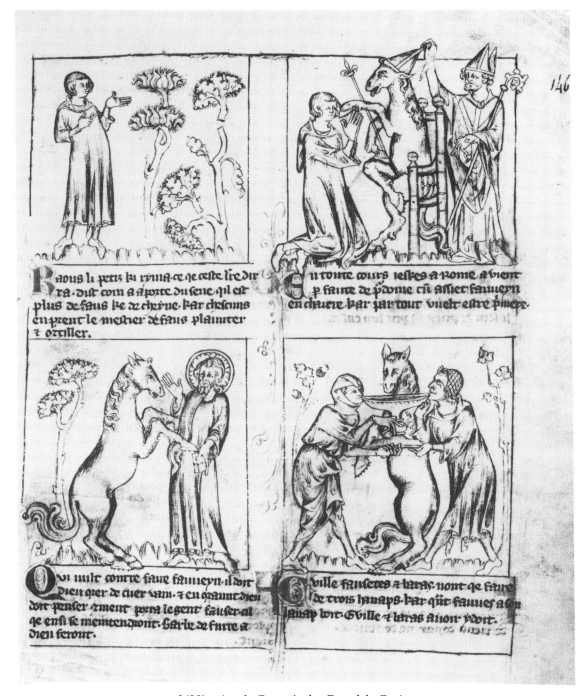

L'Histoire de Fauvain by Raoul le Petit.

The composers of the newer pieces are not named, but among the Motets are possibly five by Philippe de Vitry,[20] who became renowned as a statesman and churchman, was a friend of Petrarch, and Bishop of Meaux from 1351 until his death in 1361. Typical of the biting tone of *Fauvel* and of several of Vitry's politically-motivated Motet texts is No 129 *In nova fert/ Garrit Gallus*. This is one of a group of three Vitry pieces on the corruption of government and weakness of the King; characteristically, no-one is named and a deal of symbolic interpretation is required:

Motetus: The evil dragon that glorious Michael in days to come will completely defeat by the power of the cross, lives on by every device of intrigue: now endowed with the grace of Absalom, now with the eloquence of Ulysses, now armed with wolfish teeth like a soldier of

A Motet brought up to date to celebrate the coronation of Louis X (1314): 'Ludowice prelustris Francorum/ Servant regem misericordia/ REX REGUM'. In Fauvel the Motet commences 'O Philippe', that is Philippe IV (1285–1314).

Tersites' clan, now disguised as a fox whose cunning gains the blind King's obedience whilst in effect the fox reigns. He has filled himself with the chickens and sucks the blood of the sheep. Alas, he does not cease sucking; he still is thirsty and ravenous for prey. Now woe to the chickens, woe to the blind lion; but in the end woe to the dragon when he faces Christ!

Triplum: The cockerel sobs, crying in pain: for all the assembly of cockerels is in mourning because, while in the service of vigilance, it is treacherously betrayed to the Satrap. And the fox, like a violator of sepulchres, vigorous with the astuteness of Belial, reigns as the King, with the very consent of the lion – alas, what a slavery. Once again Jacob's people have been put to flight under another Pharaoh; they weep, for they cannot, as once before, enter the promised land. In the desert they are stricken by hunger; they have no armed help; though they cry aloud they are still robbed; perhaps they will soon die. Woeful voice of the wretched exiles, pitiful lament of the cockerels since the lion, totally blind, submits to the fraud of the fox, the traitor. You who suffer the brazenness of the fox's misdeed, arise, or what is still left of your honour perishes and will continue to perish. The avenger is slow and guilt quickly accrues.[21]

It is thought that the blind lion represents Louis X, who succeeded Philippe le Bel in November 1314; the fox would be Enguerran de Marigni, the King's chief counsellor.

Musically, Vitry's Motet is notable for its use of isorhythm in the Tenor part; indeed, Vitry seems to have been responsible for the introduction of this idea, of using repetitions of a set rhythmic pattern, and which was to become so important after him. None of his works is completely isorhythmic in all voices, though, for this was a later development. The Tenor chant *NEUMA* is divided across three repetitions of the ten-bar pattern (*talea*); the whole of this is then repeated with no change of speed but quite different writing in the Motetus and Triplum above.

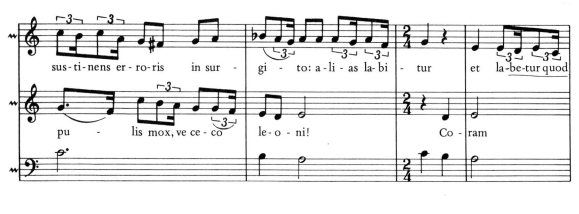

(Philippe de Vitry/*Fauvel*: In nova fert/Garrit Gallus/NEUMA — bars 51 - 59)

It is clear from the preceding examples that, although there were no abrupt changes, by the early years of the fourteenth century improved notations were being evolved, which then made possible far greater fluidity and independence of part-writing in polyphony than had been known before. The invention of more time values, smaller notes, more logical groupings and divisions led to an escape from the dullness and limitation of the traditional rhythmic modes. As the conservative Jacobus of Liège put it c.1330: 'The new art . . . uses all sorts of imperfections (i.e. duple instead of triple durations) in notes, modes, measures, indeed nearly everywhere.' A new approach to harmony developed and the compositional method of composing upper parts separately to fit the Tenor sometimes caused remarkable clashes when all the parts were played or sung together. Freedom from the shackles of modal rhythm gave greater scope for individuality between the voices and melodic style became more flowing.

Several theorists codified these events in the early years of the fourteenth century: Johannes de Muris, for instance, in his *Ars novae musicae* of 1319, or the Italian Marchettus da Padua, who formulated a separate Italian system while showing awareness of the French, in his *Pomerium* of 1318. Most famous of all, now at least, is Philippe de Vitry, who in 1320 wrote his treatise entitled *Ars Nova*, from which the period in modern scholarship takes its name. The essential feature of this otherwise not terribly exciting notation manual is the introduction of imperfect (binary) divisions in time, thus overthrowing the earlier dominance of the perfect number 3 (the Trinity and magic numbers enter much into medieval thought). Combinations of perfect or imperfect *tempus* (breve measure) with perfect or imperfect *prolation* (semibreve measure) gave the equivalent to modern $\frac{9}{8}\frac{3}{4}\frac{6}{8}\frac{2}{4}$; very important was the introduction of a new smaller note value, the minim. The minim is also said, by Simon Tunstede, a Franciscan from Oxford, in his *Quatuor principalia musicae* (1351), and by the writer known as Anonymous I (c.1350)[22] to have been invented in Navarra. The dot had a number of uses including addition (like the modern dot), division of one perfection of notes from another and marking passages of syncopation – a new device much to be exploited. A further innovation was the use of coloured notes, either red or left hollow, to show a shift in prolation.[23]

Guillaume de Machaut

Of all the poets and musicians of fourteenth-century France, Guillaume de Machaut is certainly the most important. He was the outstanding genius both in music and in poetry, and the main determining influence on the development of lyric poetry for more than a century after him.

Machaut was born in 1300 in or near Reims, in Champagne, and was probably cathedral educated. His first appointment as a young man from c.1323 into the 1330s was as 'secretary' to Jean de Luxembourg, King of Bohemia, which involved frequent travelling across Europe, especially between France, Luxembourg and Prague, and much experience of brilliant Court life. By the 1340s Machaut found a calmer existence as a Canon in the cathedral at Reims, where he sang and composed, though did not abandon his contacts with many distinguished patrons, in particular members of the royal House of France. He died, much lamented by his contemporaries, in 1377.[24]

It is important to realise that Machaut's output falls into two halves, one of which is purely literary.[25] He composed nine long narrative *Dits* and four shorter ones, in a tradition emerging from the thirteenth-century *Roman de la Rose*, together with *La Prise d'Alexandrie*, a verse chronicle of the crusading exploits of the King of Cyprus, Pierre de Lusignan, whom Machaut much admired. Altogether, his narrative verse comes to nearly 45,000 lines, and his influence on his contemporaries and successors, especially Froissart and Chaucer, was enormous.[26] Even before the musical side of his craft is taken into

Guillaume de Machaut at Work

consideration, Machaut may seriously be compared with Chaucer, Petrarch, Boccaccio or Dante.

Machaut's musical compositions fall into various categories: Motets, the *Messe de Nostre Dame,* Lais, and shorter lyrics, above all Ballades, Rondeaux and Virelais.[27] In addition, there are lyric interpolations in two of his narrative works.[28]

Twenty-four Motets are left to us. Their main characteristics are much as they were in the thirteenth century: a rigid structural scheme based on some reiterated rhythm using a melody derived from a pre-existent source, usually the liturgy but sometimes popular song; the simultaneous presentation over this instrumental foundation of two or more vocal lines using *different* texts related in theme but usually quite different in metrical structure.

Of Machaut's twenty-four Motets, eighteen are for two voices and one instrument, four are more long and complex pieces for two voices over two instrumental lines, while two may be sung by three voices. Significantly, these latter two examples are based on popular ditties, with three simultaneous French texts. Apart from these, of the remaining twenty-two examples with two simultaneous texts, sung by voices labelled *Motetus* and *Triplum* respectively, fourteen have two French texts, two have one French and one Latin text, six have two Latin texts. The fundamental instrumental line is called *Tenor;* when a further instrumental line is added, it is called *Contratenor.* Apart from the two three-voice French examples and one other based on secular material, all twenty-one remaining Tenors are liturgy-derived,[29] each bearing a cryptic identifying *incipit* under its first notes: AMARA VALDE; SUSPIRO; QUARE NON SUM MORTUUS.

'Helas! ou sera pris confors/Hareu! le feu/OBEDIENS' is an example of the type for two voices singing French texts over a liturgy-derived instrumental Tenor.[30] The Tenor here, OBEDIENS USQUE AD MORTEM, from the Gradual 'Christus factus est pro nobis', is divided isorhythmically first into three rhythmic repetitions using long notes, and then into three repetitions using notes exactly one half the value, that is double the speed. Above this the *Motetus* and *Triplum* run independently, each with its own separate French texts, though both, appropriately, give the unrequited lover's lament. The *Triplum* text contains twenty-four decasyllabic lines neatly structured into a rhyming pattern: a a a a bb c c c c bb d d d d bb etc. This amounts to a large number of words and the consequent setting as a fast-moving part treated mostly one note to one syllable. The *Motetus* text is shorter, fourteen lines in octosyllabic rhyming couplets, and has as a consequence relatively more sustained notes, rests and melismas. The doubling in tempo of the *Tenor* after its three slow appearances finds an echo in the characteristic hocketing figure which first appears in the *Triplum* and thereafter occurs several times in both voices, adding to a sense of rising excitement:

(Guillaume de Machaut: Hareu! hareu!/Helas, ou sera pris confors/OBEDIENS — bars 73 - 84)

The *Messe de Nostre Dame* is important both because it is a very great work of art and also because of its historical position as the first complete preserved polyphonic Mass known to be the work of a single author. Given a musician of Machaut's talent in cathedral choir surroundings, it is a little surprising that ecclesiastical music is much the smaller part of

Machaut: Kyrie from the Messe de Nostre Dame

his output: the Mass, a textless and possibly instrumental piece entitled *Hoquetus David*, and a few Latin Motets. The Mass is thought by some to have been composed for and performed in the brilliant coronation ceremony in Reims cathedral of the French King Charles V, in 1364. Machaut was almost certainly present; he describes the ceremony very briefly in the *Prise d'Alexandrie* (lines 799–820), but says not a word about his Mass being performed there. Even if the coronation idea has to be discarded, nevertheless, Machaut's Mass is of a stature and brilliance when properly performed that would admirably have graced such an occasion and 1364 is stylistically about right for its composition. One might draw parallels between the structure of the Mass and the Gothic architecture of the cathedral in which it was probably sung. The forces required are a small four-part choir, preferably containing some brilliant soloists, and, almost certainly, a group of instrumentalists. The manuscript sources, however, as is typical of early music, say nothing of these dispositions.

The use of soloists and of instruments is a matter of controversy, which explains why no two performances are alike.[31] The high tessituras of the voices suggest the use of boys and counter-tenors, and also reveal the shift of pitch at least one tone upwards which has occurred since Machaut's day.

There are six movements, the usual five of the Ordinary of the Mass (*Kyrie, Gloria, Credo, Sanctus, Agnus Dei*), plus a closing *Ite, Missa est*. The *Gloria* and the *Credo* are written in a homophonic '*conductus*' style for the most part, all four voices moving in block harmony to make the long texts comprehensible, though both end in a freer, contrapuntal *Amen*:

(Guillaume de Machaut: Gloria — bars 14 - 17)

The other movements are composed in contrapuntal 'Motet' style throughout and each is highly organized, especially in the rhythmic sense. Understanding of the underlying structure is essential for full appreciation of such a piece. As Safford Cape expressed it: 'Fascinatingly mysterious, glowing with a strange beauty . . ., the *Messe de Nostre Dame* offers a hermetic visage. Its isorhythmic architecture (or symmetrical rhythmic patterning), which must be grasped if the work is to become intelligible, lies hidden.'

Let us examine the *Kyrie* briefly by way of example. For his *cantus fermus* or foundation melody, Machaut took a Gregorian Chant Kyrie *Cunctipotens genitor deus*. In the first *Kyrie* he organizes this into a pattern in modern transcription four bars long. In the *Tenor* this comes seven times in all, making a section twenty-eight bars long, or twenty-seven really, since the final bar is silent. The element used here in the *Tenor* contains four notes, making twenty-eight notes altogether with the seven repetitions. The Gregorian Chant contains twenty-six notes only, so Machaut adapted it slightly, by repeating enough notes in the melody to bring it up to the necessary total, but otherwise chopped it up into the brief, repeated rhythmic units regardless of any original melodic structure inherent in the *Chant*. Its function is simply to form a foundation, a starting point.

The *Contratenor* in the first *Kyrie* section employs a free melody meant to harmonize with the *Tenor* and fill in with moving notes the bars where the *Tenor* is silent. The *Contratenor* is also organized on an isorhythmic basis: this time, however, the units are longer, of twelve bars. The rhythm of bars 1–12 is repeated, with some small alterations, in bars 13–24. This leaves three bars over to complete the twenty-seven bar section, and so a third appearance of the rhythm is begun.

The *Triplum* has an approximate isorhythmic structure and falls into two distinct halves, bars 1–13 and bars 15–26, separated by a silent bar 14. The *Motetus* alone lacks this high degree of rhythmic organization. Its function is to complete what is essentially three-part harmony above all every fourth bar when the *Tenor* has its long rest. The iambic (short-long) pattern of bar 2 in the *Tenor* affects the other parts and is found in all three other voices from time to time, aiding the sense of unity.

Similar procedures, but with different patterns and numbers, are to be found in the following *Christe* and the closing two versions of the *Kyrie*.

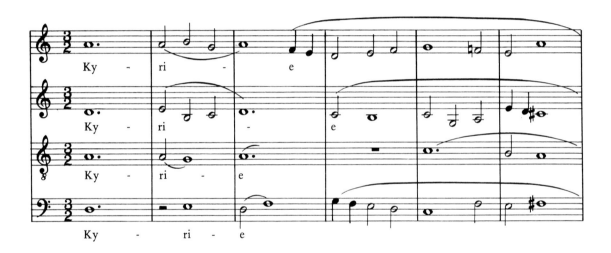

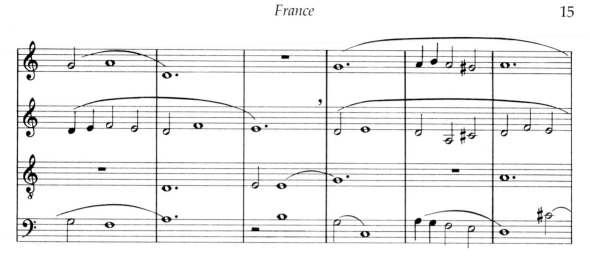

(Guillaume de Machaut: Kyrie — bars 1 - 27)

The polytextual effect characteristic of the Motets was occasionally taken over into the shorter lyric fixed forms. Machaut tried this in his double Ballade 'Quant Theseus/Ne quier veoir' and in a few other pieces including a three-voice canonic Ballade. Landini imitated this idea, as did several of Machaut's followers in the late fourteenth century. Normally, though, the Ballades and Rondeaux in particular were for a solo voice plus a few instruments; which instruments precisely, as always, is a matter for conjecture and practical expedience. We should note that Machaut's largest collection of lyrics in the *formes fixes*, 282 under the title *La Louange des Dames*,[32] contains no music, an indication of the divorce already taking place in the fourteenth century, even within Machaut, the last great exponent of a traditionally double art. Twenty-two of these poems do reappear with settings[33] in the music fascicles of his collected works in the beautiful illuminated manuscript sources, and altogether we have musical settings of 42 Ballades, 22 Rondeaux and 33 Virelais. If we take Machaut's lyrics as a whole, although musicologists discern stages of development and advancement in style,[34] the same cannot really be said for the texts alone. The *Louange des Dames* is a collection which must have been composed over most of Machaut's creative life, from about 1324 into the 1370s. Nevertheless, there is no very noticeable development in thematic material of structural procedure from what seem to be the earlier parts of the collection to the later. In some later poets, Christine de Pisan or Charles d'Orléans, for instance, this is not always the case. But striking originality in theme was not the quality most admired in medieval art. It was the subtle varied treatment of established themes which was especially prized, and here Machaut has much to offer. It is true that Jehan de Lescurel, at the very opening of the fourteenth century, gives polished examples of the Ballade, Rondeau and Virelai forms, but it was certainly Machaut who put them 'on the map' and showed how these forms, though fixed in their musical infra-structure, were capable of all manner of change and embellishment on the surface. Jehan de la Mote made an important contribution too, as we have seen, but in the absence of any surviving music known to be his it is difficult fully to assess his rôle. The same could be said of lesser early fourteenth-century figures such as Jehan Acart de Hesdin.[35]

The **Ballade** has three stanzas. Each of these is built on the musical structure I I II (each Roman figure represents a distinct and self-contained section). Typical of the way in which text fits music is 'Gais et jolis', used for the Chaucer setting No 5 in *Chaucer Songs*:

Music: I   I   II
Text: $a_{10}b_{10}$ $a_{10}b_{10}$ $b_{10}c_{10}C_{10}$

A comparable example is 'De toutes flours':

Music: I   I   II
Text: $a_{10}b_{10}$ $a_{10}b_{10}$ $c_{10}c_{10}d_{10}D_{10}$

The last line in each stanza is the same, being a refrain. Metrical patterns may vary[36] but the fundamental musical design is fixed.[37] In 'De toutes flours' we see the characteristic Machaut mid-fourteenth-century features: a single voice accompanied in this case by three instruments, one above and two below, in complex polyphony; great flexibility in word-setting in the vocal line, which has long melismas or embellishments on single syllables, such as the first syllable and especially penultimate syllables before cadence points.

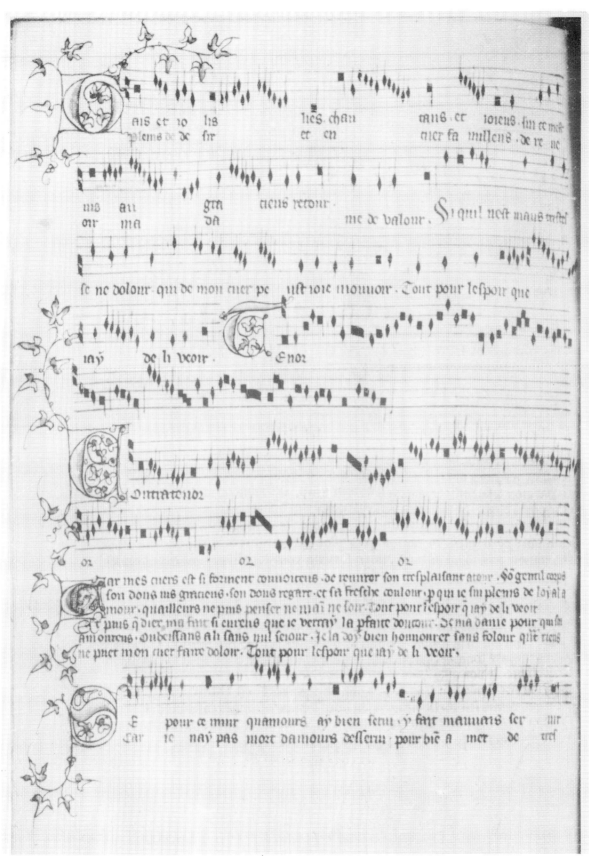

Machaut: Gais et jolis

(Guillaume de Machaut: De toutes flours — bars 22 - 30)

Characteristic also are: the use of alternative first (*ouvert*) and second (*clos*) – time cadences modulating differently at the end of the first, repeated section; the 'musical rhyme' whereby the closing phrase of section I also closes section II; the sharpening of the fifth as well as the leading note in the typical cadence:

All this is a far cry from Adam de la Hale's cautious note-against-note movement for three voices in *conductus* style at the close of the thirteenth century, or from Lescurel's monodies, florid though occasional passages may have been.

In the fourteenth century the Ballade was the dominant of the three main *formes fixes*, the more substantial and serious form, prone to more sophisticated and serious treatment both in its text and in its musical setting. Virelais were always less common, while the

Rondeau emerged to take the ascendancy in the musical context in the fifteenth century, though both Ballades and Rondeaux are numerous in the pure poetry of the time. Chaucer, writing on the French model in mid-fourteenth-century, left four Rondeaux but over a dozen Ballades.

The basic pattern for the music of the **Rondeau** is always: I II I I I II I II. In the fourteenth century the eight-line type is most popular, with one line of text per music section. Eleven and thirteen-line types are found, though, and the sixteen and twenty-one-line types flourished in the fifteenth century. It is simply a matter of how many lines of text are fitted to each music section, e.g.:

Music:	I	II	I	I	I	II	I	II
Text:								
8	A	B	a	A	a	b	A	B
11	A	BB	a	A	a	bb	A	BB
13	AB	B	ab	AB	ab	b	AB	B
16	AB	BA	ab	AB	ab	ba	AB	BA
21	AAB	BA	aab	AAB	aab	ba	AAB	BA

The refrain (indicated by capital letters) always occupies both sections I and II, the first half returning at mid-point as well as the whole to open and to close. An example of the thirteen-line type in Machaut is 'Dame, se vous n'avez aperceü', the music of which is used in the Chaucer setting No 14 in *Chaucer Songs*.

An especially curious example from the musical point of view is Machaut's eight-line Rondeau 'Ma fin est mon commencement'.[38] The text is basically a list of instructions for performance – similar pieces are known from later in the century – and reads in translation: 'My end is my beginning and my beginning is my end and *Tenor* truly; my end is my beginning. My third voice three times only comes retrograde and thus closes. My end is my beginning and my beginning is my end.' Here we see a splendid piece of ingenuity. In a number of works Machaut shows a liking for number puzzles, acrostics, anagrams and the like. The manipulation of isorhythm and overlapping rhythmic and melodic patterns in some Motets and in his Mass called for a mastery of numerical relationships. The text of 'Ma fin est mon commencement' is the explanation in words of the basic musical idea, a 'non-retrogradeable' piece in that it would read in exactly the same way from either end. In the manuscript sources the *Tenor* is laid out only to its midway point; the remaining half is the retrograde of this. The *Cantus* (vocal line) is read backwards, the text being written upside down. The same lines read the normal way round give the *Triplum*. On closer examination this ingenuity is found to go further, for the second half of the *Triplum* is the retrograde of the first half of the *Cantus* and *vice-versa*. This will be made plain by an example showing a few bars on either side of the central point:

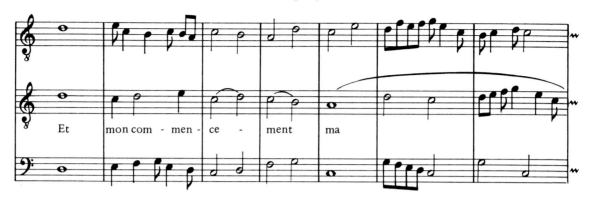

(Guillaume de Machaut: Ma fin est mon commencement — bars 14 - 27)

Again, there are very extended melismas in the vocal line, particularly on the penultimate syllable of the second music section, which covers fifteen bars.

Machaut's **Virelais** are markedly more simple in style than most of his Ballades and Rondeaux. Twenty-five of them are monodic, in the old tradition, mostly in lilting $\frac{6}{8}$ time and folk-like in character. Seven are for voice with an instrumental *Tenor*, while one only is for voice and two low instruments. This simplicity in style is no doubt a reflection of the usual level of the subject matter of Virelai texts, which are normally amorous ditties with no claims to the type of erudition encountered in the Ballade. After Machaut the Virelai was developed polyphonically as a brilliant showpiece, especially in the colourful 'realistic' type.[39] Musical simplicity in Machaut's Virelais is, however, more than compensated by intricacy of metre in the text; the extensive use of varied metres is, indeed, a feature which marks the Virelai off from the Rondeau and most Ballades in the fourteenth century.

The basic musical form here is: I II II I (I). The refrain, several lines long, occupies the whole of the initial section I and must recur to complete the piece. The form may be followed through several times over and Machaut sometimes does this to create a long song with sixty or seventy lines of text. A particularly appealing example is 'Douce dame jolie', a catchy tune with characteristic mixed metres in the verse:

Music: I   II   II   I
Text: $A_6A_6A_6B_7$ $a_6a_2b_6$ $a_6a_2b_6$ $a_6a_6a_6b_7$ etc.

Machaut goes round the form three times:

(Guillaume de Machaut: Douce dame jolie — bars 1 - 16)

Least known of Machaut's musical compositions, though possibly to him his most important pieces, are the **Lais.** The Lai is an extended lyric form with a long history.[40] Distinct from the Celtic form, traditionally sung to an improvised harp accompaniment, by Machaut's day the form had developed into a highly sophisticated test of a poet-musician's skill. To write and compose a Lai was considered to be something of a *tour de force* and Froissart (who wrote no music) reckoned that several months were needed to bring one to perfection. Machaut left twenty-five examples, nineteen of them with musical settings. The essential feature of the fourteenth-century Lai from the structural point of view is that it should normally fall into twelve sections or stanzas (which might each contain internal repetitions), all of which should be different in rhyme and metre except that the twelfth section should recall the first. The musical setting, as was the case with Machaut's Virelais, was normally monodic, probably performed by an unaccompanied soloist. In four cases, however, Machaut made polyphonic or part-polyphonic settings. In two instances (*Lay de Confort* and *Lay de la Fonteinne*) the polyphonic element is clearly indicated in the manuscript sources. In two further instances it has been discovered quite recently that hidden polyphony is present.[41] The *Lay de Consolation* turns out to be in two-voice polyphony since each stanza is divided into two musically and the two halves fit each other vertically in harmony. 'En dementant et en pleurant' is more complex, since it is now known that stanzas 1, 2 and 3 fit together in polyphony for vertical simultaneous performance.[42] These examples thus show an application to the Lai of the polytextual effect characteristic of the Motet, though occasionally also applied to the shorter lyric forms. The implication is also that, in these examples at least, two or three singers must be involved, since each line is equipped with its own full stanza or half-stanza of the Lai text. The *Lay de Confort* has twelve separate three-voice canonic settings to match the twelve divisions of the text. The *Lay de la Fonteinne*, on the other hand, is made out of alternate monodic settings and three-voice canons labelled *Chaces*: six monodies and six *chaces,* the last of which is a canonic version of the opening solo. Canonic writing is an essential feature of the few preserved French *Chaces* from earlier in the fourteenth century and also of the related Italian Trecento *Caccia,* so full of bustle and imitations of hunting calls.[43] Although the subject matter of the Lai was generally amorous and in keeping with the themes of the courtly love lyric, the *Lay de la Fonteinne,* like the monodic *Lay de Nostre Dame,* is religious, in praise of the Virgin Mary. It is natural that Machaut, as a man of the Church, should at times have laid his courtly preoccupations aside to allow his religious convictions to come to the fore. At the opening of the *Lay de la Fonteinne,* however, we find the two important sides of Machaut linked and we seem at first to be in the amorous world of, say, his *Dit de la Fonteinne,* for he speaks of his unrequited love for a heartless lady. But if this earthly lady will give him no comfort, he will seek everlasting joy elsewhere, and the long poem in praise of Our Lady ensues. The scheme is simple but subtle and effective in its contrasts. The *Chaces* in the *Lay de la Fonteinne* make particularly brilliant use of syncopation and hocket:

(Guillaume de Machaut: *Lai de la Fonteinne*, Chace 1, – bars 7 - 15)

Machaut's output of Lais does contain some exceptions to the characteristic twelve-stanza construction: 'J'aim la flour de valour' has only seven stanzas, while 'Loyauté, que point ne delay' has only one set of music to which all twelve stanzas fit, since they are identical in metre though not in rhyme. However, these are special cases.

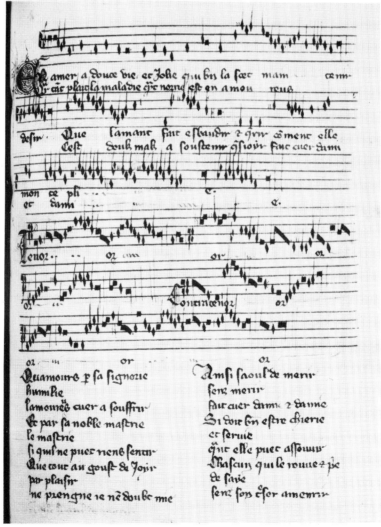

Machaut: En amer a douce vie, from Le Remède de Fortune

A frequent feature is the giving of a title to the Lai, summing up its theme or some principal image. To those already mentioned we may add: *Lay des dames, Lay mortel, Lay de l'Ymage, Lay de bonne Esperance, Lay de la Rose* etc., titles often reminiscent of those Machaut also gave to his narrative verse *Dits amoureus* which so influenced followers such as Froissart and Chaucer.

Two of the **Dits amoureus** have particular interest in that they include musical lyrics within the framework of the narrative and thus bridge the two main halves of Machaut's creativity, offering the possibility of adaptation for concert or dramatized performance. *Le Voir Dit* (c.1365) contains several songs said to be exchanged between the ageing poet and his young admirer Péronne d'Armentières, besides many possibilities for the introduction of extra incidental and background music.

Le Remède de Fortune (c.1340) has woven into it seven songs, each of which is a fine example of a separate formal type important in Machaut's day. The sequence of Lai, Complainte, Chanson roial, Baladelle, Balade, Virelai and Rondeau thus presents a practical 'art poétique' preceding the first formal versification treatise in French, Deschamps' *Art de Dictier* of 1392.

The Post-Machaut Generation

Machaut dominated the mid fourteenth century. No-one before or after him could display such mastery of the double lyric art. The extant secular repertory[44] from the later years of the fourteenth century shows nevertheless that the now ancient tradition of composers providing their own texts and setting them was far from dead. There are examples of composers setting verse known to be by an independent poet, but this practice was still the exception rather than the rule.

The three main manuscript sources of the late fourteenth-century art are: Chantilly, Musée Condé 564 (*olim* 1047 : *Ch*); Paris, B.N., n.a.fr. 6771 (*PR* : 'Codex Reina'); Modena, Bibl. Estense, ∝ .M.5.24 (*olim* 568 : *Mod*).[45] In each case it is demonstrable that the manuscript was copied in S. France or N. Italy and that the works contained largely relate to southern milieux. Machaut's music was still revered and performed, but from the 1370s, and even perhaps a little earlier, all the French musician-poets of note, as distinct from minstrels and mere performers, seem to have emigrated southwards. Many of them hailed originally from the North, as their names alone can show: *Pykini, J. de Senleches*; P. de *Molins, J. de Noyon*.[46] For many of them the move to the South was in itself a way of identifying with new developments, an 'avant-garde' spirit which, if not in conscious reaction against Machaut, at least took many of his compositional ideas to extremes in an 'Ars subtilior' devoted to complexity. Their spirit is reflected very well in a satirical Ballade by the composer Guido, who probably worked in Aragon:

> *Or voit tout en aventure*
> *Puis qu'ainsi me convient fayre*
> *A la novelle figue*
> *Qui doyt a chascun desplayre;*
> *Que c'est trestout en contraire*
> *De bon art qui est parfayt:*
> Certes, ce n'est pas bien fayt!

Nos faysoms contre Nature
De ce qu'est bien fayt deffayre;
Que Philipe qui mais ne dure
Nos dona boin exemplaire.
Nos laisons tous ses afayres
Por Marquet le contrefayt:
Certes, ce n'est pas bien fayt!

L'art de Marquet n'a mesure
N'onques riens ne sait parfayre;
C'est trop grant outrecuidure
D'ansuïr et de portrayre
Ces figures, et tout traire
Ou il n'a riens de bon trayt:
Certes, ce n'est pas bien fayt!

[Now everything is uncontrolled since I have thus to follow the new fashion which is bound to displease everyone; for it is quite the contrary of good art which is perfect: indeed, this is not well done! / We are acting against Nature, undoing what was well done; Philippe (de Vitry), who is no more, gave us a good example. We are abandoning all his ideas for Marchettus (da Padua) the counterfeiter: indeed, this is not well done! / The art of Marchettus has no measure and does not know how to perfect anything; it is too self-opiniated for one to follow and portray these figurations, and derive everything where nothing is of good design: indeed, this is not well done!][47]

This text could almost be taken as a 'manifesto' for the new School, employed in the courts of the South and absorbed by the possibilities above all for rhythmic subtlety offered by new refinements in notational techniques.

One of the principal attractions in the South was the splendour of the Papal Court, established in **Avignon** during the Exile (1305–78) and seat of the anti-Popes during the Schism (1378–1417). The frescoes of the 'Tour de la Garderobe' in the Papal Palace are purely secular in nature, mostly hunting scenes, symbolic of the worldly and luxurious preoccupations of the Pontiff and his Court, especially in the time of Clement VII, who is celebrated in Mayhuet de Joan's Ballade with Latin text 'Inclite flos Gebenensis', as well as in Egidius' Ballade 'Cortois et sages', probably written when Robert de Genève was elected as Avignon Pope in 1378. It was a general feature of both noble and ecclesiastical households to employ musicians in a double function, as Chapel singers for religious occasions and as secular performers for entertainment at banquets and on state occasions; if these versatile artists showed ability in composition also, this was a bonus for the patron and a useful accomplishment for the musician, who might thereby hope to hold more securely to his position in a notoriously insecure profession. Avignon was no exception and archives show the names of several members of the Papal choir also known to be composers in the secular sphere. The Motet 'Alma polis/Axe poli'[48] contains a list of twenty members of a choir in all probability that of Avignon. Included are a number of *Augustini de Florentia*, two professors of theory (*professores teorici*), singers from as far away as Cologne or Cyprus (Girardus de Colonia, Ydrolanus, *modulator Ciprianus*), and in particular Egidius de Aurolia, who may well be the composer of three French Ballades contained in the principal source manuscripts listed above. About forty isorhythmic Motets of this type, so skilfully imitated by the Englishman John Aleyn (Alanus),[49] survive in the manuscripts *Ch*, *Iv*[50] and *Mod.*[51] Their Latin and French texts are often packed with topical information and allusions, in the Vitry manner.[52] 'Alma polis/ Axe poli', which probably dates from the 1380s, is typical in its isorhythmic construction and makes much use of simultaneous independent metres in the various voices, also a feature of much of the late secular repertory:

(Alma polis/Axe poli — bars 1 - 10)

It would be pleasant to think that it is just such a band of musicians who are portrayed so vividly at the foot of f.37r in the Chantilly manuscript.

Their faces all show highly individual character; they are tonsured and wear monks' robes, yet have been sketched in after an amorous Ballade, Galiot's 'Le sault perilleux'. Or perhaps they are the 'doulce compaygnie' so regretted on f.47r of the same manuscript in an anonymous Ballade written by one who was forced to depart:

> *Adieu vous di, très doulce compaygnie,*
> *Puisque de vous departir me convient*
> *Par Fortune . . .*

Records from Aragon show that both singers and instrumentalists from Avignon were in demand.[53]

Second only to Avignon was the court of **Gaston Febus,** comte de Foix (1343–91) at Orthez. This cultured if impetuous nobleman, a poet in his own right but famed above all for his love of hunting, was perhaps the most important of all the patrons of 'Ars subtilior'. As Froissart tells us:

> *Il prenoit grant esbatement en menestraudie, car bien s'i congnoissoit;*
> *il faisoit devant lui ses clercs volontiers chanter chançons, rondiaux et virelaiz.*

[He much enjoyed minstrelsy, for he knew much about it; he gladly had his clerks sing songs, rondeaux and virelais before him.][54]

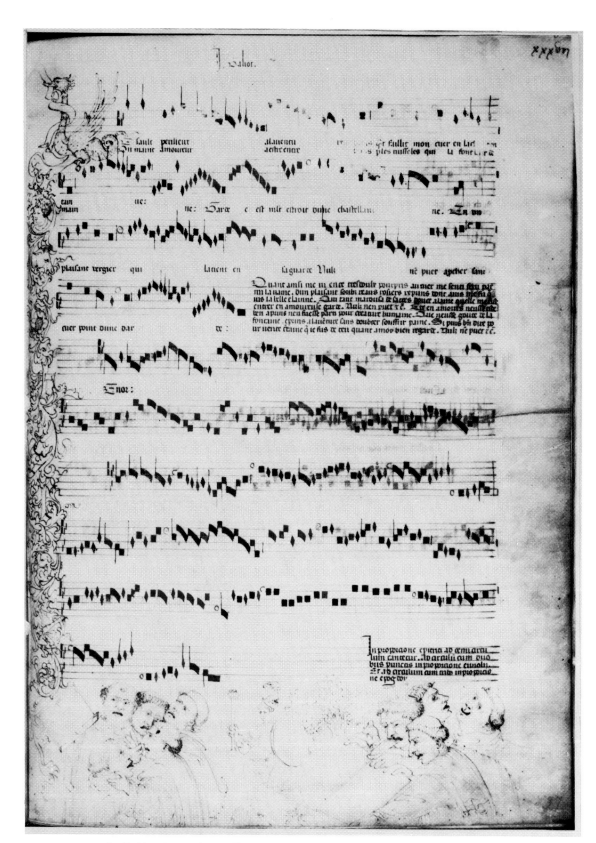

J. Galiot: Le sault perilleux, with drawing of 'La doulce compaygnie'

Gaston Febus is honoured in four Ballades in *Ch*, a manuscript which certainly centres on his circle: Franciscus' 'Phiton, Phiton', the anonymous 'Le mont Aön de Trace', Cuvelier's 'Se Galaäs' and Trebor's 'Se July Cesar':

> *Se July Cesar, Rolant et Roy Artus*
> *Furent pour conqueste renoumez ou monde,*
> *Et Yvain, Lancelot, Tristan ne Porus*
> *Eurent pour ardesse los, pris et faconde,*
> *Au jour d'ui luist et en armez tous ceuronde*
> *Cyl qui por renon et noble sorte*
> 'Febus avant' en sa enseigne porte.

[If Julius Caesar, Roland and King Arthur were famed worldwide for their conquests, and Yvain, Lancelot and Porus had praise, rewards and wealth for their courage, today there shines out and surpasses all others in arms one who, famed for his noble ways, bears 'Febus forward' on his arms.]

Julius Caesar with Courtiers,
from 'The Nine Heroes Tapestries'

Classical, biblical and other literary references are very frequent, many prompted by the popularity of the 'Nine Heroes', celebrated in Jaques de Longuyon's *Voeux du Paon* of 1310 and in many tapestries of the period.

The comte de Foix had further works composed in his honour, for example the Motets 'Inter densas' (*Ch*) and 'Altissonis' and 'Febus mundo oriens' (*Iv*).[55]

Almost as important as a centre fostering the late fourteenth-century 'avant-garde' was the Court of **Aragon** in Barcelona under Peter IV (1335–87), John I[56] (1387–96) and Martin I[57] (1396–1410). Musical life was very active there and constant exchanges of composers, singers and other performers took place across the Pyrenees with Orthez and with Avignon.[58] Of the post-Machaut generation of poet-musicians Trebor, Senleches, P. de Molins, Grimace, J. de Noyon, Gacian Reyneau, Taillandier, Galiot and Philipoctus de Caserta are known to have worked in the Aragon Court in Barcelona, as well as at Gerona, the residence of Martin I during the reign of his brother John I, and at the Court of Castile, where Queen Eleanor, sister of John I of Aragon, was much loved by her musicians, as Senleches' Ballade 'Fuions de chi', written upon her death in 1382, clearly shows. Navarra also had its share of minstrelsy. John I of Aragon is celebrated in Trebor's 'Quant joyne cuer' and 'En seumeillant', the latter Ballade being composed on the occasion of the expedition to Sardinia in 1388–89.

The late fourteenth-century repertory may be divided into a number of categories according to musical style. The earliest works contemporary with Machaut differ little from him. Some, indeed, are positively derived from him, such as Franciscus' Ballade 'Phiton, Phiton, beste très veneneuse' which is closely related to Machaut's 'Phyton, le mervilleus serpent', or the anonymous Ballade 'Dame qui fust si très bien assenée', based on Machaut's 'De Fortune me doy plaindre'. The subtle setting by F. Andrieu, possibly Franciscus or otherwise unknown, of Deschamps' two Ballades on the death of Machaut (1377), 'Armes, Amours, Dames, Chevalerie/ O flour des flours de toute melodie', quotes from the *Gloria* of Machaut's Mass in the thrilling held chords at the opening of the refrain;[59] the music is used in Chaucer setting No 9 in *Chaucer Songs*. As a further example of straightforward Machaut-derived style, we may cite P. de Molins' Ballade 'De ce que fol pensé',[60] a song which apparently knew exceptional popularity in its day, for it has survived in six sources and is known to have been in at least two others now lost.

The style is restrained, with only extremely limited use of syncopation or hocket:

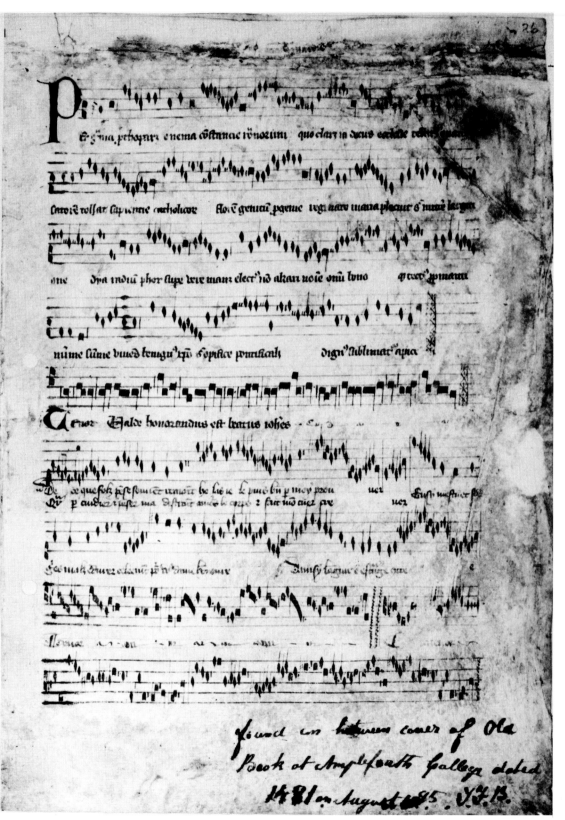

P. de Molins: De ce que fol pensé

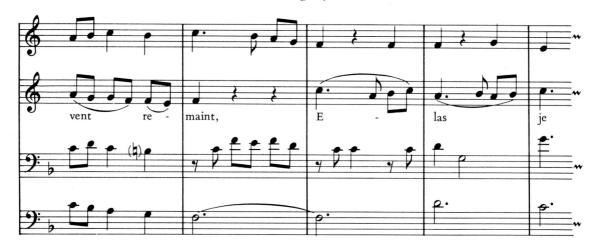

(P. des Molins: De ce que fol pensé — bars 1 - 9)

The piece also appears in keyboard transcription in the early fifteenth-century Faenza manuscript (*Fa*)[61] and its continuing appeal is attested by its appearance in an Arras tapestry of c.1420.

Le Concert (P. de Molins: De ce que fol pensé)

Relatively straightforward still but rather more exciting, is the fast-moving **'realistic virelai'** style, which above all exploits colourful effects much in the manner of the Italian Caccia. Grimace's 'Alarme, alarme',[62] for instance, opens with a fanfare figure and a call to arms in the lover's defence. Vaillant's 'Par maintes fois' is a particularly appealing piece which makes much use of stylised bird-song as the nightingale calls all the other birds of the air to put the intrusive cuckoo to death.

The anonymous 'Or sus, vous dormés trop' calls lovers out to the meadows early in the morning with exciting trumpet-like motifs:

(Or sus, vous dormez trop — bars 65 - 74)

Far more complicated is the so-called 'manneristic style'[63] in which syncopation, subtle division and dissonance become extreme. Solage gives good examples of this, his Ballade 'S'aincy estoit', for example, or Trebor, and especially three composers apparently Italian in origin, Matheus de Perusio, Anthonello and Philipoctus de Caserta. Despite the evident Italian connection – Caserta was in the Angevin Kingdom of Naples – their absorption of French 'Ars subtilior' is complete. Typical is the following passage from P. de Caserta's Ballade 'En remirant vo vouce pourtraiture':

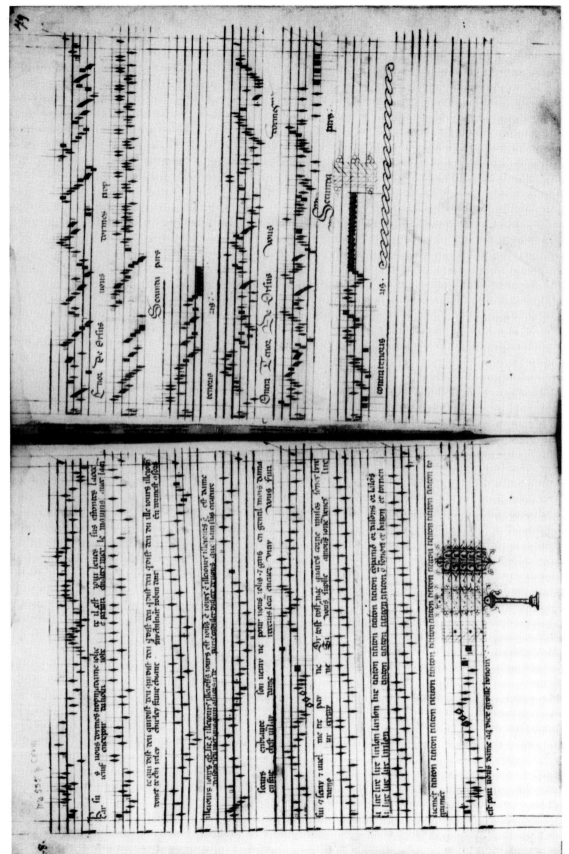

Anon.: Or sus, vous dormés trop

(P. de Caserta; En remirant vo douce pourtraiture — bars 12 - 20)

Such music can leave no doubt as to the technical competence and brilliance both of those who wrote it and those who performed it in the Courts of the fourteenth century.

A further development, possibly reflecting the invention of new or larger instruments, was the introduction of music in a lower tessitura than before. The opening of Senleches' 'Fuions de chi', for example, shows both *Tenor* and *Contratenor* descending to low Bb:

(J. Senleches; Fuions de ci — bars 1 - 5)

The extreme in this direction, exploited certainly for comic purposes, comes in Solage's Rondeau 'Fumeux, fume', where the exaltation of grumpiness descends into the depths with an accompanying disintegration of tonality:

(Solage : Fumeux fume — bars 16 - 22)

Inevitably, there was a reaction against this relatively 'difficult' music. In a sense, it is surprising that the 'Ars subtilior' composers were able to find and maintain such sympathetic patronage for so long. The return to simplicity and moderation, in anticipation of the song styles of Dufay and Binchois in the early fifteenth century, and not so far removed from Machaut style again, is illustrated by a piece such as the anonymous Virelai 'Le gay plaisir' contained in *PR* but also copied with interesting modifications into the mixed French-English collection of the manuscript Cambridge University Library Add.5943 at the turn of the century.[64]

The influence of French music in the fourteenth century was all pervasive. As we shall see, music and musicians from France were favoured alongside the native repertory in Trecento Italy. In Britain French influence was paramount, as it was in Aragon, Castile and Navarra. 'French' songs are found with Flemish texts, for example in *PR* the Ballade 'En wyflic beildt ghestadt van sinne', or the Virelai with mixed French, Latin and Flemish text 'En ties, en latim, en romans'. There were German imitations and *contrafacta*; Oswald von Wolkenstein, for instance, substituted a German text 'Der May' for Vaillant's 'Par maintes foys',[65] and the manuscripts *WolkA* and *WolkB* (Vienna, Nationalbibl. MS 2777 & Innsbruck, Univ. Lib., no call no.) contain two Ballades 'Du ausserweltes schöns, mein herz' and 'Wolauff, gesell' to the music of 'Je voy mon cuer' and 'Fuiiés de moy, amie', respectively. A group of late fourteenth-century repertory manuscripts seems to have further Northern and possibly German connections: the lost Strasbourg manuscript (*Str*),[66] and fragments in Vorau, Villingen, Munich (Codex Monacensis)[67] and Prague.[68] This latter manuscript, Prague, Univ. Lib. XI.E.9, probably bears witness to a taste in Bohemia for French music, hardly surprising in the wake of Jean de Bohème's patronage of Machaut, and further fragmentary sources, some from Central and Eastern Europe, continue to appear.[69]

Most striking of all the evidence of French musical culture outside France, however, is certainly the **Cypriot-French repertory.** This is contained solely in the manuscript *TuB* (Turin, Bibl. naz., J.11.9) and contains a large and rich collection from the French Court in Cyprus around the turn of the fourteenth and fifteenth centuries. There are well over 200 polyphonic pieces, including Mass movements, 41 isorhythmic Motets, 102 Ballades, 43 Rondeaux and 21 Virelais, yet no composer is named and no item is found elsewhere in Continental sources.[70] The manuscript was probably compiled c.1413 in the reign of King Janus (1398–1432) under the influence of his second wife Charlotte of Bourbon, who arrived in the island in 1411 with a retinue of sixty persons including musicians. Although there exist no detailed descriptions of the musical establishment in Cyprus, R. Hoppin mentions a number of influences and contacts of note, including Machaut's celebration of the widely travelled King Pierre I de Lusignan in his *Prise d'Alexandrie* (c.1370); the friendship from 1361 between the same King and his chamberlain Philippe de Mézières, who later became advisor to the French King Charles VI and who speaks favourably of Cuvelier in his *Songe du vieil Pelerin;* the visit to Cyprus in 1389 of the distinguished French noblemen Jean, Sénechal d'Eu and Jean Boucicaut, who had just been composing their *Livre des Cent Ballades* during captivity in Egypt; the visit in 1393 by the poet Oton de Granson, in the company of Henry Bolingbroke. Hoppin also notes a reference to a gift of eighty francs in gold made by the newly-crowned French King Charles V 'to the minstrels of the King of Cyprus'; the presence in Pierre de Lusignan's chapel in 1363 of a 'Henricus de Mossa, clerk of the diocese of Liège, organist and singer'; the naming of a composer 'Ydrolanus, modulator Ciprianus' in the *Ch* musician Motet 'Alma polis/Axe poli';[71] the presence of a Kyrie in a manuscript in Apt (Library of the Chapter) headed by the word 'Chypre'.

The style of much of the Cypriot-French music is that of the straightforward 'modernists' of the early fifteenth century, though there are many instances of manneristic writing. If the manuscript was copied c.1413, it nevertheless clearly contains music dating back across the previous thirty years. The music of the anonymous Cypriot-French Ballade 'Sous un bel arbre' is used for the Chaucer setting No 10 in *Chaucer Songs*.

Music for the Mass

The Mass movements in the Cypriot-French repertory are interesting in that they are set in song style, for solo voice and accompanying instruments; similar settings are to be found in England in the Old Hall manuscript.[72] The *Christe* opening below will serve to show a characteristic passage of 'modern' style, flowing and even a little ornate in the vocal line, rather in the Italian manner, but simple in its rhythms and outline:

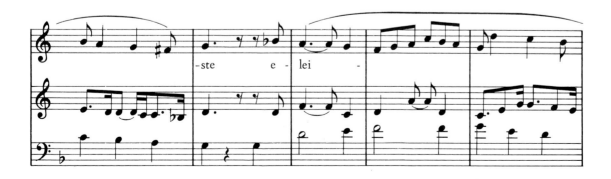

(Cyprus Kyrie, *TuB* f. 139v/140r — bars 21 - 40)

Apart from the *Messe de Nostre Dame,* Machaut's masterpiece which towers over all others in this century, there remains a considerable body of Mass music, particularly that from Avignon preserved in the Apt and Ivrea manuscripts.[73]

Before Machaut and the roughly contemporary *Tournai Mass,* all known settings are single line only. The *Tournai Mass,* which is anonymous and probably not all the work of a single composer, lacks both the unity of design and the brilliance of effect achieved by Machaut. It contains the same six movements as the Machaut Mass, but is for three voices throughout as opposed to Machaut's four-part writing. Although there is a certain amount of $\frac{6}{8}$ quaver movement and simple hocketing in the *Gloria,* all the rest is fairly strict and archaic note-against-note writing. If we compare the opening of the *Kyrie* with that of the Machaut,[74] the contrast is made clear:

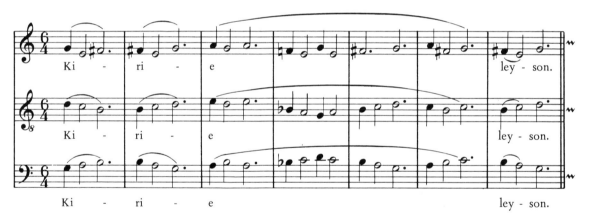

(Tournai Mass, Kyrie — bars 1 - 7)

The *Toulouse Mass* is probably of later date. It employs a certain amount of syncopation and running exchanges between the upper parts. Only four movements remain: *Kyrie, Sanctus, Agnus Dei* and *'Motetus super Ite, missa est',* all three-part writing with text under the upper line only. The first three of these movements are in duple time, a 'modern' feature, with $\frac{6}{8}$ for the close.

The *Barcelona Mass* has all five principal sections, but no final *Ite.* Curiously, four-part writing is used only for the *Agnus,* in which the outer two voices have text underlaid, while three-part writing prevails in the first four movements. The *Agnus,* at its close, displays hocketing patterns similar to those encountered in some Ballades in the last third of the century, and must probably be dissociated from the rest which consists mostly of note-against-note style.

The *Toulouse Mass*, with the *Sorbonne Mass* (or *Besançon Mass*) and Mass movements from the late fourteenth-century repertory manuscript Cambrai, Bibl. munic. 1328 (*CaB*)[75] are interrelated in some respects with the Avignon pieces in the Ivrea and Apt manuscripts.[76] H. Stäblein-Harder divides the movements into three basic compositional procedures: Motet style (on pre-established *Tenors*); Discant style (freely composed, in fairly complex polyphony); Simultaneous style (mainly note-against-note). That Mass music in Avignon could be as flamboyant as secular song, in disregard of the Papal Bull of 1324, may be shown by the following *Amen*, from an Ivrea *Credo* attributed to a composer named Orles:

(Orles, Credo – bars 131 - 138)

Music and Drama

Relatively little drama survives from fourteenth-century France compared with the rich flowering of *Passions* and *Farces* in the fifteenth century. Secular comedy is almost totally absent, probably a reminder that times were harder for the masses than for the nobility during the Hundred Years War. A few early Passion plays do survive, however, and also, of the greatest importance for our knowledge of the use of music in religious drama, forty *Miracles de Nostre Dame* which were performed by the Goldsmiths' Guild in Paris once a year on various dates in December and January between 1339 and 1382 inclusive, with breaks in 1354 and 1358–60, times of popular insurrection.[77] Music is used extensively in these plays and study of it can tell us much of the developing tradition of religious theatrical music which underlies not only the fifteenth-century French Passion cycles, but the great Northern English cycles too. No musical notation is included in the sole source,

Paris B.N. f.fr.819–820, but this is probably in part because the many Rondeaux in praise of the Virgin were *contrafacta* of already existant secular music. Motets and hymns could easily be borrowed or found in Service Books, while fanfares and minstrel performances of various kinds would probably be improvised. Altogether the plays[78] include 72 Rondeaux, 9 Motets, 5 *Te Deum*, 3 *Regina celi*, 3 *Ave Regina celorum*, 1 *Ave Maria*, 1 *Ave maris stella*, 1 *Veni, creator spiritus*, 1 *Amen*, 1 Mass Introit, 2 lesser-known Latin hymns and 4 assorted closing songs. Ten plays include performances from minstrels at dances, banquets and processions.

The main function of the Rondeaux is to give musical expression to the descent of the Virgin when she comes to intercede on the sinner's behalf or to succour those in distress. Our Lady does not sing, but is escorted by Angels, most commonly Gabriel and Michiel. Serene as the singing was meant to be, the angelic procession often occurred in most dramatic circumstances – to a woman clinging to a rock in mid-ocean during a storm, for instance. Writing for two, three and even four voices is indicated by the script. Harmony is intended, yet the predominance of eleven and thirteen-line Rondeaux types with entirely vocal performance is 'old-fashioned', implying music more in the style of Adam de la Hale, or at the most Lescurel, at the very beginning of the century.

Instrumental Music

Of purely instrumental music, on the face of it, fourteenth-century France has little to offer. On the other hand, it does seem to be perfectly authentic to give instrumental performances of pieces with vocal lines, rather in the Elizabethan way of 'apt for voices or for viols'. As Jean Lefèvre says, in his translation of Richard de Fournival's *De Vetula*, describing Ovid's youthful enthusiasm for the arts:

> *Et combien que de bouche on die*
> *Motez, balades, virelais,*
> *Comedies, rondeauls et lais,*
> *Autres instruments dont l'en use,*
> . . . .
> *Faisoie concorder souvent*
> *Par pulz de doiz, par trait ou vent.*

[And although one (normally) sings Motets, Ballades, Virelais, funny songs, Rondeaux and Lais, I performed them on all kinds of instrument, with movement of fingers, or percussion or wind.][79]

Many pieces, especially songs, appear in different sources with different numbers of parts, or with totally different parts substituted and the situation was clearly fluid, largely dependent on what forces were available at a given moment. Machaut's *Hoquetus David*, with no text, may be intended for instruments. Many French songs in particular appear in italianate sources such as the Codex Reina (*PR*) or the comparable manuscript *Pit* (Paris, B.N. ital.568) with such corrupt or incomplete texts that, from those sources, unless a singer had previously memorized the words, an instrumental performance would be the only one possible. In *Pit*, for example the Rondeau 'Esperance' is given with this initial word only at the commencement of the *Cantus* line.[80]

The Robertsbridge fragments, discussed below[81] because of their English association, might better be classed as French instrumental arrangements. This is most likely in the case of the *Estampies* which are very comparable with surviving French *Estampies* and *Danses réales* of the thirteenth century, while the arrangements of *Fauvel* Motets speak for themselves.

The best examples of instrumental music, still arrangements of vocal pieces including a vocal line and text in their original conception, are to be found in the Faenza manuscript (*Fa*). Although the manuscript probably dates from the early fifteenth century, its mixed French and Italian contents no doubt show characteristic embellishment practice current among instrumentalists in the late fourteenth century.[82] If for keyboard – portative organ, most likely – the right hand is far more active than the left, usually an embellished *Cantus* over more or less the original *Tenor*. It is perfectly possible to play these arrangements on two separate melodic instruments instead, though the compositions are written down in score form, unlike the bulk of fourteenth-century music in which the various lines are separated from each other in the manuscripts. Here is the opening of the Faenza version of Machaut's Ballade 'De toutes flours':

(De toutes flours – bars 1 - 16)

2. Italy

O tu, cara scienzia mia, musica,
O dolce melodia con vaghi canti,
Che fa' rinovellar tuttor gli amanti,

E io son corda di tuo consonanzia,
Che imaginar solea tuo bel trovato,
Or son procuratore ed avocato.

Però ritorno a te, musica cara,
Ch'ogni atto bel d'amor da te s'apara.
(Giovanni da Cascia)

A fundamental distinction may be made between the essentially simple and mellifluous character of native Italian music in the fourteenth century[83] and the complex subtlety of the French art, which nevertheless became influential and fashionable in Italy in the closing years.[84] There was a marked difference in approach, the Italian sensuous and melismatic, the French rational and highly organized. At the time few Italian composers attempted the advanced French style – Anthonellus and Philipoctus de Caserta and Matheus de Perusio are the great exceptions – and few French composers tried the Italian before Johannes Ciconia from Liège at the turn of the century,[85] though there was a Guilelmus de Francia (*alias* Frate Guglielmo di Santo Spirito),[86] an Augustine who composed Italian songs c.1365 in Florence, including a setting of Sacchetti's Madrigal 'La neve, e'l ghiaccio, e venti d'oriente'. Difficulty in assimilating Italian style is evident in his music, and it is possible that he contributed to those French elements discernable in the Florentines Landini and Andreas.[87] There are in the Trecento occasional examples of Italians using French texts, just as Northerners such as Arnold and Hugo de Lantins in the following century occasionally used Italian. But despite the popularity of the French manneristic School so clearly attested by mixed Franco-Italian repertory manuscripts originating in Italian Courts, it was the subsequent and more simple 'modern' art, especially of the Burgundian School, brought to Italy in the early Quattrocento by composers such as Dufay which fused with the native Italian sweetness to produce what is now usually referred to as 'true Renaissance' style.

Very little Italian music which may clearly be identified as such remains from the thirteenth and early fourteenth centuries. This must in part be due to the Guelf-Ghibelline strife and the consequent conditions unfavourable to artistic endeavour. After the Albigensian 'Crusade', Italy had become home for many Provençal *troubadours*, however, and it was their monodic art in the old style, parallel with that of the *trouvères* in N. France, which tended to dominate.[88] Just as in France, at the opening of the Trecento

Music and her Attendants

Fra Angelico: Christ glorified in the Court of Heaven

traditional single-line settings were normal for secular song. It was very much more common in Italy than in France at that date for poets to create verses in lyric forms independent of music,[89] or to be prepared to create both kinds.[90] The sonnet, perhaps the most important Italian poetic form of the age, was not intended for music at all, and references to 'my song' in *canzoni* may often be mere poetic convention. This seems to be the case, for example, in Dante's *La vita nuova* (c.1295), but several lines in his first Ballata do indicate a musical setting, though we have no knowledge of any ability on Dante's part to provide one:

> Ballad, I want you to find out love again
> > And go to my lady's presence,
> So my lord pleads his defence
> > Which you can sing to his strain.
> . . . . . .
> *When you meet him and ask her mercy,*
> > *While sweet sounds play,*
> *Utter this oration . . .*
> . . . . . .
> > *By the grace of my music's purity*
> *Remain here with her, . . .*[91]

Dante further distinguishes, in his *De Vulgari Eloquentia*, between forms such as the *canzone* which, whether with music or without, stand on their own and dance songs which in his view are inferior; we see here that the Ballata, just like the early French Ballade, Rondeau and Virelai, was still used *carole*-wise in Dante's day, soon after 1300:

> Moreover, whatever produces by its own power the effect for which it was made, appears nobler than that which requires external assistance; but *canzoni* produce by their own power the whole effect they ought to produce, which *ballate* do not, for they require the assistance of the performers for whom they are written; it therefore follows that *canzoni* are to be deemed nobler than *ballate*.[92]

When Dante meets his old friend, the musician Casella, in *Purgatorio*, Canto 2, and hears the setting of his own *canzone* 'Amor che nella mente mi ragiona', there can be no doubt concerning the musical context nor the solo performance:

> *'Love in my mind his conversation making',*
> *Thus he began, so sweetly that I find*
> *Within me still the dulcet echoes waking.*[93]

Hymns in very simple style, the *Laude spirituali* mostly inherited from the previous century, remained in the background on a popular level throughout the Trecento and found a new lease of life in the century following.[94] It is interesting to note that current secular songs were sometimes adapted for use as *Laude*, just as in the long-established tradition of the French *chanson pieuse*; the manuscript Vatican Chig.L.VII.266, f.291v gives a *Lauda* 'El cor mi si divide' with the instruction that it should be sung to the tune of a Ballata set by Andrea da Firenze, 'come una ballata che comincia *Cosa chrudel m'ancide*'. It seems probable that, when such adaptation was made, ornate embellishments were dispensed with to leave music in straightforward *conductus* style; an example is known from a little later, in the fifteenth century, of a piece ('Giustiniana', from Petrucci's book of *Frottole*) which appears in different sources in plain and in embellished form.[95] Perhaps it was such practices, or the popularity of artless music, which provoked the strictures against inferior meddlers in music made by Landini later in the century and Jacopo da Bologna earlier:

> *Oselleto salvazo per stasone*
> *Dolci versiti canta cum bel modo:*
> *Tal e tal grida forte, chi'i' no lodo.*
>
> *Per gridar forte non se canta bene,*
> *Ma con suave, dolce melodia*
> *Se fa bel canto e zò vol maistria.*
>
> *Pochi l'hano e tuti se fa magistri,*
> *Fa ballate, matrical e muteti,*
> *Tut' enfioran Filipoti e Marcheti.*
>
> Si è piena la terra de magistroli,
> Che loco più no trovano i discipuli.

[The little wild bird, in its season, sings sweet verses in lovely style: such as I shall not praise can only shout./ Shouting loud is not good singing, for fine song is made of soft, sweet melody, if anyone has the skill./ Few do have it, though they all call themselves masters, and make Ballate, Madrigals and Motets, embellishing (i.e. going against) Philip (de Vitry) and Marchettus (da Padua)./ The world is so full of little masters that there is no room left for any pupils.]

Much the same point is made by Sacchetti in his Madrigal 'Ben s'affatica invano chi fa or versi', which also refers to Marchettus in the ritornello:

> *Cosi del canto avien: sanz' alcun' arte*
> *Mille Marchetti veggio in ogni parte.*[96]

Similar strictures were made in France, for example by Senleches in his double Ballade 'Je me merveil aucune fois comment/ J'ay pluseurs fois pour mon esbatement'.

Jacopo is nevertheless the only one of the great Trecento composers to have left a setting of a Lauda text, his 'Nel mio parlar di questa donn' eterna / Doname Cristo grazia sempiterna', also his only example in Ballata form.

A few theoretical treatises concerning the composing of verse and which refer to musical forms and practices have survived from the early Trecento: 'De variis inveniendo et rimandi modis' in the glosses on the *Documenti d'amore* made by the Tuscan lawyer and man-of-letters Francesco da Barberino in Florence between 1313 and 1326; a small anonymous Treatise now in Venice, Bibl. Marciana (Cod. Marc. Lat. cl.12,n.97), probably the work of a Venetian c.1330; the *Summa artis rythmici vulgaris dictaminis* written in 1332 by the Paduan judge and man-of-letters Antonio da Tempo.[97] These works make mention of *Ballate, Rotundelli, Motteti, Caccie, Madriali, Sirventesi*. Ballate, Madrigals and Cacce, as we shall see, were the principal forms for polyphonic setting in the Trecento. Motets were not strongly favoured in Italy and hark back more to the preceding age, as do the *Sirventes* or *Serventois* of the *troubadours* and *trouvères*. The mention of Rondeaux (*Rotundelli*) similarly reminds one of the importance of this dance form in thirteenth-century France, and its subsequent development. Very few examples are known in Italian settings, apart from imitations on the French model in the fifteenth century, but the important manuscript Vatican Rossi 215, generally accepted as the earliest collection surviving of Trecento music, does include an example set for two voices:

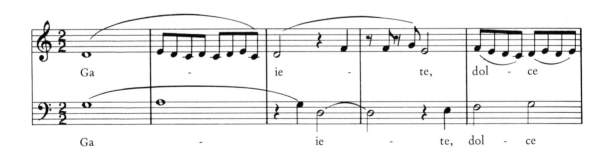

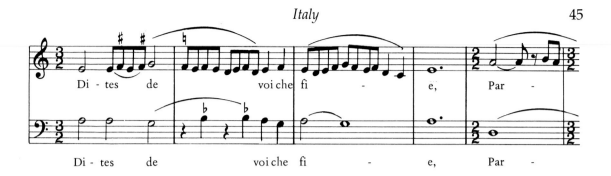

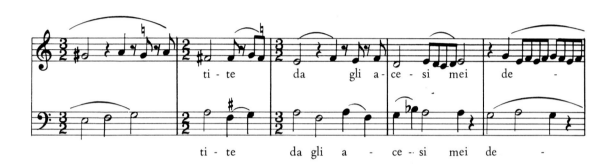

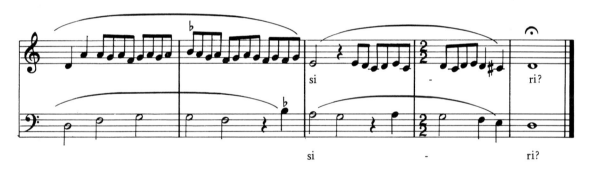

(Gaiete, dolce parolete mie – refrain)

The Rossi manuscript also contains a number of monodies, single melody settings, to be expected at the beginning of the century, if we recall their French equivalent in Jehan de Lescurel. The Ballata 'Per tropo fede talor se perigola', for example, is regular in form, but rather less ornate than many settings to follow a few years later:

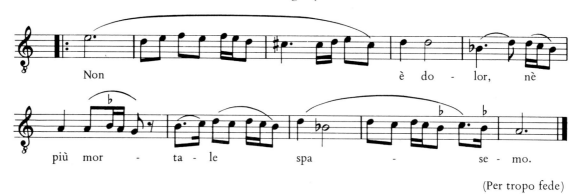

Non è do - lor, nè

più mor - ta - le spa - se - mo.

(Per tropo fede)

The Composers and their Background

The enthusiasm for music-making in Italian polite society, even if it is on a less sophisticated level, can nowhere so vividly be seen as in the interludes of Boccaccio's *Decameron*, which depicts the ten days spent in idyllic country-house setting outside Florence in 1348 by a party of seven young ladies and three young gentlemen, seeking escape from the epidemic of plague which had struck the city. Each day one of the company is elected 'Queen' or 'King' and dictates the ceremonies:

> Afterwards, the tables were removed, and the queen sent for musical instruments so that one or two of their number, well versed in music, could play and sing, while the rest, ladies and gentlemen alike, could dance a *carole*. At the queen's request, Dioneo took a lute and Fiammetta a viol, and they struck up a melodious tune, whereupon the queen, having sent the servants off to eat, formed a ring with the other ladies and the two young men, and sedately began to dance. And when the dance was over, they sang a number of gay and charming little songs.[98]

At the conclusion of the first day Dioneo again takes the lute and the rest dance while Emilia sings a Ballata in amorous tones:

> In mine own body take I such delight
> That to no other love could I
> My fond affections plight . . .[99]

Similar entertainment is enjoyed on the remaining evenings, always a mixture of singing, playing instruments and dancing. On Day II, for instance:

> When this song was finished, they sang a number of others, danced many dances and played several tunes.[100]

Both ladies and gentlemen play and sing; ladies are shown to compose also, as on Day III, when the whole company joins in the refrains:

> No sooner had the tables been removed than Filostrato, wishing to keep to the path which the ladies crowned before him had taken, called upon Lauretta to dance and sing them a song.
> 'My lord', she said, 'the only songs I know are the ones I have composed myself, and of those I remember, none is especially apt for so merry a gathering as this. But if you would like me to sing you one, I will gladly oblige.'
> 'Nothing of yours could be other than pleasing and beautiful', replied the king. 'Sing it, therefore, exactly as you wrote it.' And so, in mellifluous but somewhat plaintive tones, Lauretta began as follows, and the other ladies repeated the refrain after each verse . . . .[101]

At the Close of Day VI more boisterous dancing takes place:

> The king, however, who was in good mettle, sent for Tindaro and ordered him to bring out his cornemuse, to the strains of which he caused several reels to be danced.[102]

and on the following Day other instruments alternate with this:

> In no time at all they were dancing *caroles* beside the beautiful fountain, accompanied sometimes by Tindaro on the cornemuse and sometimes by the music of other instruments.[103]

The sheer exuberance and delight in spontaneous music-making is shown nowhere better than at the opening of Day IX, after a long country walk:

> They then rested for a while, nor did they sit down at table before half-a-dozen canzonets, each of them more lively than the one preceding it, had been sung by the young men and the ladies.[104]

though it seems that enthusiasm had at times to compensate for a less-than-perfect performance:

> They then sang countless songs, more entertaining for the words than polished in the singing.[105]

Many of the surviving works of the 'Italian Ars Nova'[106] are anonymous, though this is less serious than it is for French works. Many of the composers named remain nothing but names to us, while others reveal themselves more through their works than through slight contemporary allusions. Two distinct 'provinces' of music and poetry, and of musical notation, may be distinguished: N. Italian and Florentine. Although the latter is influenced in its notation by French usage, it is interesting to note that no corresponding difference in musical style is to be observed. If anything, the Florentine 'School' is more faithful to the essential Italian characteristics, while the N. Italian composers show a tendency to introduce intricacies of rhythm, though always without causing syncopation across the (modern) 'bar-line'. It should not be imagined, however, that Florence and the North were separate musical spheres with little contact between them. The evidence we have concerning the composers alone, scanty though it may be, indicates the contrary: Giovanni da Cascia, from the parish of Cascia a few miles from Florence and also known as Johannes de Florentia, was a celebrated organist and choirmaster in the cathedral in Florence, but his fame led to an invitation to the Court of Mastino della Scala (1329–51) at Verona. Here he must have met Jacopo da Bologna, recently come from the service of Luchino Visconti (d.1349) in Milan. Bartolino da Padova, mentioned in Giovanni da Prato's *Paradiso degli Alberti* and in Simone Prodenzani's *Saporetto,* had obvious Florentine sympathies and connections and probably accompanied Francesco Carrara into exile there from Padua in 1386.

The chronicler Villani relates that Jacopo da Bologna and Giovanni da Cascia benefited from the protection of Mastino II della Scala. However, Jacopo was certainly in the Milanese Court in August 1346, the date of the twin births of Giovanni and Luchino Novello, sons of Luchino Visconti; this event had a certain political significance, as though to confirm Milanese authority over Genova, which had been weakened by internal strife and submitted to Luchino in February of that year. This explains the linking of Liguria with Milan in a generally joyful Italy in Jacopo's Madrigal:

O in Italia felice Liguria,
E proprio tu, Milan, lauda e gloria
De' dui nati segnor, che 'l cel t'aguria.

Segno fo ben, che fo de gran vittoria,
Ch'un' aquila li trasse a cristianesmo
E Parma a lor donò da po' el batesmo.

Un venere fra sesta e terza naquero
Luca e Zuane a chi lor nomi piaquero.

Quaranta sei un emme cum tri ci
Corea e fo d'agosto al quarto di.

[Oh, in Italy, happy Liguria, and especially you, Milan, praise and glory be to God for the birth of the two lords, which heaven foretold. / It was a good sign, of great victory, that an eagle brought them to Christianity and gave them Parma after their baptism. / On a Friday between Sext and Terce were born Luchino and Giovanni, who took pleasure in their names. / This happened in 1346 on the fourth day of August.]

A further Madrigal, with mixed Italian and Latin text, by Jacopo gives an acrostic **LUCHINUS,** and probably relates to events in 1341, when a plot led by Francesco Pusterla, the only serious attempt against Luchino during his reign, failed and the ringleaders were executed. The *senhal* (hidden name, a favourite device in the genre) of ISABELLA in line 7 praises Luchino's wife Isabella Freschi, as opposed to the plotter's wife Margherita Pusterla, who had been Luchino's mistress:

Lo *lume vostro, dolce mio segnore,*
Virtute sic perfecte est ornatum,
Ch'*a rei non luce, a' boni sempr 'è chiaro.*

Hoc est notum et satis est probatum
In *quegli c'han sentito il gusto amaro*
Nascosamente per comporre errore.

Una donna vi regge, ch **'è sì bella:**
Sul ciel è posta più lucente stella.

[Your light, my sweet lord, is adorned with such perfect virtue that it does not shine on evil-doers, but for the good is always bright./ This is well known and well proved to those who have experienced the bitter taste for their treacherous plotting./ A lady rules over you who is so beautiful (**Isabella**) that there is no brighter star in the heavens.]

The events of 1346 are similarly referred to in a Luchino acrostic Motet fragment, 'Laudibus dignis merito laudatur', which may safely be attributed to Jacopo, while a further Motet of his, 'Lux purpurata radiis', has a double text in praise of Luchino and an acrostic **LUCHINUS VICECOMES**. It is quite probable that Jacopo remained in Milan until Luchino's death in 1349.

It is possible that Giovanni da Cascia, as well as Maestro Piero, a somewhat older composer, also spent some time in the Milanese Court. Like Gaston Febus, Luchino loved hunting; we read of him:

Fuit magnificus in equitaturis et equorum falleris, in asturibus, falconibus, acciptribus et magnis canibus.[107]

Both composers in contest set a spirited Caccia text 'Con bracchi assai e con molti levrieri', which describes a hunting party along the banks of the river Adda; one of the dogs named, Varino, reappears in Jacopo's Caccia 'Per sparverare tolsi el mio sparvero', and we may well wonder if this was one of Luchino's favourite animals. Maestro Piero may be identified with Magister Petrus Andreutii, recorded in 1335 in Perugia as a 'doctor comunis Perusii in arte cantus'.[108] All three great early Trecento composers were certainly present together a little later in Verona at the Court of Mastino II della Scala. As Villani records, all three took part in a contest to compose Madrigals in praise of a lady referred to as **ANNA.** In Maestro Piero's example, 'Sovra un fiume regale', the name in the ritornello is undisguised:

> **Anna**, *mio cor,* **Anna**, *la vita mia,*
> *Gli raggi tuo fatt' han d'amor la via.*

In the competing texts the *senhal* is hidden:

> ***Anna***morar mi fe' 'l suo viso umano
> E'l dolce guardo e la pulita mano.
>> (Giovanni, ritornello of 'Appress' un fiume chiaro')

> *Ahi lasso mi, non vol vegnir piè **a nave**,*
> *Ma tene 'l mio cor stretto sotto chiave.*
>> (Jacopo, ritornello of 'O dolze apres' un bel parlaro fiume')

The lady makes reply in a further setting by Giovanni:

> *Donna già fui leggiadr'* ***anna***morata

and, indeed, a whole story in Madrigal sequence is revealed, always centred on the lady ANNA who dwells by a *fiume* (i.e. the river Adige), by a *perlaro* tree, as again in Piero's:

> *A l'ombra d'un perlaro.*[109]

or Giovanni's:

> *O perlaro gentil.*

Both Piero and Jacopo set a Madrigal text 'Si come al canto della bella Iguana' in praise of a lady MARGHERITA, who appears also in Jacopo's Madrigal 'Lucida petra, O **Margherita** cara', possibly an illegitimate daughter of Luchino, though marguerite symbolism was a poetic commonplace of the time.[110] The *Iguane* or *Euguane* are also to be found in Giovanni's Madrigal 'Nascose el viso stava fra le fronde', and are fairies or nymphs 'said to inhabit the hills near Padua which are still today called the Colli Euganei'.[111]

Three further Madrigals link Jacopo and Giovanni, all concerning a lady, or so it seems, who, metaphorically, has been transformed into a poisonous serpent. Jacopo's double-length text 'Soto l'imperio' opens with a reference to the eagle emblem borne by the Scaligeri as representatives of the Holy Roman Emperor in Italy:

> *Soto l'imperio del posente prince,*
> *Che nel so nom' ha le dorate ale,*
> *Regna la bisa el cui morso me vince*

> *Si, che da lei fugir nula me vale.*
> *La me persegue e 'l cor mio segnoreza;*
> *Poi come dona instesa se vageza.*

> *Come ch'io la remiro pur s'acorze,*
> *I ochi doneschi e chiude e via sen fuze;*
> *Ma come serpe tosicosa porze*
>
> *De foco fiama che m'aceca e struze.*
> *L'animo ha crudo e sì aspra la scorza*
> *Ch'amor en lei per mi più non ha forza.*
>
> *Custei me fe' zà lume più che 'l sole;*
> *Cum più zò me recordo più me dole.*

[Beneath the sway of the powerful prince who in his name bears golden wings, reigns the snake whose bite overcomes me / So that flight from it avails me nothing; it pursues me and masters my heart; then it charms me just like a woman. / The more I look at it, the more it shrinks away, closes its womanly eyes and flees; but like a venomous serpent it gives out/fiery flame which blinds and consumes me. Its spirit is cruel and its appearance so fierce that Love has no power over it to help me. / Indeed, it shines more brightly on me than the sun; the more I think of it, the more I grieve.]

Much the same story is related in another of Jacopo's Madrigals, with a precise Veronese setting by the Adige, 'Nel bel zardino che l'Atice cenge', and in Giovanni's 'Donna già fui leggiadra innamorata', in which it is the lady who speaks: she had been changed into a serpent solely in order to kill a false lover; when she has tormented him enough, she will return to her female form and have mercy on him!

Piero was certainly the oldest in this trio. His works, particularly contained in the earliest, Rossi manuscript, bear a close resemblance in notation to the recommendations of Marchettus da Padua in his *Pomerium* of 1319.[112] Jacopo was in all probability the youngest and was probably still writing in about 1381, for his Madrigal 'Fenice fu' e vissi pura e morbida' seems to refer to a marriage between a lady from Verona, symbolised by the phoenix (*fenice*), the device of Antonio della Scala, left in control of Verona after the death of his brother Bartolomeo in 1381, and a gentleman from Milan, represented by the turtle-dove (*tortora*), on the arms of Gian Galeazzo Visconti, the Count of Virtù, who succeeded his father Galeazzo in 1378.[113] Donato da Cascia's Madrigal 'Dal cielo scese per iscala d'oro' similarly refers to a 'donna fenice, umile e pia', that is Samaritana da Polenta, wife of Antonio della Scala. The anonymous Madrigal 'La nobil scala' is clearly a further such work in praise of the Scaligeri, but certainly from the later part of the century, to judge by its musical style.[114]

Musical events and personalities in Florence are better recorded and observed especially in works by Franco Sacchetti, Simone Prodenzani d'Orvieto and Giovanni Gherardi da Prato. In a long poem composed about 1388 Sacchetti lists many prominent citizens of Florence he had known, and includes two musicians, Lorenzo Masini da Firenze and Gherardello da Firenze:

> *Chi avesse avuto in musica diletto*
> *Lorenzo ritrovera e Gherardello,*
> *Maestri di quella sanza alcun difetto.*

[Whoever took pleasure in music used to seek out Lorenzo and Gherardello, perfect masters of that art.]

(*Il libro della rime*, 290)

When Gherardello died, Francesco di Messer Simone Peruzzi addressed to Sacchetti a sonnet in lament, 'Ralegratevi, Muse, or giubilate', to which Sacchetti made reply in like form, 'Come in terra lasciò sconsolate';[115] the chronological disposition of Sacchetti's manuscript allows this event to be dated between 1362 and 1365. Sacchetti heads several of his poems with information on the composer of any musical setting and includes Ballate and Madrigals by Gherardello, his son Giovanni and his brother Giacomo.[116] Some of the pieces so indicated, by Niccolò del Proposto or da Perugia, Donato da Cascia, Ottolino de Brixia, Lorenzo, Gherardello and his family, for instance, as well as one by Sacchetti himself, have failed to survive in any musical source.[117] It is evident from this that the setting, not only of verses by Sacchetti, but of independent poets in general, was fairly widespread and probably more frequent than in France, though the lack of identification of separate authors for texts in most French sources leaves an element of uncertainty. Boccaccio was set by Lorenzo and Niccolò; Soldanieri by Donato, Lorenzo, Gherardello, Paolo (tenorista) da Firenze and Landini. Bartolino da Padova set Giovanni da Ravenna's Madrigal 'Imperiale sedendo', Griffoni's Ballata 'Chi tempo a' and Dondi's Ballata 'La sacrosancta carità'; Landini set Steffano di Cino, Rinuccini, Malatesta, Soldanieri, Bindo d'Alesso Donati and Sacchetti. Indeed, Sacchetti's *Il Libro delle rime* (p.284) includes an exchange of sonnets between himself and Landini in which the poet asks for a musical setting for his verses:

> *Priego ch'adorni le parole nove*
> [I beg you to adorn these new words]

and the musician returns the lines duly clad:

> *Vestita la canzon, che 'l cor commove,*
> *Rimando a te, sì ch'omai per la terra*
> *Cantando potrá gire qui ed altrove.*

[The song is clad, so as to move hearts, and I return it to you so that henceforward throughout the world anyone who finds it can go around singing it.]

It is surprising, perhaps, that there should have been so little inclination to set the greatest lyricist of all: Petrarch. Only one contemporary setting is known, by Jacopo, of the Madrigal 'Non al suo amante più Diana piaque'. A Florentine feature comparable with that of the Veronese ANNA competition was the writing of a number of pieces in praise of a young lady prominent in the sophisticated society which gathered round the wealthy enthusiast for the arts, Antonio di Niccolò degli Alberti, in his lovely villa aptly named 'Il Paradiso'. Her name was Niccolosa, **Cosa** for short. Both Lorenzo and Vincenzo da Rimini set a Madrigal, the first line of which contains an obvious allusion to the home of their host:

> *Ita se n'era a star nel 'Paradiso'*

and in which **Cosa** is depicted as Proserpina singing and plucking flowers before she was carried away by Pluto. Lorenzo's Madrigal 'Vidi ne l'ombra d'una bella luce', Andrea da Firenze's Ballata '**Cosa** crudel m'ancide', Paolo da Firenze's Ballata 'Una **cosa** di veder tutta beleza' and Landini's Ballata 'Che **cosa** è questa, Amor, che 'l ciel produce', all celebrate the beauty of the lady **Cosa.** The most delightful picture of the meetings where these songs must have been sung is given in Giovanni da Prato's *Il Paradiso degli Alberti* (c.1426),[118] a work unlike Boccaccio's *Decameron* in that the framework tends to become more important than the novelle contained within. Above all, Francesco Landini is depicted as the supreme virtuoso, unequalled in music's art:

Fioriva ancora in que. tempo Francesco delli Organi, musico teorico e pratico, mirabil cosa a ridire; il quale, cieco quasi a nativià, si mostrò di tanto intelletto divino che in ogni parte più astratta mostrava le sotilissime proporzioné de' suoi musicabili numeri, e quelle con tanta dolcezza col suo organo praticava ch 'è cosa non credibile pure a udilla; e non istante questo, elli con ogni artista e filosofo gío disputando non tanto della sua musica, ma in tutte l'arti liberali, perché di tutte quelle in buona parte erudito si n'era.

[At that time there still flourished Francesco the Organist, a musician in both theory and practice, which is something remarkable; he was blind almost from birth but showed such divine intelligence that on the most abstract level he could demonstrate the subtlest proportions of musical numbers and could play them on his organ with such sweetness that it seemed impossible even when one heard it; nevertheless, he enjoyed discussion with artists and thinkers not only about music, but about all the liberal arts, for he was well versed in them all.][119]

Posto a ssedere i valenti uomini, Francesco, che lietissimo era, chiese il suo organetto e cominciò sí dolcemente a ssonare suoi amorosi canti che nussuno quivi si era che per dolcezza della dolcissima ermonia no.lli paresse che 'l cuore per soprabondante litizia del petto uscire gli volesse.

[When the good men had sat down, Francesco, who was in high spirits, took his little organ and began to play so sweetly his songs of love that there was no-one present who did not feel, through the sweetness of this sweetest harmony, as if overflowing joy would make their hearts burst from their breasts.][120]

E prestamente con piacere di tutti, e singularmente di Francesco musico, due fanciullette cominciarono una ballata a cantare, tenendo loro bordone Biagio di Sernello, con tante piace-volezza e con voci sí angeliche che non che gli astanti uomine e donne, ma chiaramente si vide e udí li ucelletti, che ssu per li cipressi erano, farsi più pressimani e i loro canti con più dolcezza e copia cantare. Le parole della ballata son queste:

> *Or su, gentili spirti ad amor pronti,*
> *Volete voi vedere il 'Paradiso'?*
> *Mirate d'esta* **cosa** *suo bel viso . . .*

[And soon, to the pleasure of the assembly, especially of Francesco the musician, two girls began to sing a Ballata, accompanied by Biagio di Sernello, in such pleasing tones and with such angelic voices, that not only the men and women looking on, but also the birds watching and listening up in the cypress trees, gathered closer and sang their own more sweetly and more abundantly than before. The words of the Ballata were these:

> *Rise up, gentle souls, eager for love,*
> *Would you like to see 'Paradise'?*
> *Just look upon the lovely face of that* **Cosa** *. . .*][121]

Dopo quest novellare, sendo già il sole montato e cominciando a riscaldare, standosi alle dolcissime ombre la compagnia, cantando mille ugelletti fra lle verzicanti frondi, fu comandato a Francesco che tocasse um-poco l'organetto per vedere se il cantare dell 'ucelletti menomasse o crescesse per lo suo sonare. E cosí prestissimo facea; di che grandissima maraviglia seguío: ché, cominciato il suono, si vidono molti uccelli tacere e, quasi come attoniti faccendosi più dapresso, per grande spazio udendo passaro; dapoi ripresso il lor canto, radoppiandolo, mostravano inistimabile vaghezza, e singularmente alcuno rusignuolo intanto che apresso a uno braccio sopra il capo Francesco . . .

[After this story, since the sun had already risen and it was becoming hot, the company stood in the pleasant shade while a thousand birds sang amid the green foliage. Francesco was asked to play a little on his organ to see if his playing would make the birds sing more or less. And this he did straightway, and something marvelous then happened. As soon as he had begun playing many of the birds were seen to fall silent and, as if amazed, they came closer and stayed to listen in great delight; then they took up their song again with redoubled vigour and unimaginable charm, and, amazingly, a nightingale came and settled on a branch just over Francesco's head.][122]

Francesco Landini

Landini's life is, indeed, better documented than any other musician of the century, thanks especially to the historian of Florence, Villani.[123] Landini lived from 1325 to 1397 and was born in Fiesole and died in Florence, where he was buried in the Basilica of S. Lorenzo. His brilliance as an organist, theoretician and philosopher led him to high consideration among the most important citizens of Florence. His blindness, which resulted from a childhood illness, is symbolized in his Madrigal 'Mostrommi Amor già fra le verdi fronde', in which a blinded peregrin falcon struggles in darkness for freedom and aspires to reach great heights.[124]

Prodenzani's *Saporetto*[125] shows, in a section on the *Mundus Placitus* (Life of Pleasure) a society much like that at the 'Paradiso', though a little later in the century and even more addicted to musical enjoyment, dancing, playing and singing. Invaluable are the numerous passages in which composers, performers and a wide repertory of pieces and types of music are named, some of which are known no longer today. In the Court of Pierbaldo, the musical hero Sollazzo dazzles with his brilliance and versatility. At Vespers, for instance:

> *Solaço nel principio fe' dimoro*
> *Con tenoristi e 'l biscantor sostenne;*
> *Puoi de sonar gli orgheni gli convenne,*
> *Chè pregato ne fo da tucti loro . . .*

[Sollazzo first stayed with the Tenors and took the lower line; then it pleased him to play the organ, since everyone had asked him to . . .][126]

or on a less restrained occasion:

> *Con la chitarra fe' suoni a tenore*
> *Con tanta melodia, che a ciaschuno*

Per la dolceça gli alegrava 'l core.
Con la cetara ancor ne fece alcuno,
Puoi venner pifar sordi cum tenore:
Solaço incontinente ne prese uno.

[He played the Tenor on the gittern so melodiously that he gladdened the hearts of all who heard him. Then he tried a little on the citole; after that came muted shawms (?) for the Tenor: straightway Sollazzo took one up.][127]

Sollazzo follows this display with a show on bowed instruments:

Rubebe, rubechette et rubecone.[128]

Most interesting is the demonstration both of the equal taste for French and Italian music and of the possibility of giving an instrumental performance of pieces usually regarded as songs:

Una arpa fo adducta assai reale
Ove Solaço fe' La dolce cera,
Ucel de Dio con Aquil altera,
Verde buschetto et puoi Imperiale,
Agniel so' bianco et anco 'l Pelegrino,
Orsus madame, da par desperança
Et fecie Monfiante et l'Ansellino . . .[129]

It is the prominent presence of Landini's younger contemporary Bartolino da Padova which marks this description off as one of the closing two decades of the century. The passage above, which is only one of several such mines of information, shows Sollazzo performing on a splendid harp pieces including Jacopo's triple Madrigal 'Aquil altera ferma / Creatura gentil / Uccel di dio' in celebration of the visit to Italy by the Emperor Charles IV in 1354,[130] Giovanni's Madrigal 'Agnel son bianco', the anonymous Ballata 'Io sono un pellegrin che vo cercando' and two pieces by Bartolino, as well as, probably, the French Virelai 'Or sus, vous dormés trop, ma dame joliete'[131] and maybe the Rondeau 'Esperance ky en mon cuer'.[132] 'Imperial sedendo fra più stelle',[133] to a text by Giovanni da Ravenna, is a Madrigal in praise of the Carrara family, probably composed before the death of Francesco il Vecchio in 1388, although the arms depicted, a chariot surmounted by a winged Saracen, passed on to the son Francesco Novello, who escaped from the Viscontis and established himself in Florence in 1389, from whence he planned a military come-back against Milan:

Imperial sedendo fra più stelle
Dal ciel desese un carro d'onor degno
Soto signor d'ogni altro ma' benegno.

Le rote soi guidavan quatro done,
Justicia e Temperencia con Forteza
Ed an' Prudenza tra cotanta alteza.

Nel mezo un Saracin con l'ale d'oro
Tene 'l fabricator del so tesoro.

[Seated imperially among many stars, from the sky there descended a chariot worthy of honour, and on it a lord kinder than any other./ Its wheels were guided by four ladies: Justice and Temperance with Strength and Prudence of such great distinction./ In their midst a Saracen with golden wings was bearing the maker of his riches.]

'La douce cere d'un fier animal',[134] italianized by Prodenzani, was an attempt by Bartolino to use a French Madrigal text, though the corrupt state in which it stands suggests that his abilities in the language were insufficient. Similarly, the Madrigal 'La fiera testa che d'uman si ciba', set by both Bartolino and Niccolò del Proposto, has a French refrain as well as alternate lines of Italian and Latin in the body of the text. A heraldic piece again, the reference is to the Visconti threat to Florence in 1397,[135] a threat resolved only by Gian Galeazzo's sudden death in 1402. The Treaty concluded in 1403 is no doubt the theme of Bartolino's Madrigal 'Alba colomba con sua verde rama', the dove of peace. Bartolino may not have lived to see the sad end of Francesco Carrara, attacked by Venice after his repossession of Verona, taken prisoner and executed in 1405, while his sons Francesco and Giacomo were strangled in prison in 1406, sad events lamented by Ciconia in his Ballata 'Con lagrime bangnandome 'l viso'.

Composers such as Bartolino, Paolo, Andrea dei Servi and Zaccara were still at work in the first decade of the Quattrocento. Zaccara seems to have had some contact with England;[136] Paolo celebrated the victory of Florence over Pisa in his Madrigal 'Godi, Firenza, po' che se' sì grande' in 1406.[137]

Manuscript Sources

As we have observed, some of the most important sources of Italian Trecento music, all copied in Italy, contain a double repertory of contemporary French and Italian pieces. Very often the Italian scribe had an imperfect knowledge of French and badly distorted, or even omitted the French texts; the Italian has, on the whole, survived in a much more satisfactory state. Of the major sources we should list:

1. (*PR*) 'Codex Reina', Paris, B.N., n.a.fr.6771.[138] Late fourteenth-century, copied probably in Padua, as is suggested by the high incidence of works by Bartolino, Jacopo and Giovanni. Part I (Italian) contains 40 Madrigals, 62 Ballate and 1 Caccia; Part II (French) contains 43 Ballades, 7 Rondeaux and 28 Virelais.[139] There is also a fifteenth-century supplement.[140]

2. (*Mod*) Modena, Biblioteca Estense, ∝ .M.5,24 (*olim* lat.568).[141] N. Italian. Two main sections: fascicles 2, 3 and 4, copied in the late fourteenth-century, more elaborately copied and illuminated, contain mainly French Ballades, with Latin and Italian compositions interspersed; fascicles 1 and 5 are almost entirely devoted to Matheus de Perusio and are probably early fifteenth century.

3. (*Pit*) Paris, B.N., ital 568.[142] N. Italian, late fourteenth-century. Contains 163 Italian, 35 French and 9 sacred Latin works. Apparently one of the main sources for the Squarcialupi Codex.

4. (*Lo*) London, B.M., Add.29987.[143] N. Italian, late fourteenth-century. The only source to indicate the form at the head of each work, e.g. *ballata, chaccia, madriale*. There are 45 Ballate, 35 Madrigals, 8 Caccie, 15 Dances and a small number of religious pieces; in addition there are three French Virelais, 'Or sus' and two others attributed to Donatus and to Franciscus de frorençia (Landini?).

5. (*FP*) Florence, Bibl. Naz. Centrale, Panciatichi 26.[144] N. Italian, early fifteenth-century. Contains 151 Italian and 24 French compositions.

6. (*Sq*) 'Squarcialupi Codex'. Florence, Bibl. Laurentiana, Palat.87.[145] A 'collector's piece' in its own time, compiled for the Florentine organist Antonio Squarcialupi, who died in 1470. Each composer has a separate section devoted to his works, each preceded by his portrait in an illuminated Initial. Nearly every one of the great Trecento composers is well represented, apart from the early Piero and Giovanni and the late Paolo.

7. (*Luc*) 'Codex Mancini'. Lucca, Archivio di Stato and Perugia, Bibl. Communale and Pistoia, Archivio Capitolare del Duomo.[146] A late fourteenth-century manuscript separated into fragments, the vellum being reused for legal documents.

8. (*PadA*) Padua, Bibl. Universitaria, MSS 1475 & 684 and Oxford, Bodleian Library, Canonici Pat. lat. 229.[147] Fragments of a larger late fourteenth-century manuscript originating from the Abbey of St. Justin in Padua, and later used by the monks for bookbinding.

Principal Trecento Song Forms and Styles

The three main forms of Italian Trecento lyric poetry set to music were the Madrigal, the Ballata and the Caccia. Taste changed from a preference for the Madrigal in the earlier part of the century, reflected in the works of Giovanni da Cascia and Jacopo da Bologna, for instance, to a bias towards the Ballata in the later years, as we find them in Francesco Landini or Bartolino da Padova. The Caccia was less common at all times. Each of the forms, as was the case in France,[148] may be divided into two principal sections of music I and II.

The **Madrigal**[149] has stanzas which must always contain three or multiples of three lines, usually of eleven syllables each although seven-syllable lines do occur. The ritornello, which is *not* a refrain, completes the form and contains only two lines which rhyme with one another; for this the music usually changes time. Occasionally there is text for two ritornelli to be performed consecutively at the close. As is the case with the French 'fixed forms', the possibility of surface variation is considerable. For example, in Jacopo:

Music: I I II
Text: $a_{11}b_{11}a_{11}$ $b_{11}c_{11}b_{11}$ $c_{11}c_{11}$ ('Non al suo amante')

Music: I I II
Text: $a_{11}b_{11}b_{11}$ $a_{11}b_{11}b_{11}$ $c_{11}c_{11}$ ('Nel bel zardino')

Music: I I II
Text: $a_{11}b_{11}b_{11}$ $b_{11}c_{11}c_{11}$ $b_{11}b_{11}$ ('Di novo è giunto')

Music: I I I II
Text: $a_{11}b_{11}b_{11}$ $a_{11}c_{11}c_{11}$ $d_{11}d_{11}d_{11}$ $d_{11}d_{11}$ ('Oselleto salvazo')

Music: I I I
Text: $a_{11}a_{11}a_{11}a_{11}b_{11}b_{11}$ $a_{11}a_{11}a_{11}a_{11}b_{11}b_{11}$ $a_{11}a_{11}$ ('Soto l'imperio')

In a few instances in the Codex Reina (*PR*) a return to the first stanza is indicated at the end of the ritornello; either this is an error on the part of the scribe, imagining that he was copying a Ballata, or, more likely, it is an indication that the entire song should be sung through twice. In the case of Jacopo's 'Aquil' altera / Creatura gentil / Uccel di dio' the ritornello is equipped with only one line of text, but has an *ouvert* and a *clos* ending; either the whole form has to be repeated or else the ritornello alone performed twice. That greater exceptions could occur is illustrated by Jacopo's 'O in Italia', in which four lines of text are set to the first music section. Madrigals are set for two voices more often than for three, all lines with text and therefore sung, contrary to the usual French practice. They are often characterised by florid embellishment, while the texts, as we have seen, are normally serious and expressive in nature, with much use of allegory and reference to classical antiquity. Fairly common is the device of delaying the entry of the second voice, as in Jacopo's 'Di novo è giunto un cavalier errante', a delightful allegory of Winter as a knight on prancing steed shod with ice.

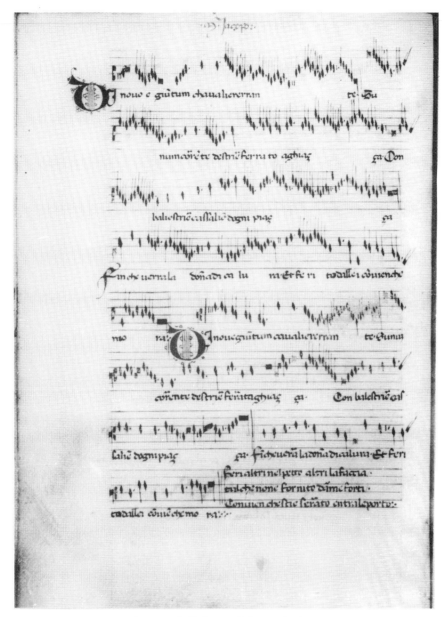

Jacopo da Bologna: Di novo è giunto

(Jacopo da Bologna: Di novo è giunto — bars 1 - 14)

From the later years we may compare Bartolino's 'Imperial sedendo', for two voices plus an inner, apparently instrumental line with no text:

(Bartolino da Padova, Inperiale sedendo — bars 1 - 20)

Deservedly the most famous Madrigal of all, perhaps, is Landini's triple setting, after Machaut and the Motet tradition, of three texts reminiscent of Jacopo's 'Oselleto salvazo', lamenting a decline in both musical and moral standards:

I *Musica son, che mi dolgo piangendo*
   Veder gli effetti mi' dolci e perfetti
   Lasciar per frottol' i vaghi intelletti.

   Perchè 'gnoranza 'n viçi ognun costuma;
   Lasciasi 'l buon e pigliasi la schiuma.

II *Già furon le dolcezze mie pregiate*
    Da cavalier', baroni e gran signori.
    Or son imbastarditi i genti cori.

    Ma di musica sol non mi lamento
    Ch'ancor l'altre virtù lasciate sento.

III *Ciascun vuoli narrar musical note,*
     E compor madrigal, cacce, ballate,
     Tenendo 'gnun in la so autenti carte.

     Chi vuol d'una virtù venire in loda
     Conviengli prima giugner' alla proda.

[I am Music, and I grieve and weep to see my sweet and perfect effects abandoned for frivolity by fine minds. / For Ignorance invades every sphere; they leave what is good and take the froth.

Once my delights were praised by knights, barons and great lords. Now noble hearts have been corrupted. / But I grieve for more than music, since all other virtues have been abandoned.

Everyone wants to compose music, and write madrigals, cacce and ballate, and all have a high opinion of their own creations. / Whoever wishes to receive praise for his talent must first have some worthwhile achievement!]

(Francesco Landini: Musica son/Già furon/Ciascun vuoli — bars 1 - 18)

The **Caccia**[150] is similar to the Madrigal in that it closes with a ritornello, again normally in contrasting mood with the body of the text. Jacopo made two different settings of his 'Oselleto salvazo', one of which uses canon in the first music section, a feature essential to the Caccia. Normally the Caccia is for three voices or two voices plus a lower instrumental line and exploits hunting calls and similar dramatic effects to an even greater extent than the French 'realistic Virelai'. It is debatable whether the Italian Caccia was derived from the French *Chace*, a relatively early example of which appears in the Ivrea manuscript.[151] The canonic element was all that survived into Machaut's *Chaces* in his *Lay de la Fonteinne*. Certainly hunting poems, boisterous in intention, were commonly written in Trecento Italy, whether in the usual lengthy Caccia stanza form or not. Giovanni Sercambi, for example, in his *Novelle*, quotes a Madrigal by Niccolò Soldanieri marked by characteristic vivacity, a skittish piece in which the lady is the huntress and much play is made on cuckoo cuckoldry:

A fornivol vo. Cu cu un cucul fammi . . .[152]

Six out of eight pieces by Maestro Piero, nearer the beginning of the century, use canon and may be considered as a transitional stage from Madrigal towards Caccia; for example, Piero's two-voice 'Chavalcando per un giovine accorto':

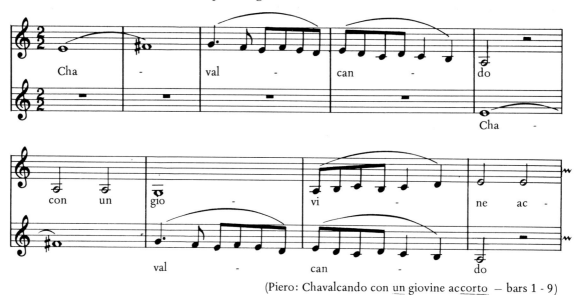

(Piero: Chavalcando con un giovine accorto — bars 1 - 9)

To a Soldanieri text, Lorenzo's 'Apposte messe veltri e gran mastini' is for two voices in the body of the piece, making spirited use of calls to the dogs:

(Lorenzo: Apposte messe — bars 23 - 26)

but falls into a single line, presumably for the two singers in unison, or answering each other, for the ritornello, where the sounds of hunting horns are heard:

(Lorenzo: Apposte messe — bars 78 - 84)

A similar effect, but in polyphonic form, may be heard in Niccolò's 'Dappoi che 'l sole', in which the lover's heart catches fire. Alarm bells are rung, and warning trumpets sounded:

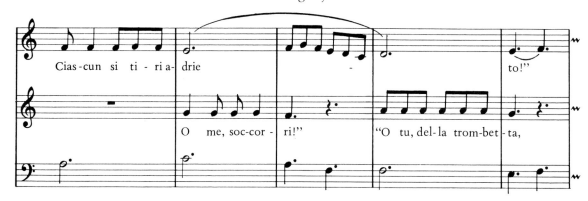

(Niccolo: Dappoi che 'l sole — bars 110 - 119)

Other works in Caccia form similarly stray from the original hunting context, be it for quail or partridge, deer or chamois, and depict exciting fishing scenes (e.g. Landini's 'Così pensoso'), sailing (e.g. Piero's 'Con dolce brama'), or bustle in the market-place (e.g. Vincenzo da Rimini's 'Nell' acqua chiara').

Of particular interest is an anonymous Caccia in the manuscript *FP* for two voices and instrument but with French text 'Quan ye voy le duz tems venir'. This seems to be a rare example of a late fourteenth-century French composer attempting the Italian canonic form:

(Quan ye voy le duç tens — bars 1 - 8)

The **Ballata** is similar to the French Virelai in its underlying pattern I II II I. The number of lines set to each section may vary, as may the number of syllables to each line and also the rhyming scheme. If sufficient text is available, the form is repeated, always recommencing with the refrain, that is the text first sung to section I. It is usual also to end with the refrain, though in the manuscript this may not always be indicated. The second section of music often has an *ouvert* and a *clos* ending for the first and second-time bars, but this is not always the case. As examples of typical structures, we may take:

Music: I   II   II   I   ⌠I
Text: A_{11} b_{11} b_{11} a_{11} ⌊A_{11} (Bartolino, 'Sempre se trova in alta dona amore')

Music: I   II   II   I   ⌠I
Text: $A_{11}A_{11}$ $b_{11}a_{11}$ $b_{11}a_{11}$ $a_{11}a_{11}$ ⌊$A_{11}A_{11}$ (Henricus, 'Il capo biondo, li capilli d'oro')

Music: I   II   II   I   ⌠I
Text: $A_{11}B_7B_{11}$ $b_{11}c_{11}$ $b_{11}c_{11}$ $c_{11}b_7b_{11}$ ⌊$A_{11}B_7B_{11}$ (Joh. Baçus Correçarius, 'Se questa dea de vert d'onestate')

Music: I   II   II   I   ⌠I
Text: $A_{11}B_{11}B_5A_7$ $c_{11}c_7d_7$ $c_{11}c_7d_7$ $d_{11}e_{11}e_5a_7$ ⌊$A_{11}B_{11}B_5A_7$ (Landini, 'Donna, che d'amor senta, non sì mora')

More three-part Ballate than Madrigals are known, but the two-part type predominates. The presence of untexted voices no doubt indicates that instruments took part in their performance, as in one of the loveliest, Landini's 'Gram piant' agli ochi e grave dogli al core':

(Francesco Landini: Gram piant' — bars 1 - 9)

Francesco Landini: Gram piant' agli ochi

A further Ballata of Landini's, 'Questa fanciulla', is of particular interest since a probably fourteenth-century instrumental arrangement of it appears as an interpolated page in the Codex Reina (*PR*). The opening of the arrangement is quoted below (p. 69), but we give here the first bars of the song version to facilitate comparison:

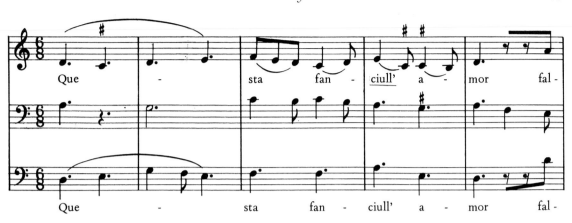

(Francesco Landini: Questa fanciull' amor — bars 1 - 11)

An excellent example of a more complex Ballata setting, in a style similar to Bartolino's, is 'La nobil scala', which contains exciting passages of imitation and hocketing, as in the closing bars of section I, on the penultimate syllable of the line:

(La nobil Scala — bars 44 - 53)

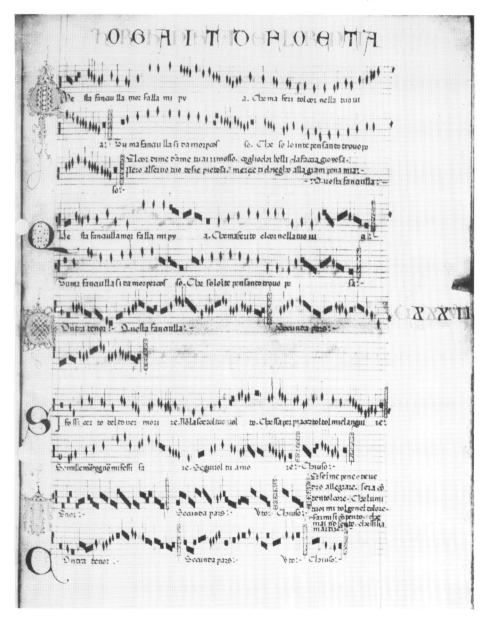

Francesco Landini: Questa fanciulla

Motets and Church Music

The Motet was not fostered in Italy and few example are known. Jacopo's example, 'Lux purpurata / Diligita justiciam', on the LUCHINUS V(I)CECOMES acrostic, is for two texted voices over an instrumental *Tenor*. There seems to be relatively little in common between this and, say, the roughly contemporary and highly-organized Motets of Machaut. The *Tenor*, apparently, is not liturgy-derived, nor is it treated isorhythmically. Rather, the piece is through-composed almost in *conductus* style, though rests of a bar or more each time are distributed through all parts to produce two-part writing most of the time. Rhythmically the piece is not adventurous, but French influence may be detected in the exchanges between voices in the closing bars:

(Jacopo da Bologna: Lux purpurata/Diligite justiciam— bars 51 - 67)

Some of the more advanced late fourteenth-century Motets with Latin text in the manuscript *Mod*, if not those in *Ch* only, should perhaps be included among Italian compositions.[153] The problem here, apart from anonymity, is to determine the origin of Latin works among a mixed Franco-Italian repertory. At the very least the *Mod* examples again demonstrate a taste for such pieces in the French style among certain, though probably limited, circles in Italy.

Music for the **Mass**[154] is similarly less abundant in Trecento Italian sources, no doubt in part due to the absence of the Papacy in Avignon during the Exile, for much of the surviving French Mass music comes from this source. No complete Mass by any single composer is known; the movements most favoured for polyphonic setting were the *Gloria* and the *Credo*, mostly straightforward settings for two voices. From the earlier part of the century we may take a *Credo* by Bartholus de Florentia, a composer probably slightly senior to Giovanni da Cascia. The style is simple but flowing, the upper part embellished a little:

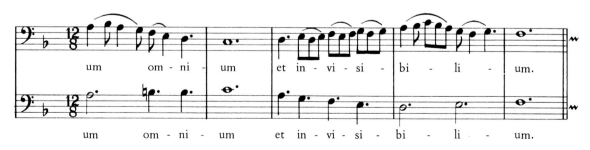

(Bartholus de Florentia: Credo — bars 1 - 15)

Later in the century Mass settings, like those from Cyprus,[155] tended to adopt secular song styles akin to the Ballata and the Caccia. Lorenzo Masini, for instance, mentioned by Villani[156] as an important predecessor of Landini active c.1350–70, gives a *Sanctus* in which faster movement is sometimes given to the lower voice and imitation is exploited:

(Lorenzo: Sanctus – bars 20 - 27)

Instrumental Music

In the field of instrumental music Italy can provide more of interest than England or France. Purely instrumental performances of songs were acceptable, as we saw in Sollazzo's versions using a harp, and some manuscript sources omit or give only the first few words of the text, making a vocal performance impossible unless the singer had already memorized the text. The Codex Reina (*PR*) contains on folios 85r and 85v two pieces apparently for keyboard, probably added before the turn of the century. The second of these is incomplete and unidentified; the first is an arrangement of Landini's 'Questa fanciulla', the opening of which may be compared with the original on p.65 above:

(Questa fanciulla (*PR*) — bars 1-21)

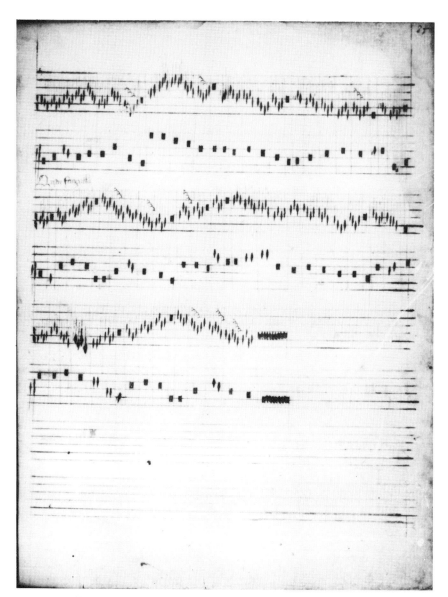

Francesco Landini: Questa fanciulla (Keyboard version)

Similar arrangements, though mostly more ornate, are contained in the manuscript *Fa* (Codex Bonadies, Faenza, Bibl. communale 117), from which we have already seen a French example, p.39 above. For further comparison we may take the *Fa* version of Bartolino's Madrigal 'Imperial sedendo',[157] already quoted on p.58 above. The *Tenor* line remains unchanged, but a new and embellished upper part is added. The style of this embellishment indicates the type of ornamentation which no doubt was frequently practised in performance in the fourteenth and fifteenth centuries:

(Imperial sedendo *(Fa)* — bars 1 - 6)

Particularly valuable is the collection of Trecento dances preserved in the manuscript *Lo* (London, B.M., Add. 29987). These are all single-line melodies obviously instrumental in character; unwritten are the drone accompaniments and parts for drums usually added in modern performance and which seem to constitute the intended effect. The eight initial dances may be classed as *Estampies* much in the thirteenth-century French tradition, with up to five sections always alternating with the refrain which begins the piece. The titles are colourful: 'Goia', 'Isabella', 'Tre Fontane', 'Belicha', 'In pro' etc. and the first confirms the *Estampie* connection: 'Istanpitta Ghaetta':

(Istanpitta Ghaetta — bars 1 - 14)

The dances following include four *Saltarelli* full of springing movement, e.g.:

(Saltarello — bars 1 - 14)

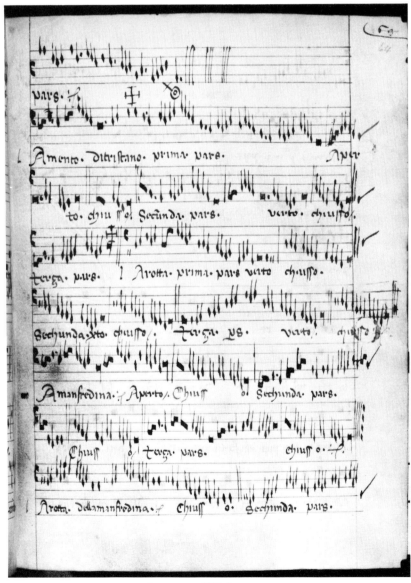

Lamento di Tristano

There is a spry 'Trotto', like an *Estampie* but much abbreviated, and two pieces, 'Lamento di Tristano' and 'La Manfredina' which begin slowly but are each followed by a spirited 'Rotta' based initially on the slow dance melody:

(Lamento di Tristano — bars 1 - 10)

(La Rotta — bars 1 - 7)

These are dances of a popular nature, somewhat mechanical in their repeated motifs, removed from the flow and graceful sophistication of the great monuments of Trecento song.

3. Britain

Religious Polyphony

The largest extant repertory of English polyphonic music of the thirteenth and early fourteenth centuries is comprised of fragments recovered from bindings of manuscripts originating in Worcester, no doubt part of the repertory once sung in the Cathedral there. The fragmentary nature of the sources makes assessment difficult, but the impression is strong that Worcester Cathedral was one of the most important centres of music in 'ars antiqua' style.[158] Some of the pieces certainly originated in France, whereas others seem to be original English compositions. When the influence of the more advanced French Ars Nova style, best represented for Britain by the Old Hall manuscript, was felt, the Worcester repertory was abandoned and suffered the common fate of outmoded writings; the precious manuscripts were cut up for use in bookbinding.

The repertory consists mainly of Gradual and Alleluia compositions for the Mass and Responds for the Offices, Conducti, Organa, Hymns, Sequences and Motets. Some of the Motets are based on identified chants, others are freely composed. Most of the repertory is for three voices, though there are some examples of two and four-part writing. A typical procedure is interchange between the top two voices over a repeated foundation, as for example in No 92, the Conductus 'Salve rosa florum', bars 43–70. The top voice in bars 43–56 reappears in the second voice bars 57–70 and *vice-versa,* with a small modification in bars 68–69:

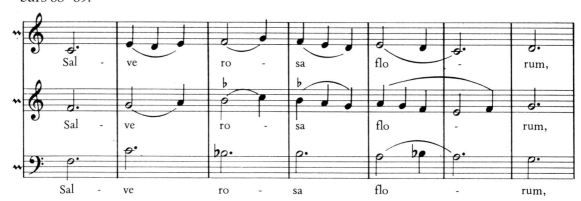

Sa - lu - tis pu - er - pe - ra,

Sa - lu - tis pu - er - pe - ra,

Sa - lu - tis pu - er - pe - ra,

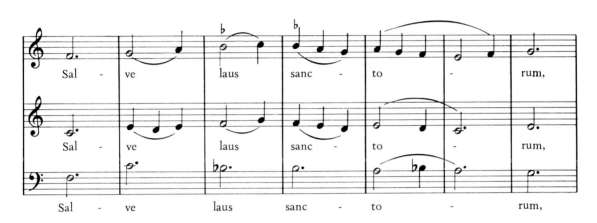

Sal - ve laus sanc - to - rum,

Sal - ve laus sanc - to - rum,

Sal - ve laus sanc - to - rum,

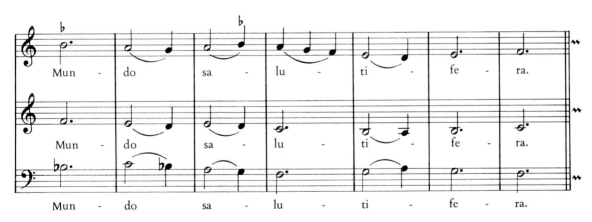

Mun - do sa - lu - ti - fe - ra.

Mun - do sa - lu - ti - fe - ra.

Mun - do sa - lu - ti - fe - ra.

(Salve rosa florum — bars 43 - 70)

The harmonic style of this piece is described as *fauxbourdon*, that is a predominantly parallel movement in fourths with frequent $\frac{6}{3}$ chords; this is typical of many English compositions of the period.

Not far from Worcester, in Evesham Abbey from 1298, the Benedictine monk Walter Odington composed his important theoretical treatise, the *Summa de speculatione musicae*.[159] In Odington's day, under the rule of Abbot John de Brockenhampton, the Abbey was considerably enlarged, in particular by the addition of a great and beautiful chapter-house, which was decorated by a painter brought especially from London.

Although there is no direct evidence for the performance of polyphonic music in Evesham, this setting and the example of nearby Worcester makes it very probable that the latest polyphony was heard there.

The *Summa* reflects very clearly the academic theoretical approach to music inherited from the great theorists of the past, and the continuing importance of plainchant as musical foundation for an early fourteenth-century monastic writer. There are six parts: I and II are concerned above all with proportion and number, part of the traditional University instruction in the *quadrivium;* III combines theory with practice and describes the construction of organs, bells and monochords; IV is a very brief discussion of metrics; V is an extended description of plainchant, its tones and its notation; VI concludes with a chapter on harmony, a reflection of contemporary polyphonic mensural writing and comparable with discussions in treatises by Anonymous IV, Johannes Garlandia, Franco of Cologne and Johannes de Grocheo. As F. Hammond describes the overall structure of the *Summa:*

> 'The logical arrangement of these six parts mirrors the author's concern for sufficient articulation of his material. Part I considers number itself, while Part II uses abstract number for the consideration of harmonic proportions, number expressed in sound. The instruments of Part III furnish audible demonstrations of these relationships. Part IV considers the same harmonious mathematical relationships demonstrated in time rather than in pitch, while Parts V and VI discuss plainsong and polyphony, the two kinds of sounding music.'

Although complete identification is difficult, there can be no doubt that many British monastic centres, like Worcester, used music from France with additions of their own invention throughout the thirteenth and well into the fourteenth centuries. A good example is the Priory of St. Andrews in Fife, where music of the Paris Notre Dame School was performed amid the great grey stones of that lovely cathedral by the sea; but new pieces were added too. The St. Andrews manuscript, one of the most important collections of Leonin, Perotin and Notre Dame Motets, was certainly in use in the fourteenth century, bearing witness to the continued employment of the *ars antiqua* repertory, especially in more remote areas, outmoded though it had become in France itself.[160] Especially interesting are two purely local Responds in praise of St. Andrew: 'Vir perfectus' and 'Vir iste'. Here is a short section from the first of these, showing very simple two-part writing, the upper voice faster moving, the lower in sustained notes:

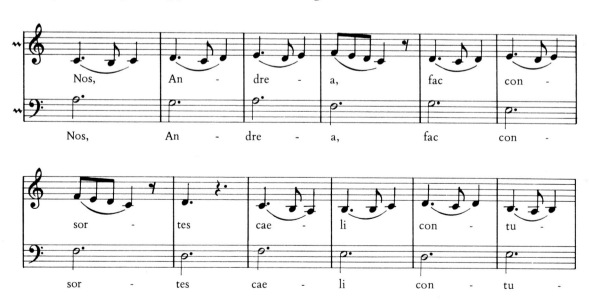

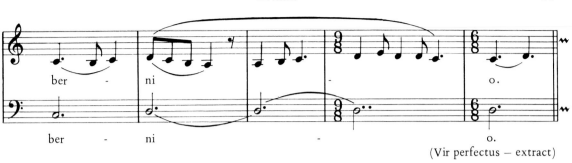

ber - ni - o.

(Vir perfectus — extract)

Pipe & Tabor, Psaltery, Fiddle, Trumpet

Much further south, in East Anglia, the Abbey of Bury St. Edmunds used a similarly mixed local and Continental repertory. The manuscript Oxford, Bodleian Library E Mus.7 certainly came from the Abbey, as a fourteenth-century inscription tells us, and this is confirmed by the discovery among the works of polyphonic music bound in at the front of two early fourteenth-century Motets in honour of St. Edmund.[161] Each is based on the Sarum antiphon *Ave rex gentis Anglorum,* itself identical musically and in part textually with the Marian antiphon *Ave regina caelorum, mater regis,* which may possibly be derived from it. The treatment of this foundation in the two St. Edmund Motets is, however, quite different. In 'Deus tuorum militum / De flore martyrum / AVE REX' the chant melody (*color*) comes twice in the *Tenor,* each appearance broken into three repetitions of a seven-bar rhythmic pattern (*talea*), giving a composition 42 bars long. The *Triplum* voice moves steadily, but the *Motetus* is faster moving and more adventurous:

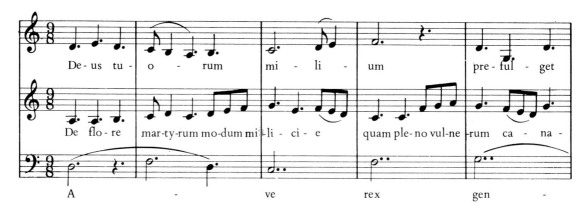

(Deus tuorum/De flore martyrum/Ave rex — bars 1 - 15)

'Ave miles celestis / AVE REX' is for four voices, more homophonic in style but exploiting the device of interchange interestingly within the upper and the lower pairs. It seems more likely that the interchanging sections without text are intended to be played on instruments than sung:

(Ave miles/Ave rex — bars 1 - 29)

Leaves bound at the back of the St. Edmunds manuscript include four Motets of later date, towards the mid-fourteenth century, all of French origin. Two use French texts, one has known French concordances, all employ Ars Nova devices such as diminution in *Tenor* repetitions, and in one case the use of isorhythm in upper voices.[162]

Other important, though fragmentary remains cannot be linked so positively with particular centres. The manuscript Oxford, New College 362, however, which preserves in full or in part fourteen Motets and four Conducti from an originally much larger collection, contains one work in common with the Worcester repertory and one with a Missal probably from the Augustinian Abbey of St. Thomas the Martyr in Dublin, B.M. Add.24198.[163] Among the incomplete items is one voice of the Motet 'Balaam inquit vaticinans/BALAAM', possibly of English origin[164] and present in its complete three-voice form in the great Notre Dame manuscript at Montpellier (Bibl. Univ. H 196), in its eighth fascicle which is thought by its editor to date from the early fourteenth century.[165] The simple style of this piece represents well the prevalent nature of Motet writing before the more adventurous innovations of Vitry and Ars Nova. There are four appearances of the five-bar *Tenor*, derived from four verses of the Epiphany Sequence *Epiphaniam Domino canamus*, with repeat and interchange in the upper voices each time; a varied four-bar refrain follows each of the four main ten-bar sections:

BALAAM

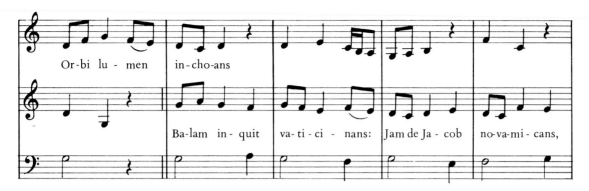

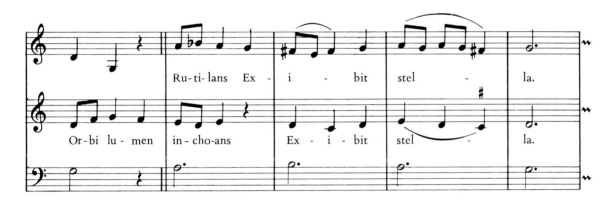

(Balam inquit/BALAAM — bars 16 - 29)

The surrounding bars 1–15 and 31–58 are textless and could be given a purely instrumental performance.

Also from the binding of a book now in the Bodleian Library is the manuscript Hatton 81, leaves containing two complete Motets, two complete and one incomplete Conducti[166] of a similar nature to those we have considered.

Generally recognized as a hall-mark of native 'English' style is the fondness for parallel movement especially using thirds and sixths. Particularly good examples of this procedure, which was to continue as a dominant feature of fifteenth-century carol writing, are to be found in the manuscript B.M. Sloane 1210, the initial and final binding leaves of which include settings of a troped *Kyrie,* a *Gloria* and *Credo,* and the hymn 'O lux beata Trinitas'. Here is the opening of the *Kyrie*:

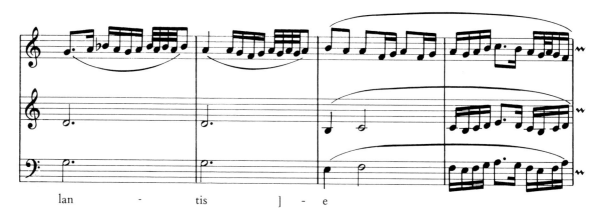

(Kyrie – bars 1 - 10)

Numerous fragmentary sources remain to show these same easy-going, pleasant-sounding characteristics in fourteenth-century Sequence settings, for example this section from an incomplete source, Cambridge, Pembroke College, MS 228:[167]

(Nos ergo labiles – bars 1 - 6)

The most famous musical collection of all from medieval England, the Old Hall manuscript, now B.M. Add.57950, is a nearly complete and beautifully copied repertory mostly of Mass music used by the royal Household Chapel in the early fifteenth century. For the first time in the history of English music a long list of composers are named. Most of them: Byttering, Cooke, Lambe, Power, Pycard, Sturgeon, Tyes, for example, were active in the early years of the fifteenth century; more advanced pieces by Dunstable and Forest were added in a later hand. It is evident from recent research, however, that some of this music was composed in the late fourteenth century and, indeed, much of it bears the stamp of French Ars Nova style.[168]

A *Gloria* and a *Sanctus* are attributed to 'Roy Henry'; this was once thought to mean Henry VI, then Henry V, but there is good reason to suppose that Henry IV (1399–1413) is the true solution. At all events, a section from Roy Henry's *Gloria* will show at once the entirely different nature of this music in comparison with earlier English examples we have examined and its great similarity with late fourteenth-century French song style, in particular, it might be said, with similar song-style Mass settings in the French-Cypriot repertory. The French fondness for hemiola, syncopation and hocket are all here in some degree:

Citole, Fiddle. Psalter of Robert de Lisle

(Roy Henry: Gloria — bars 35 - 45)

Further confirmation both of the late fourteenth-century dating of part of the collection and of Continental influence, comes from the identification of two of the composers, one from France and the other from Italy. The Frenchman Mayshuet appears as 'Mayhuet de Joan' and 'Matheus de Sancto Johanne' in certain Continental sources.[169] He is known in all for three Ballades including 'Inclite flos', a Latin text in praise of the Avignon Pope Clement VII, two Rondeaux and the Motet 'Ave post libamina / Nunc surgunt' in Old Hall. He is known to have been a singer in the service of Louis, duc d'Anjou in 1378, and was attached to the Chapel of Clement VII from 1382--86. Part of the rather odd Latin 'Triplex I' text of his Motet indicates that he also found employment in England:

> The active, distinguished Frenchman composed this song on French melodies: but after he revised it with the Latin language it more often became sweet to the English . . .[170]

His indictment of singers who 'seek their best song' and 'multiply the short notes' when they see some important person in church, rather than to the glory of God, together with his recommendation of 'careful movement of the voice' possibly accompanied by 'stringed instruments', all this being worth more than 'ignorance, blind assumption and complicated vulgarity' implies a certain conservatism in his approach. His Ballade 'Science n'a nul annemi'[171] follows a similar theme in its protestations against amateurism and a too facile approach to musical composition. His Old Hall Motet[172] is isorhythmic in all parts, but with a limited use of syncopation and no really florid passages:

(Mayshuet: Are post libamina/Nunc surgunt — bars 1 - 7)

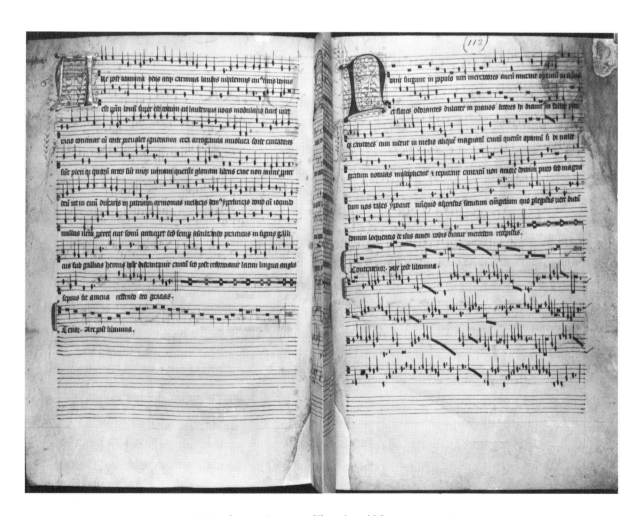

Mayshuet: Are post libamina / Nunc surgunt

The Italian Zacar is represented by an incomplete version of a three-voice *Gloria* with added text 'Gloria, laus, honor' in Motet style in the *Contratenor*. He is no doubt to be identified with Magister Zacharias, a singer of the Papal chapel featured in a place of honour as composer in the sumptuous collection of Trecento music in the Squarcialupi Codex, though there seem to have been several musicians of that name and the position is a little confused.[173] The best candidate must be Antonio Zachara da Teramo who left another *Gloria* specifically labelled *anglicana*.[174] The Italian origin of this Old Hall composer is certain, and much of the later Old Hall repertory bears witness to Italian influence.[175] His *Gloria*, which is found in six sources, including one now in Warsaw, is best preserved in the manuscript Bologna, Bibl. G.B. Martini, Q 15. The initial entries of the voices are staggered; the style is simple and much more part of 'early Renaissance' music, anticipating Dufay, than of the florid dissonance of 'Ars subtilior'. As in Italian song, the *Tenor* has a text:

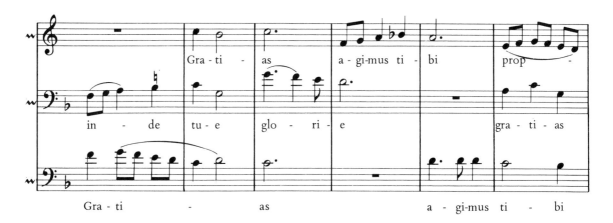

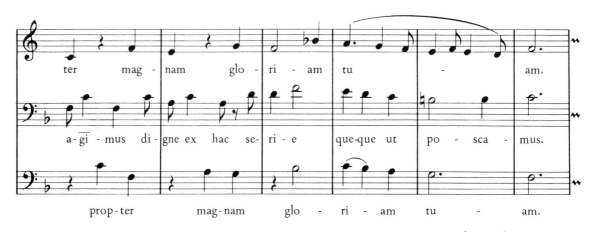

(Zacar: Gloria — bars 18 - 29)

The Chapel Royal

The English royal Household maintained an important chapel choir throughout our period, a choir Chaucer must have had many an occasion to hear. A memorandum from the slightly later *Household Book of Edward IV*[176] shows that the 'Chapleyns and Clerkes of Chapell' also had it as their duty to entertain on certain Feast days:

Memorandum that the King hath a song before him in his hall or chambre uppon All-Halowen-day at the later graces, by some of these clerkes and children of chapell, in remembraunce of Christmasse, and so of men and children in Christmasse thorowoute; but after the song on All-Halowen-day is don, the steward and thesaurer of household shall be warned where hit likith the King to kepe his Christmasse.

The names of many of the members of the Chapel Royal, as well as of minstrels, are to be found among such documents as the Wardrobe Book and Livery Roll, Issue Rolls of the Exchequer and Household Accounts.[177] The names of the singers often betray their place of origin; for example the Accounts between 1342 and 1374 in the reign of Edward IV show payments to: John de Wodford, Robert de Kyngeston, John de Maidenston, John de Leek, William de Lambhoth, William de Yepeswich, Robert de Bury, Edmond monachus de Bury, Robert de Walton, John de Corby, Richard de Medford, John de Kendale, John de Salesbury, John de Grantham, John Excestre. Among the separate Queen's Chapel we find, for example, Richard de Raundes, Thomas de Chynham, John de Derby. By far the most important name, musically speaking, preserved in Chapel Royal accounts in 1364–5, 1366–8, 1370 and 1372–4 is that of John Aleyn. He was without doubt the composer of the famous 'musician Motet', 'Sub Arturo / Fons citharizancium / IN OMNEM TERRAM', which lists the names of thirteen of his Chapel Royal contemporaries.[178] This brilliant composition survives in the important late fourteenth-century French repertory manuscript *Ch*, which is intimately connected with the circle of Gaston Febus, comte de Foix, at Orthez. It is most likely that he journeyed there in the entourage of the Black Prince, who may have been served by John Aleyn, as he certainly was by some of Aleyn's contemporaries, and who came into contact with Gaston several times during his residence in Bordeaux from 1363 as Prince of Aquitaine.[179] The composer's name is given in this manuscript and in one further source, the Italian Bologna, Bibl. G. B. Martini, Q 15, as Alanus, and he signs himself in the closing stanza of his *Motetus* text as 'J. Alanus minimus', recommending himself humbly and trusting that praise of others will protect him from envious tongues. B. Trowell's invaluable researches led him to the conclusion that John Aleyn 'was obviously a trusted servant of Edward III and was well rewarded for his work'. He was nominated to a prebend in St. Paul's cathedral in London in 1361 as 'King's clerk, John Aleyn'. In 1362 he became a canon of Windsor. He died in 1373.[180] It was B. Trowell's suggestion that Aleyn's ceremonial Motet was written for an especially magnificent meeting of Garter Knights at Windsor Castle in 1358, on St. George's Day. Edward III was celebrating the Black Prince's victory over the French at Poitiers in 1356, and for the occasion completed the Round Tower, to house his Round Table, since the Order imitated the ideals of the legendary King Arthur. Early though this date seems for the musical style in question, it would be nice to think that Chaucer was present and met some of the musicians named: John of Corby, Richard Blith, William Mugge, Nicholas of Hungerford, William Tideswell, Simon Clemens, for instance. Much later, in 1390, Chaucer was in Windsor in a different capacity, as Clerk of the King's Works, supervising repairs to St. George's Chapel.

Aleyn's Motet is an outstanding monument to medieval ingenuity in its own right, and a striking demonstration of how it was possible for an Englishman to master the most sophisticated late fourteenth-century French isorhythmic techniques. The list of Chapel Royal singers in the *Triplum* text is balanced in the *Duplum* by a list of famous musical authorities: Tubal, Pythagoras, Boethius, Pope Gregory I, Guido, Franco of Cologne:

Fontes hii sunt seculi,
adhuc quorum rivuli
cuncta regna rigant.

[They are springs from which streams flow to irrigate every kingdom in the world.]

Furthermore, the penultimate of the six stanzas of the *Duplum* text describes the musical structure of the composition:

> *Huius pes triplarii*
> *bis sub emiolii*
> *normis recitatur,*
> *ut hii pulsent Dominum,*
> *quorum numeri nonum*
> *triplo modulatur.*

It emerges from this that the *Tenor* (*pes*) is to be performed three times with a diminution of two-thirds on each occasion, that is a change from $\frac{9}{8}$ to $\frac{6}{8}$ to $\frac{4}{8}$, represented in the Bologna manuscript by the conventional signs ⊙ ₵ and C. in addition, each section of the *Tenor* and *Triplum* involves an internal triple repetition, giving a ninefold structure in all. The example shows the eighth of these divisions, with the *Tenor* in its shortest values, quite independent of the different metres running above it:

(Alanus: Sub Arturo/Fons citharizantium/IN OMNEM TERRAM — bars 113 - 128)

Instrumental Music

It is likely that the many dance-like textless passages in the linking *caudae* of thirteenth-century church *conducti* were either derived from contemporary dance or intended for instrumental performance.[181] As in France and Italy, the possibility was always present of giving purely instrumental performances of pieces originally involving voices. The manuscript Bamberg IV.6,[182] copied just after 1300, even contains a wordless piece specifically called 'In saeculum viellatoris', this being one of a group of five variations in three parts on the 'In saeculum' theme from the Easter Gradual Verse 'Confitemini'.[183] An extended and lively dance-tune in the manuscript Oxford, Bodleian Library, Douce 139 suddenly bursts into three parts.[184] The *estampies* and *danses royales* of the thirteenth century[185] were doubtless still popular in the fourteenth century and are comparable with the fourteenth-century Italian repertory in the manuscript *Lo*.[186] Robert de Handlo, writing in England in 1326, mentions the *estampeta*.

Robertsbridge Fragments

The specific contribution of an English source to fourteenth-century instrumental music consists of four pieces for portative organ keyboard or clavichord, on two folios bound with a Register from the Abbey of Robertsbridge in Sussex. The 'Robertsbridge Fragments' are notated in a special way, with letters indicating the lower of the two lines, the earliest known example of so-called 'German organ tablature'.[187]

The first and last pieces contained in this source are incomplete. Of the four remaining pieces, the first two are *estampie*-like in character, divided into the traditional sections or *puncta*, with fast-moving and obviously instrumental figuration:[188]

(No. 2 (f. 43r) — bars 27 - 34)

(No. 3 (f. 43v) — bars 1 - 9)

The next two pieces are comparable with the Faenza Codex arrangements of fourteenth-century French and Italian song,[189] but relate to an earlier date, for they are versions of two Motets by Philippe de Vitry from the *Roman de Fauvel*. Since the *Fauvel* musical interpolations were made in 1314 and the Robertsbridge Fragments are generally admitted to date from c.1330, this is a particularly good example of the close contact between England and France and the speed of transmission of such material in the fourteenth century. The first of these, found in three sources altogether, '[Adesto] Firmissime, fidem teneamus',[190] is the *Motetus* of the *Fauvel* Trinity Motet 'Firmissimi, fidem teneamus / Adesto, Sancta Trinitas / ALLELUYA':[191]

to   ]   Fir -   mis - si -

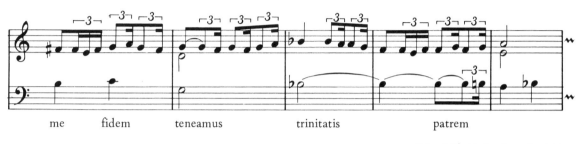

me   fidem   teneamus   trinitatis   patrem

(No. 4 (f. 43v) — bars 1 - 14)

This Motet is quoted in Vitry's own *Ars Nova* treatise and in the Erfurt *Compendium*.[192]

The second, 'Tribum, quem non abhorruit', is basically the *Triplum* of Philippe de Vitry's Motet 'Tribum, quem non abhorruit / Quoniam secta latronum / MERITO'.[193] This was the most popular of the *Fauvel* interpolations, for it occurs in six sources altogether, including the fifteenth-century *Rostocker Liederbuch*,[194] and was quoted three times by contemporary theorists, including Philipoctus de Caserta.[195] The opening of the Roberts-bridge version[196] is given below:

Tri - bum   quem   non ab -   hor - ru - it

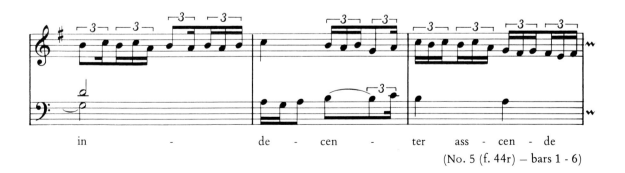

in -   de - cen -   ter   ass - cen - de

(No. 5 (f. 44r) — bars 1 - 6)

It is noteworthy that the arranger simply took the first upper voice to enter in the Vitry original as his upper line, *Motetus* in the one case, *Triplum* in the other. Both pieces, in the vocal form, also appear in the manuscript Brussels, Bibl. roy. 19606.

An obvious feature of the Robertsbridge arrangements of these Vitry Motets, though one which commentators seem generally to overlook, is the presence of a line of text with the music in the manuscript. This strongly suggests the continued involvement of a singing voice, perhaps doubled by the instrumental line, though underlay in the source is far from accurate.

Latin Song

The fourteenth century, in England as on the Continent, inherited a great repertory of Latin verse, both secular and sacred,[197] and continued to add to it. As is the case with vernacular verse of the period, it is not always certain that music was involved, since in so many cases the verse alone has been preserved. Some forms are more obviously song styles than others and these probably were intended to be sung, especially since, in the English context, we are mainly concerned with simple and traditional types, far removed from the complexities of late fourteenth-century French style which, as we have seen, confirmed a divorce between musicians and poets.

Hymns from the past were still favoured, while new hymns were created. The *Alma redemptoris* which forms the main theme of Chaucer's *Prioress's Tale* was composed by Hermanus Contractus (1013–1054) in the Abbey of Feichenau. He also composed the equally felicitous *Salve Regina* and was an important theorist. The *Alma redemptoris* melody was often used later in the Middle Ages incorporated into the texture of polyphonic compositions:

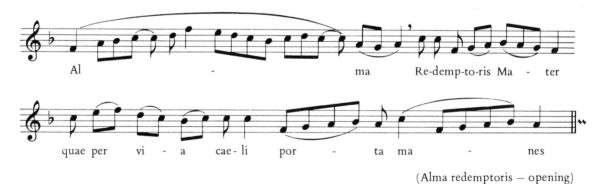

(*Alma redemptoris* — opening)

An English translation of this was made by William Herebert, a Franciscan Friar who died in 1333 at Hereford:

> *Holy moder, þat bere Cryst*
> *Buggere of monkunde,*
> *Þou art ȝat of hevene blisse*
> *Þat prest wey ȝyfst and bunde.*
> *Þou sterre of se rer op þe volk*
> *Þat rysing haveht in munde.*
> *In þe þou were after and raþer,*
> *Whar-of so wondreth kunde.*
> > *Of Gabrieles mouþe*
> > *Þou vonge þylke 'Ave';*
> > *Lesne ous of sunne nouþe,*
> > *So woe bisecheth þe.*[198]

Herebert made English versions of seventeen 'hympnos et antiphonas' in all, mostly of Latin texts but a few from Anglo-Norman French, in the transposition of which he seems more at ease. One of these:

> *Bysoeth ʒou in þys ylke lyf*
> *Of lyflode in þat oþer lyf*

is a paraphrase of part of a long poem or song probably composed by Nicolas Bozon:

> *Vous purveez en ceste vie*
> *De soustenaunce en l'autre vie.* [199]

Bozon, similarly a Franciscan Friar, probably from Nottingham, like many other of his colleagues in England and on the Continent, included vernacular verses or songs in some of his attractive sermons,[200] no doubt a ploy to hold the attention of his lay congregation and help instill his teaching. His name appears with a separate small collection of religious verses in B.M. Add.46919 and we know that one of his songs, at least, was actually sung in the course of one of his sermons.[201]

Angelus ad Virginem

Most important for the Chaucer context is the hymn 'Angelus ad virginem', sung by Nicholas in the *Miller's Tale*. Although this began its life as a monody in the thirteenth century, it was sometimes performed polyphonically, as the two versions (with incomplete text) in Cambridge University Library, MS Add 710 show.

The transcription below follows the first of these, in three voices; it also provides the complete text, which is known from earlier sources, and the middle English translation from B.M. Arundel 248, f.154r, 'Gabriele fram evene king'. The melody is in the middle voice:

An - ge-lus ad vir - gi - nem sub - in-trans in con-cla - ve, Vir-gi-nis for - mi - di-nem de-
Ga - bri-el fram e - vene king sent to the mai-de swe - te, Brou-te hire blis-ful ti-ding and

mul-cens, in-quit: "A - ve, A - ve, re-gi-na vir - gi - num, Coe - li ter-rae-que do-mi-
faire he gan hire gre - ten: "Heil, be thu ful of grace a - rith, for go-des sone this evene

num Con - ci- pi- es Et pa-ri- es In-tac - ta Sa - lu-tem ho - mi-
lith for ma - nes loven wile man bi comen and ta - ken fles of the mai-den

num: Tu por - ta coe - li fac - ta, Me - de - la cri - mi - num."
brith, man - ken fre for to ma - ken of senne and dev - les mith."

(Angelus ad Virginem)

The reverse of transposition into the vernacular is found in the now celebrated case of the *Red Book of Ossory*.[202] This contains sixty Latin religious *cantilenae* modelled on popular songs in both English and French. The transpositions were mostly composed by the Canterbury-trained Richard de Ledrede (i.e. Leatherhead in Surrey), who was Bishop of Ossory, in the Palace of Kilkenny, an English enclave in southern Ireland, from 1317 to 1360. He voices the opinion, often expressed by senior medieval churchmen, that for priests the singing of secular ditties constitutes a form of spiritual pollution, and his aim is to help them over their evident inclinations by providing more suitable words. The all-important explanation of this appears as a memorandum at the foot of the first page:

Attende, lector, quod Episcopus Ossoriensis fecit istas canytilenas pro vicaris Ecclesie Cathedralis sacerdotibus et clericis suis ad cantandum in magnis festis et solaciis, ne guttura eorum et ora Deo sanctificata polluantur cantilenis teatralibus, turpibus et secularibus, et cum sint cantores provideant sibi de notis convenientibus secundum quod dictamina requirunt.

[Know, reader, that the Bishop of Ossory made these songs for the vicars, priests and clerics of the Cathedral Church to sing on important holidays and celebrations, so that their throats and mouths, which are consecrated to God, be not polluted by frivolous, lewd and worldly songs; and, since they are singers, let them provide themselves with suitable tunes according to what these ditties require.]

Striking here is the acceptance by the Bishop of the possibility of using the original, worldly tunes for his *contrafacta*; it is the words of the popular songs which offend him, not their rhythms or melodies. The tunes are, indeed, identified for the would-be-singer, in sixteen cases, by the inclusion of the opening few words or lines of the original English or French:

> *Have mercie on me frere,*
> *Barfore that y go*

[Used three times]

> *Alas, how shold y synge?*
> *Yloren is my playinge:*
> *How shold y with that olde man*
> *To leven and let my lemmon*
> *Swettish of al thinge?*

[Very much in the twelfth and thirteenth-century tradition of the *chanson de la mal mariée*]

> *'Do, do', nyghtyngale synges wel ful murye,*
> *'Shal y nevre for thyn love lenger kary'*

[In the tradition of the French *rossignolet* who so dominates Spring openings and *envois* in *trouvère* poetry, and whose singing features importantly in several of the late fourteenth-century 'realistic' Virelais]

> *Harrow! Jeo sui trahy,*
> *Par fol amour de mal amy*

[Again, in the *mal mariée* tradition and bearing witness, by its direct use of French, to the trilingual ability expected of educated Englishmen in the fourteenth century]

Sadly, only one of these fragmentary *incipits* has been able to be completed, from B.M. Rawlinson D.913, a half-leaf probably from Coggeshall, Essex. This song, however, 'Maiden in the mor lay', a folk-like Rondeau related to the dance-song patterns of the *carole* so important in the French and English lyric traditions of the thirteenth, fourteenth and fifteenth centuries, almost makes up for this loss by its fresh simplicity. Here is the first stanza, together with the Bishop's version, a Nativity song 'Peperit virgo':

Maiden in the mor lay,	*Peperit virgo,*
In the mor lay,	*Virgo regia,*
Sevenyst fulle,	*Mater orphanorum,*
Sevenyst fulle;	*Mater orphanorum;*
Maiden in the mor lay,	*Peperit virgo,*
In the mor lay,	*Virgo regia,*
Sevenyst fulle,	*Mater orphanorum,*
Sevenyst fulle	*Mater orphanorum*
Ant a day . . .[203]	*Plena gracia . . .*[204]

Additional confirmation of the secular and dance origin of this song, even though the moor becomes a wood, comes from an interesting reference in a fourteenth-century Latin sermon in Worcester cathedral library MS F.126:

Et quis putus? Responditur in quodam cantico, viz. **Karole** 'þe mayde [in] þe wode lay'

to which is added the marginal explanation

þe cold water of þe well spryng.[205]

A more severe reaction, with assistance from above, to the intrusion into church of popular song, is found in the tale of the singers of Kölbigk who disturbed Mass and were condemned to dance and sing for a year, in Robert Manning's *Handlyng Synne*:[206]

> *þ'ese wommen ȝede and tolled here oute*
> *Wyþ hem to karolle þe cherche aboute.*
> *Beune ordeyned here karollyng;*
> *Gerlew endyted what they shuld syng:*
> *þis is þe karolle þat þey sunge,*
> *As telleþ þe latyn tunge,*
> *'Equitabat Bevo per silvam formosam,*
> *Quid stamus, cur non imus?'*

The *chanson pieuse* had been an important genre in thirteenth-century France. In the fourteenth century, as we have seen, popular religious songs, in Latin or in the venacular, were an extremely important part of the British musical scene. Likewise, we may note *en passant* comparable movements in Germany,[207] in Italy[208] and in Spain. Especially striking is the case of the red-bound *Liber Vermell*[209] copied in Montserrat c.1400 and which, like the *Red Book* of Ossory, has an explanatory introduction to its collection of ten Latin and Catalan hymns:

> Quia interdum peregrini quando vigilant in ecclesia beate marie de Monte Serrato, volunt cantare et tripudiare et etiam in platea de die. Et ibi non debeant nisi honestas ac devotas cantilenas cantare. Idcirco superius et inferius alique sunt scripte. Et de hoc uti debent honeste et parce ne perturbent perseverantes in orationibus et devotis contemplationibus in quibus omnes vigilantes insistere debent pariter et devote vaccare.

> [Since sometimes pilgrims, when they keep vigil in the church of Holy Mary in Montserrat, wish to sing and dance, and even in the street in daytime, but should sing there nothing but decent and pious songs, for that reason the various [songs] above and below have been written. And these should be used properly and with moderation so as not to disturb sermons in course and devout contemplation in which all pilgrims alike should dwell, and spend their time in devotion.]

Clearly, dancing as well as singing was expected among the pilgrims, and the same may well have been true at Kilkenny. Not only is the music present in the *Liber Vermell* collection, but four of the items are polyphonic in two or three parts, including a Motet with Catalan texts. Here is the first of nine stanzas in the final item, a monodic dance-song in Latin which, as Greene describes it,[210] has the 'burden-and-stanza structure of the vernacular dance-song'.

(Ad mortem festinamus)

We must remember that the Black Death ravaged most of Europe in the fourteenth century, and see this song as an early item on the theme of the 'Dance of Death', which assumed such macabre proportions in the literature and art of the fifteenth century.

English Song

That many of the clergy, despite the elevated intentions of their elders, remained addicted to popular secular song and dance music is beyond doubt. In 1388, for instance, the Dean and Chapter of Wells cathedral promulgated Statutes which alleged that Canons, apart from singing their psalms too fast, were:

present personally, hunting, fowling and fishing; caring nothing for the clerical state, they take part in dances and masques and day and night prowl round the streets and lanes of the city leading a riotous existence, singing and shouting.[211]

Dancing even went on in church grounds, reminiscent of the Kölbigk legend, as we know from the rebuke which Ralph Baldock, Bishop of London, issued in April 1308 to the people of Barking who had held dances, wrestling and 'lascivious sports' in the cemetery, 'to the scandal of the Church and the peril of souls'.[212]

Although a very large number of Middle English lyrics from the thirteenth to the fifteenth centuries have been preserved – about 2,000 in over 450 manuscripts – and fragmentary clues such as we have already seen in the *Red Book of Ossory* show us the prevalence of secular song, nevertheless the vast majority of lyrics which have come down to us are religious in nature.[213] This must partly be to do with the nature of the sources, most of which are monastic, and also with the archaic, folk-like nature of many of the songs, often reminiscent of French popular and dance song of the twelfth and thirteenth centuries; the musical settings were doubtless single-line, melodious, easily remembered and more normally transmitted by mouth rather than written down. Nevertheless, the almost total absence of native English song with extant musical setting in the fourteenth century is dismaying and, really, rather strange, even though we must remember the continuing currency and importance of Anglo-Norman French. Perhaps many of the surviving English lyrics are meant to be sung to French settings of a comparable type; we have seen how common *contrafacta* were, and it is certainly the case for Ballades and Rondeaux in the French model from Chaucer onwards.[214] Our extant examples, with the possible addition of a carol and a small Anglo-French repertory,[215] amount to a scrap of a song copied on the back of a legal document, 'Bryd one brere':

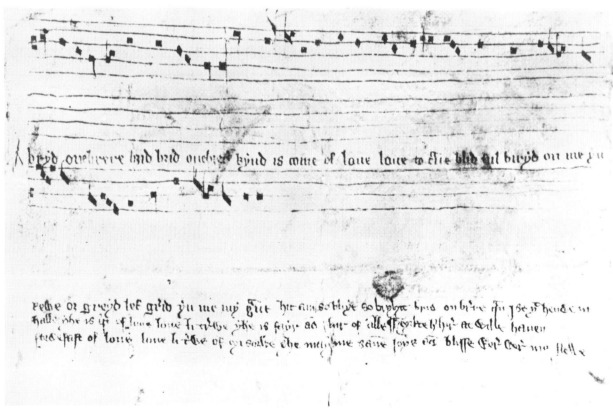

Bryd one brere

Bryd one bre - re, brid, brid one bre - re Kynd is come of

love, love to [cra - ve] Blid - ful biryd, on me yu

re - we, Or greyd, lef, greid yu me my gra - ve.

(Bryd one brere)

and the upper voice of what is possibly a late thirteenth-century Motet in the binding of Corpus Christi College, Cambridge, MS 8, 'Worldes Blisce'. This is the only English Motet text so far found.[216] The Tenor line has now been slightly clipped in the manuscript; a third voice is absent from the fragment:

Worldes Blisce

[BENEDICAMUS DOMINO]

Worl - des blis - ce have god day! Nou fram min her - te wand a - way; him

for to lo-ven min hert his went, þat þurȝ his si - de spe - re rent

(Worldes blisce/BENEDICAMUS — bars 1 - 16)

One of the richest sources for early Middle English lyrics, B.M. Harley 2253,[217] is problematic in that, although it was copied in the early fourteenth century, most of the texts contained in it probably date from the century before. This is a collection which again includes pieces in Latin and in French, and seems to have been compiled by monks at Leominster in Herefordshire. The contents are varied and often make the musical context evident. For instance:

> *I sike when I singe*
> *For sorowe that I se,*
> *When I with wipinge*
> *Beholde upon the Tre,*
> *And se Jesu, the swete . . .*

[f.80r, a Passion song]

> *Alle, that beth of herte trewe*
> *A stounde herkneth to my song:*
> *Of del that Deth hath dight us newe,*
> *That maketh me sike and sorewe among . . .*

[f.73r, a song in the *Planctus* tradition, on the death of Edward I, and possibly derived from a French piece in the same metre][218]

Chosen by R. Greene[219] as possibly the earliest English carol, with its typical burden (or refrain) and stanza form, is:

> Blowe, northerne wind,
> Send thou me my sweting,
> Blow, northerne wind,
> Blow, blow, blow!
>
> *I chot a burde in bowre bright*
> *That sully semly is on sight,*
> *Menskful maiden of might,*
> *Fair and fre to fonde.*
> *In all this wurhliche won*

> *A burde of blod and of bon*
> *Never yet I muste non*
> *Lussomore in londe . . .* (f.72v)

Greene suggests[220] that the initial burden was once an independent folk song later added to the main song in stanza form in order to adopt it to *carole* pattern.

Perhaps, rather than lament the loss of music for these lovely words, we should revert to *contrafactum* and devise a setting 'de notis convenientibus' along the lines suggested for Chaucer lyrics in *Chaucer Songs*.

The vellum fragment B.M. Rawlinson D.913 which provided us with the text of 'Maiden in the mor lay' contains other pieces of similar fairy-like and ritual character. One can almost see the leprechauns in:

> *Ich am of Irlaunde,*
> *Ant of the holy londe*
> *Of Irlande.*
>
> *Gode sire, pray ich the,*
> *For of saynte charite,*
> *Come ant daunce wyt me*
> *In Irlaunde.*[221]

Similarly dance-like in form and spirit is the Hawthorn Tree song:

> *Of everykune tre –*
> *Of everykune tre –*
> *The hawethorn blowet suotes*
> *Of everykune tre.*
>
> *My lemmon sse ssal boe –*
> *My lemmon sse ssal boe –*
> *The fairest of erthkinne,*
> *My lemmon sse ssal boe.*[222]

Carols

We have already met dance-songs in *carole* form, such is the importance of the type; it has a long history extending back to the Provençal *Ballada* via the late thirteenth-century French *Pastourelle*[223] and the *Ballette*, a mid-way form between the *Ballade* and the *Virelai*.[224] It has close parallels with the French Ballade, Rondeau and Virelai,[225] the thirteenth-century *Cantigas* of Alfonso the Wise,[226] early fourteenth-century Italian *Laude*,[227] the later fourteenth-century Italian Ballata[228] and the fifteenth-century Italian *Frottola* and Spanish *Villancico*. The reader cannot do better than to refer to the fine introduction to R. Greene's *The Early English Carols*[229] for a complete summing-up. The *carole* or round-dance was traditionally a song with refrains, possibly sung with alternation between a soloist and a group, and normally sung by the dancers themselves to mark their movement. This widespread form of courtly entertainment is described in many an idyllic scene in thirteenth-century romance, including *Guillaume de Dôle*,[230] *Le Roman de la Violette*[231] and *Le Roman de la Rose*.[232]

In Middle English literature there are similarly many comparable references. It seems possible to make a distinction, however, as the fourteenth century progresses, between *carole* in the traditional sense of sung dance music and a later usage signifying song alone. For the implication of dance with the song we may cite:

The Carol of Deduit (Roman de la Rose)

a) *Cursor Mundi* (c.1300)[233]

> *To Jerusalem þat heved bare þai*
> *Þer caroled wives be þe way.*
> *Of þair carol such was þe sange*
> *Atte þai for joy had amonge.*

b) *Sir Gawain and the Green Knight*, 11. 1025–26

> *Forþy wonderly þay woke, and þe wyn dronken,*
> *Daunsed ful dreȝly wyth dere carolez.*

c) Chaucer, *Legend of Good Women*

> *That never wakynge, in the day or nyght,*
> *Ye nere sut of myn hertes remembraunce,*
> *For wele or wo, for carole or for daunce.*

d) Chaucer, *Knight's Tale* – portrayed on the wall of the Temple of Venus are:

> *Festes, instrumentz, caroles, daunces,*
> *Lust and array, and all the circumstances*
> *Of love . . .*

e) Chaucer: *Canon Yeoman's Tale* – in which the 'sotted preest' is so described:

> *Was never noon nightingale that lust bet to synge,*
> *Ne lady lustier in carolynge . . .*

f) Gower, *Confessio Amantis*[234]

> *. . . whanne her list on nyhtes wake*
> *In chambre as to carole and daunce.* (Bk.IV, 2778–9)

> *There was Revel, ther was daunsigne,*
> *And every lif which coude singe*
> *Of lusti wommen in the route*
> *A freissh carole hath sunge aboute.* (Bk.VI, 141–5)

> *And if it nedes so betyde,*
> *That I in compainie abyde,*
> *Whereas I muste daunce and singe*
> *The hove dance and carolinge,*
> *Or forto go the newefot.* (Bk. V, 3143–6)

And for *carole* later meaning song without dance:
Gower, *Confessio Amantis*

> *Bot Slowthe mai no profit winne,*
> *Bot he mai singe in his karole*
> *How Latewar came to the Dole.* (Bk. IV, 250–2)

> *And if it so befalle among,*
> *That sche carole upon a song,*
> *When I it hiere I am so fedd,*
> *That I am fro miself so ledd,*
> *As though I were in paradis.* (Bk. VI, 867–71)

The vast majority of surviving Middle English carols, some of which have Latin or macaronic texts and many of which are set polyphonically to enchanting music,[235] date from the fifteenth century. It is perfectly possible, though, that some of these, though contained in fifteenth-century manuscripts, may have been composed in the late fourteenth century, just as the early fourteenth-century Harley lyrics manuscript is thought to hold a mainly thirteenth-century repertory. Apart from this possibility, other carols dateable before 1400 include:

a)

> *Of on that is so fayr and bright,*
> *Velud maris stella . . .*[236]

in the thirteenth-century B.M. Egerton 613 but adapted by the insertion of an initial burden in the fifteenth-century Bodleian Library, Ashmole 1393:

> Enixa est puerpera
> *A lady that was so feyre and bright,*
> *Velut maris stella . . .*[237]

b)

> *Honnd by honnd we schulle ous take . . .*

from some Franciscan sermon notes written c.1350, in Bodleian, Bodley 26.[238]

c)

> *Mayde and moder, glade thou be . . .*

written on the flyleaf of a Psalter, Yale University Library, Osborn Collection, Osborn Shelves a.l.[239]

d)

> *Nou sprinkes the sprai . . .*

in Lincoln's Inn, Hale 135.[240]

e) Four pieces preserved in the National Library of Scotland, Advocates' Library, 18.7.21:

Maiden and moder, cum and se[241]

Luveli ter of loveli eyghe[242]

Lullay, lullay, la, lullay,
Mi dere moder, lullay[243]

Lullay, lullay, litel child,
Qui wepest thou so sore?[244]

This manuscript, copied in 1372, was the work of yet another Franciscan Friar, John Grimestone, who probably came from Yorkshire.[245] The last two carols are representative of the important lullaby genre, as the Virgin sings to the Christ Child in his manger cradle. The burden and first stanza only of the first of these, with music attached and which possibly like the text dates from the fourteenth century, reappears as the single melody lullaby towards the end of the 'transitional' Franco-English collection in Cambridge University Library, Add. 5943:[246]

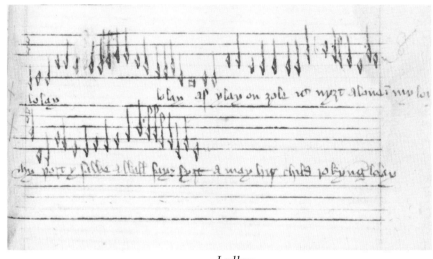

Lullay

Lullay, lullay, la, lullay
Mi dere moder, lullay.

Als I lay upon a nith
Alone in my longging,
Me thouthe I saw a wonder sith,
A maiden child rokking.

Lul - lay, [lul - lay, lul - lay, lul - lay, my de - re mo - der] lul - lay.

As I lay on Yo - le - is night a - lone in my long - ing, me -

(Lullay I)

We may compare this with the more sophisticated, though utterly serene two-voice setting of a lullaby in a further early fifteenth-century manuscript, B.M. Add.5666:[247]

Lullay, lullow, lully, lullay,
Bewy, bewy, lully, lully,
Bewy, lully, lullow, lully,
Lullay, baw, baw, my barne,
  Slepe softly now.

I saw a swete semly syght,
A blisful birde, a blossum bright,
That murnyng made and mirth of mange;
A maydin moder, mek and myld,
In credil kep a knave child
That softly slepe; scho sat and sange.

(Lullay II — bars 1 - 16)

Lyrics on the French Model

Apart from the obvious example of Chaucer, whose French-style Ballades and Rondeaux are discussed separately below and in Volume II, the influence of the French 'fixed forms' on English poetry in the late fourteenth and fifteenth centuries is well attested. Poets from the Continent such as Froissart and Granson had circulated for extended periods in the English Court. Just as Froissart's patron Wenceslas de Bohème, or the great French Dukes of Berry, Burgundy and Orléans (both father Louis and son Charles), with all the attendant nobles of the Orléans circle almost lived and breathed these lyrics, just so their English counterparts, who after all mostly spent much time during the Hundred Years War south of the Channel, vied with each other in such sophisticated pastime. Gower was perhaps not being complimentary when he thus portrays Vain-Glory:

> *And ek he can carolles make,*
> *Rondeal, balade and virelai.*[248]

But his lover boasts the same accomplishments:

> *And also I have ofte assaied*
> *Rondeal, balade and virelai*
> *For hire on whom myne herte lai*
> *To make, and also forto peinte*
> *Caroles with my wordes qweinte*
> *To settle my pourpas alofte;*
> *And thus I sang hem forth ful ofte*
> *In halle and ek in chambre aboute,*
> *And made merie among the route.*[249]

It is not always clear whether we are concerned with purely poetic accomplishment or still wth the musical art of song.[250] Christine de Pisan described Sir John Montagu, Earl of Salisbury and Knight of the Garter (born c.1350) as 'a gracious knight, loving poems, and himself a gracious poet', which is amplified by Creton into 'Right well and beautifully did he also make ballades, songs, roundels and lays'.[251] Henry of Lancaster, in the pious work of his later years, *Le Livre de Seyntz Medecines*,[252] although he does not confess to composing, had at least done some singing in his youth:

Et par ma bouche sont issu meynt chanceon amerouse qe m'ount sovent trait a pecché et altres.

[And from my mouth have come forth many a love song which often led me and others into sin.][253]

He sees music as a bad influence, or so he professes, but obviously took great delight in it:

Mes mult bien y entre un delicious chant fait d'homme ou de femme, ou de Russinol ou d'autre oisel ou estrumentz . . .

[[My ears willingly] admit a delightful song performed by a man or a woman, or by the nightingale or other bird, or on instruments.][254]

Later, in the fifteenth century, though here surely divorced from the musical context, we know that the Duke of Suffolk, who had married Chaucer's grand-daughter Alice, could make French verse almost as easily as his famous prisoner, Charles d'Orléans in exile, could turn out immaculate Ballades and Rondels in English.[255]

A transitional Anglo-French Repertory

The manuscript Cambridge University Library, Add.5943, which has already come to our attention through its inclusion of a carol, the text of which is attested well within the fourteenth century, contains a small mixed English and French repertory of songs, some of which undoubtedly also stem from the fourteenth century, more demonstrably so than those in the Bodleian Library sources sometimes compared with it, Douce 381, Ashmole 1393 and Ashmole 191,[256] though Douce 381 does contain on folio 21r a three-part French song 'Mon cuer en averoye' in fourteenth-century black notation, as opposed to the later white notation of the surrounding five English, one French and one Latin pieces. Cambridge University Library, Add.5943, besides containing the text of four further carols printed by Greene, has on folios 162r–169r a collection of secular and sacred songs in French, Latin and English.[257] The usual assertion is that this group is the earliest repertory of Continental-style songs in England. That the songs are heavily French-influenced is clear, but certainly they were not all composed in England. Of the four French pieces, all with corrupt text probably copied by an English scribe unfamiliar with French, two undoubtedly come from late fourteenth-century France: 'Esperance, ky en mon quer s'embath' and 'Le grant pleysir'. The first of these is also found in the Continental sources *Pit, Pr, Vorau* and the lost *Str*; the Cambridge version is two-part, but in *Pit* and *Vorau* a *Contratenor* is provided. The *Pit* version is almost identical with the Cambridge version and reconstruction of the three-part composition is simple:

(Esperanse ky en mon quer — bars 1 - 9)

The piece as it stands, with two lines of text only, may well be the refrain (that is the first two lines) of an eight-line Rondeau.

'Le grant pleysir' also occurs in a Continental concordance, the Codex Reina (*PR*), slightly changed as 'Le gay plaisir'. The *PR, Pr, Vorau, Str* group of manuscripts, indeed, contains pieces which, verbally or musically, find echoes among themselves. In 'Soit tart, tempre, main ou soir' (in *PR, Mod, Pr, Vorau*),[258] for instance, line 2 'Car j'ay toute ma fiance' is very similar to the second Cambridge French song 'Jeo hay en vos tote ma fiance'; we may note the line 'Soy tart, tempre, jour ou nuit', which closes 'Fait fut', the first of the three items in the *Vorau* manuscript.[259] With the possible exception of the first Cambridge French song 'Plus pur l'enor', which seems an odd man out stylistically with constant fast running quavers in the vocal part and exceptionally heavy Anglo-Norman corruption, the remaining three seem to derive from such a group of Continental late fourteenth-century repertory manuscripts.[260]

In *PR*, f.78r the text is incomplete and Italianate, lacking lines 3–4 and 7–8, but reads:

Le gay plaisir et la doce sperance
Que ay en vous, dame que tant desir,
. . . . .

. . . . .
Car il n'est rienz que je pour vous n'endure
Mais que je puise vo gent corps servir.[261]

The Cambridge version fills out the missing lines, without too severe distortion:

Le grant pleyser et le doche esperaunce
Que je ay en vos, dame que taunt desyr,
Me fayt celyr cors de totz esgrevaunce
Et prendre joye et ma dolours morir.
Car il n'ad rien que je pur vos n'endure,
Mes que jeo puis vostre gentyl corps servir.
Je vos fiance cum leal creature
Mon amour totz jours lealment mayntenyr.

However, it is when we compare the two music settings, both for three voices, that surprises emerge. The Cambridge version is a $\frac{6}{8}$ variant of the *PR* $\frac{2}{4}$, taken up one tone. In each case the barring of section I of this *Baladelle* gives fifteen divisions, and section II 16 divisions. The *Tenor* of the Cambridge version is clearly derived from the *PR* version, with occasional variants; the *Contratenor* is basically simplified; the *Cantus* is embellished.

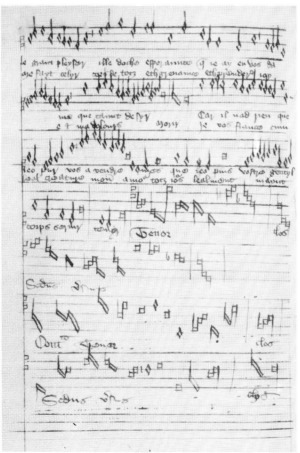

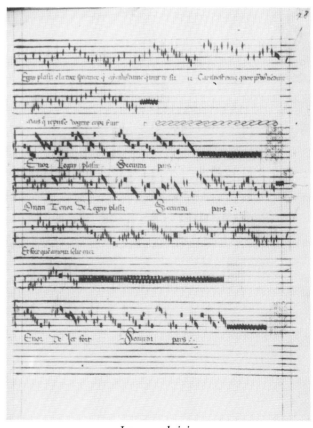

Le grant pleyser   *Le gay plaisir*

(Le grant pleyser — bars 1 - 7)

Thus at least two of the 'English French' songs in the Cambridge source are adaptations of late fourteenth-century French pieces. Maybe all the pieces are in the same case. The question is, were the adaptations made before or after the dawn of the fifteenth century and before or after the songs made the Channel crossing? At all events, the manuscript bears witness to the inextricable tangle of French and English influence and counter-influence in so many spheres of literature and music in the late Middle Ages.

A consequent question concerns the date of the English items. Could they, or at least some of them, besides the carol 'Lullay', also date from the late fourteenth century? It seems extremely possible. Here is part of the first of them:

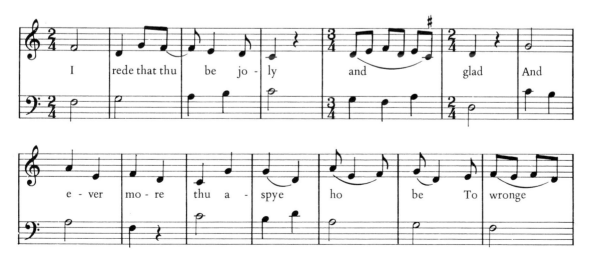

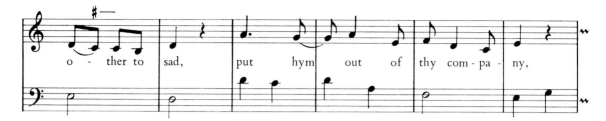

(I rede that thu be joly — bars 1 - 20)

I rede that thu be joly

The way was well paved for Walter Frye's delightful settings of 'English French' Ballades in the mid fifteenth century,[262] for John Bedyngham's setting of a Rondeau, 'Mi verry joy and most parfit pleseure', by Charles d'Orléans, or for the anonymous setting of Lydgate's Ballade 'Princesse of youthe and floure of gentylesse'.[263]

4. Chaucer

And grete wel Chaucer when ye mete
As my disciple and mi poete:
For in the floures of his youthe
In sundri wise, as well he couthe,
Of Dities and of Songes Glade
The which he for mi sake made,
The land fulfild is overal.
(John Gower, *Confessio Amantis*)

Chaucer himself was never described as a musician. No settings of his lyric works by his contemporaries or successors in the fourteenth or fifteenth centuries are known. And yet Chaucer has left us a number of poems on French models in a long-established musical tradition borrowed from France, and also makes a great number of references to musical activities in his longer works. Although these references are of a general descriptive nature, never displaying any advanced technical knowledge and often again based on Continental example, they convey more than an ordinary enthusiasm, more than simply an author's fondness for colourful material, and reflect quite clearly Chaucer's lively appreciation of everything he heard played or sung, especially in Court circles, where music was such an important ingredient in entertainment and in ceremony. Chaucer was certainly no practising musician in the way that his great French contemporary Guillaume de Machaut was; he apparently had little or no knowledge of music as a science or craft. Nevertheless, through his evident pleasure, he tells us a fair deal about the place and nature of music in the society of his time, though, to be sure, he tells us nothing that is not already well known from other sources.

Chaucer's personal involvement in the writing of songs and providing Court entertainment may have been greater than is usually supposed; his portrait of a young squire such as he himself must have been, in the *Canterbury Tales*, shows us the ideal:

Syngynge he was, or flowtynge al the day,
He was as fresh as is the moneth of May

. . . . .

He coulde songes make and wel endite,
Juste and eek daunce, and wel purtraye and write.

Geoffrey Chaucer

By 1368 Chaucer had become an Esquire of the King's Household and we see how busy he must have been in cultivating some of these talents when we read of the Duties of Squires in the happily surviving *Household Book* of Edward IV:

> These squires of household of old be accustomed, winter and summer, in afternoones and in evenings, to drawe to Lordes Chambers within Court, there to keep honest company after their cunninge, in talking of Cronicles of Kings, and of others Pollicies, or in pipeing or harpeing, synginges, or other actes marcealls, to help to occupy the court, and accompanie estraingers, till the time require of departing.

It even looks as if the young Geoffrey *sang* some of his songs, as well as told some of his stories, to keep happy the 'estraingers' at Court, if we believe what Chaucer's famous contemporary John Gower has Venus say to him in his long poem, the *Confessio Amantis*. And, of course, we cannot forget that, in the famous 'Retraccion' at the close of the *Canterbury Tales*, Chaucer begs forgiveness for:

> *many a song and many a lecherous lay.*

Chaucer did indeed 'serve Venus', in literary ways at least, in most of his works and, in *The House of Fame*, envisions his reward, as Jupiter sends an eagle to him because he has served the goddess for so long and has 'set his wit':

> *To make bokes, songes, dytees,*
> *In rime, or elles in cadence.*

Nevertheless, despite these references, there is no firm evidence to suggest that Chaucer was able to compose musical settings, and it seems certain that, even if he did collaborate with musical colleagues and even sometimes sang the results, it was the text alone which formed his main contribution. The type of sympathy he has with the spiritual effects of music seems to be conveyed in parts of his translation of Boethius' *Consolations of Philosophy*; the Lady Philosophy, an allegorical depiction which underlies so many others in medieval literature, sings to the emprisoned author, and we read:

> By this she hadde ended hir song, when the sweetness of her ditee hadde through-perced me that was desirous of herkninge.

Later, *Philosophia* tells how:

> It liketh me to showe, by subtil song, with slaklie and delitable soun of strenges, how that Nature, mighty, enclineth and flitteth the governments of things.

A further famous work which Chaucer translated rather than composed, the *Romance of the Rose*, shows how singing and playing instruments well, dancing too, are considered not simply as useful talents for entertaining visitors or whiling away the evenings, but, as the squire increases in years, as essential in his development as a courtly lover, basic requirements in the wooing of ladies. The advice to the lover is tinged with irony, nevertheless:

> *And if thy voice be faire and cler,*
> *Thou shalt maken no gret daunger*
> *Whanne to singe they goodly preye:*
> *It is thy worship for t'obeye.*
> *Also to you it longith ay*
> *To harpe and gitterne, daunce and play;*
> *For if he can wel foote and daunce,*
> *It may him greetly do avaunce.*
> *Among eke, for thy lady sake,*
> *Songes and complayntes that thou make,*
> *For that wol meven in hir herte,*
> *Whanne they reden of thy smerte.*

Ladies, too, were expected to have similar accomplishments. When the Black Knight (that is, John of Gaunt) laments his dead wife in *The Book of the Duchess*, this is an important item in his feeling of loss and bereavement:

> *I saugh hyr daunce so comlily,*
> *Carole and synge so swetely.*

In Theseus' palace too, in *The Knighte's Tale*, the poet coyly refrains from telling:

> *What ladies fairest been or best daunsynge,*
> *Or which of hem kan dauncen best and synge.*

When Chaucer lists musical instruments by name, he has certain favourites, and, although a fair number are mentioned overall, there is no attempt to reproduce the immense and virtuosic catalogues as we find them in certain works of Machaut, which Chaucer nevertheless knew well. Not all the musical scenes depicted are courtly – far from it! Often we enter into the street or the tavern – or worse – and hear music of a much more popular variety. Take *The Pardoner's Tale*, for instance:

> *In Flaundres whylom was a companye*
> *Of yonge folk, that haunteden folye,*
> *As ryot, hasard, stewes, and tavernes,*
> *Whereas, with harpes, lutes and giternes,*
> *They daunce and play at dees bothe day and night.*

Later on, we meet:

> *Singers with harpes, baudes, wayfarers.*

Nearly the same group comes into *The Maunciple's Tale*, where we read of Phebus' sorrow when told by a crow of his wife's infidelity:

> *For sorwe of which he brak his minstralcye,*
> *Bothe harpe and lute, and giterne, and sautrye.*

The small harp, so often represented in contemporary miniatures, was played with particular zest by Chaucer's Friar:

> *And in his harping, when he had songe,*
> *His eyen twinkled in his head aright,*
> *As don the sterres in the frosty night.*

Especially interesting is the description of harp playing in *Troilus*:

> *For though the beste harpour upon lyve*
> *Wold on the best souned joly harpe*
> *That ever was, with alle his fingres fyve,*
> *Touch ay o streng, or ay o werbul harpe,*
> *Were his nayles poynted never so sharpe,*
> *It shulde maken every wight to dulle,*
> *To here his glee, and of his strokes fulle.*

The gittern returns in *The Miller's Tale*, played by Absolom:

> *And Absolom his giterne hath y-take,*
> *For paramours, he thoghte to wake.*

He serenades the carpenter's wife:

> *Ful wel acordaunt to his giterninge.*

In *The Cook's Tale*, the apprentice Perkin Revelour also plays the gittern plus a second instrument, namely the rebec:

> *Al conne he pleye on giterne or ribible*

and we find that Absolom, the Parish Clerk in *The Miller's Tale*, can also turn his hand to the rebec among other tricks:

> *In twenty manere could he trippe and daunce*
> *After the scole of Oxenforde tho,*
> *And with his legges casten to and fro,*
> *And pleyen on a small ribible;*
> *There-to he song som-tyme a loud quinible;*
> *And as wel coude he pleye on his giterne,*
> *In all the toun nas brewhous ne taverne*
> *That he ne visited with his solas.*

The 'sautrye' or psaltery is used by Nicholas in *The Miller's Tale:*

> *He kist her swete, and taketh his sautrye,*
> *And pleyeth faste, and maketh melodye.*

The 'symphonye' (French 'chifonie') or hurdy-gurdy comes into Fairyland when Chaucer's absurd *Sir Thopas,* in his burlesque contribution to *The Canterbury Tales,* wanders too far:

> *Heere is the queen of Fayerye,*
> *With harpe and pipe and symphonye*
> *Dwelling in this place.*

We must add to this the 'rote' or quadrangular harp played by the wanton pilgrim Frere:

> *And certeinly he hadde a murye note:*
> *Wel koude he synge and pleyen on a rote.*

Although he names no further stringed instrument, Chaucer does give a striking description of an invisible accompaniment to the singing of the birds in *The Parlement of Fowles:*

> *Of instruments of strenges in acord*
> *Herde I so pleye a ravisshing swetnesse*
> *That god, that maker is of al and lord,*
> *Ne herde better, as I gesse.*

This is reminiscent of the 'delitable soun of strenges' in *Boethius* and suggests the more sustained effects produced by the bowed fiddle (French 'vielle').

The organ, symbol of Church as opposed to secular music, is not left out. In *The Nonne Preeste's Tale* we learn of the cockerel Chauntecleer:

> *In al the land of crowing nas his peer.*
> *His voice was merier than the merry organ*
> *On messe-days that in the chirche gon.*

It is appropriately to the background of organ music, too, that Saint Cecilia on her wedding day sings innerly of her desire to remain a virgin:

> *And while the organs maden melodie,*
> *To God allone in herte thus sang she:*
> *'O Lord, my soule and eek my body gye*
> *Unwemmed, lest that it confounded be.'*

The really rustic out-of-doors instrument, always depicted in jolly bands of dancing peasants from Books of Hours to Brueghel, is, of course, the bagpipe; this lusty instrument is used by the Miller to keep the pilgrims' feet moving as they set off on the Canterbury road:

> *A baggepype wel coude he blowe and sowne,*
> *And ther-with-al he broghte us out of towne.*

It must be a similar instrument played so horribly by Wikked-Tunge (Malbouche) in *The Romance of the Rose*, but translated rather oddly by Chaucer as 'hornpypes':

> *Discordant ever fro armonye,*
> *And distoned from melodye,*
> *Controuve he wolde, and foule fayle,*
> *With hornpypes of Cornewayle.*
> *In floytes made he discordaunce*
> *And in his musik, with mischaunce,*
> *He wolde seyn, with notes newe,*
> *That he ne found no womman trewe.*

Especially interesting, in view of Chaucer's background, are his descriptions of functional music as an important part of Court and ceremonial occasions. *The Knighte's Tale*, as we might expect, is a fruitful source of pageant music, full of bright colour and clarion calls woven into the duel of death between Arcite and his once bosom friend Palamon for the fair Emily. At the preceding banquet we read of:

> *The minstralcye, the service at the feeste.*

When the fighting begins, the brass instruments and drums come into their own:

> *Pypes, trompes, nakers, clariounes,*
> *That in the battle blowen blody sounes.*

It must be the same loud music which awakes Theseus:

> *The grete Theseus, that of his sleep awaked*
> *With minstralcye and noyse that was maked.*

It is *heralds*, rather than minstrels or private individuals, who exercise their métier here on the battlefield:

> *The heraudes left hir priking up and doun;*
> *Now ringen trompes loude and clarioun.*

It is striking to find, in *Sir Thopas*, that minstrels were to entertain the knight while he was in the process of being armed:

> *'Do come,' he seyde, 'my mynstrales,*
> *And geestours for to tellen tales,*
> *   Anon in myn armynge.'*

Trumpets and horns likewise brighten a royal wedding, in *The Man of Lawe's Tale,* though Chaucer refrains from expanding in detail:

> *What sholde I tellen of the royaltee*
> *At mariage, or which cours gooth biforn;*
> *Who bloweth in a trompe or in a horne?*
> *The fruit of every tale is fer to saye:*
> *They ete, and drinke, and daunce, and singe, and pleye.*

Similarly, in *The Clerke's Tale,* the marquis sets out to fetch Griseldis as his bride:

> *With many a soun of sondrye melodye.*

Even in the Tartar Court, according to *The Squire's Tale,* music rules the day. The King sits:

> *Herkeninge his minstralles hir thinges pleye*
> *Biforn him at the bord deliciously.*

Quite often we have to be on our guard when we read literary descriptions of musical events, just as we have to be sharply critical of hosts of angelic instrumentalists or idealized instrumental groupings in painting. The writer or the artist often let fantasy or aesthetic considerations take over and present ensembles which in no way reflect true contemporary practice. The number of different musical instruments available in the Middle Ages was superior to that in the modern symphony orchestra, but even Machaut, who lists thirty-five of them in his description of a banquet in his verse chronicle *La Prise d'Alexandrie,* would never have contemplated using more than a handful at any one time in normal performance. Exaggeration for artistic effect enters in and Chaucer occasionally succumbs to this impulse. Simply calling the music 'heavenly' is not very extreme, of course, as in that same *Squiere's Tale* description of the Court of Cambinskon, King of Tartary:

> *Toforn him gooth the loude minstralcye.*
> *Til he cam to his chambre of parements,*
> *There as they sownen diverse instruments,*
> *That it is like an heven for to here.*

More extravagant is the claim made for the feast held by Sarpedon for Troilus and Pandarus:

> *Nor in this world ther is non instrument*
> *Delicious, thorugh wynde or touche of corde,*
> *As fer as any wight hath evere ywent,*
> *That tonge telle or herte may recorde,*
> *That at that feeste it nas wel acorde.*

How like this is to Machaut's lines from the *Remède de Fortune:*

> *Et certeinnement, il me semble,*
> *Qu'onques mais tele melodie*
> *Ne fu veüe ne oïe,*
> *Car chascuns d'eaus, selonc l'acort*
> *De son instrument, sans descort,*
> *Viële, guiterne, citole,*
> *Harpe, trompe, corne, flajole,*
> *Pipe, souffle, muse, naquaire,*
> *Taboure, et quanque on puet faire*
> *De dois, de penne et de l'archet*
> *Oÿ j' et vi en ce parchet.*

In *The House of Fame* in particular, however, the vision is taken much further: a vision of great and famous harpers, some of antiquity, with little, lesser harpers beneath them, much in the way important and less important figures are often depicted in medieval miniatures; and vast assemblies of wind players using instruments of many kinds from the most sophisticated to the downright primitive. This is the nearest Chaucer comes to the kind of listing given by Machaut:

> *And eek in ech of the pinnacles*
> *Weren sondry habitacles,*
> *In which stoden, al withoute –*
> *Ful the castel, al aboute –*
> *Of alle maner of minstrales,*
> *And gestiours, that tellen tales*
> *Both of weping and of game,*
> *Of al that longeth unto Fame.*
> *Ther herde I pleyen on an harpe*
> *That souned bothe wel and sharpe,*
> *Orpheus ful craftely.*
> *And on his syde, faste by,*
> *Sat the harper Orion,*
> *And Eacides Chiron,*
> *And other harpers many oon,*
> *And the Bret Glascurion;*
> *And smale harpers with her gleës*
> *Seten under hem in seës,*
> *And gonne on hem upward to gape,*
> *And contrefete hem as an ape,*
> *Or as craft countrefeteth kinde.*
> *Tho saugh I stonden hem behinde,*
> *A-fer from hem, al by hemselve,*
> *Many thousand times twelve,*
> *That maden loude menstralcyes*
> *In cornemuse, and shalmyes,*
> *And many other maner pype,*
> *That craftely begunne pype*
> *Bothe in doucet and in rede,*
> *That bene at feestes with the brede;*
> *And many floute and lilting-horne,*
> *And pypes made of grene corne.*

The Nine Muses, in heavenly chorus, complete this vision on the grand scale:

> *And, lord! the hevenish melodye*
> *Of songes, ful of armonye*
> *I herde aboute her trone y-songe*
> *That al the palys-walles ronge!*
> *So sang the mighty Muse, she,*
> *That cleped is Caliopee,*
> *And hir eighte sustren eke,*
> *That in her face semen meke;*
> *And evermo, eternally,*
> *They songe of Fame, as tho herde I:*
> *'Heried be thou and thy name,*
> *Goddesse of renoun and of fame.'*

Chaucer's greatest musical flight of fancy, still in *The House of Fame*, is his description of the two trumpets of Eolus, the God of Wind, one black and tempestuous, the other golden and serene. Chaucer elaborates the symbolism of good renown or ill fame at length and with brilliance. First, Fame summons Eolus:

> *And bid him bring his clarioun*
> *That is ful dyvers of his soun,*
> *And hit is cleped Clere Laude*
> *With which he wont is to heraude*
> *Hem that me list y-preised be.*
>
> *And also bid him how that he*
> *Bringe his other clarioun*
> *That highte Sclaundre in every toun,*
> *With which he wont is to diffame*
> *Hem that me list and do hem shame.*

The hellish attributes of the black trumpet of ill-fame are grim indeed. Eolus:

> *Took out his blakke trumpe of bras*
> *That fouler than the devil was,*
> *And gan this trumpe for to blowe,*
> *As al the world shulde overthrow;*
> *That throughout every region*
> *Wente this foule trumpes soun,*
> *As swift as pelet out of gonne,*
> *Whan fyr is in the poudre ronne,*
> *And swiche a smoke gan out-wende*
> *Out of his foule trumpes end,*
> *Blak, blo, grenish, swartish reed,*
> *As doth wher that men melte leed,*
> *Lo, al on high fro the tuel!*

But when the second, golden trumpet sounds, balmy fragrance wafts over the world:

> *And out of his trumpe of gold he brayde*
> *Anon, and sette hit to his mouthe,*
> *And blew hit est, and west, and south,*
> *And north, as loude as any thunder,*
> *That every wight had of hit wonder,*
> *So brode hit ran, or that it stente.*
> *And, certes, at the breeth that wente*
> *Out of his trumpes mouth smelde*
> *As men a pot-ful bawme helde*
> *Among a basket ful of roses.*

Although Chaucer does not mention a great number of specific musical pieces by name, as we find in the near contemporary *Paradiso degli Alberti* by Giovanni da Prato, for instance, he does include a few titles, some identifiable and others not. The most famous of these is certainly the popular hymn *Angelus ad virginem* sung by Nicholas, the poor Clerke of Oxenforde, in *The Miller's Tale*:

> *And al above there lay a gay sautrye,*
> *On which he made a nightes melodye*
> *So swetely that all the chambre rong;*

> *And* Angelus ad virginem *he song;*
> *And after that he song the kinges note;*
> *Ful often blessed was his merry throte.*

What the 'Kinge's Note' was, is a mystery. *Angelus ad virginem,* on the other hand, dates from the thirteenth century; it survives in five manuscripts as a single melody, in one manuscript in a two-voice version, and in one manuscript in two three-voice versions. Two Middle English versions are known, 'Th'angel to the vergyn said' and 'Gabriele, fram evene king'.[264]

The popular (and entirely secular) song sung by Chauntecleer and Pertelote in *The Nonne Preeste's Tale,* 'My lefe ys faren in a lond', is preserved in a manuscript at Trinity College, Cambridge, but with no music and preceded by the words 'And for your love evermore wepyng I syng this song.' Chaucer smiles as he imagines this farmyard duet:

> *But such a joye was it to here hem singe,*
> *Whan that the brighte sonne gan to springe,*
> *In swete accord, 'my lief is faren in londe'.*
> *For thilke tyme, as I have understonde,*
> *Bestes and briddes coude speke and singe.*

As we shall see, the theme of singing birds is taken up with a vengeance in *The Parlement of Fowles.*

One of Chaucer's stories hinges totally on a hymn: *Alma redemptoris,* in *The Prioress's Tale* of the young Christian boy who was so enraptured by the words and the music that he memorized it and always sang it on his journey to and from school:

> *Ful murily than wolde he synge and crie*
> *O* Alma redemptoris *evermo.*

This journey lay through a Jewish quarter of the town, where the boy had his throat cut and his body thrown into a pit. When his mother sought him, the body continued to sing:

> *There he with throte ykorven lay upright,*
> *He* Alma redemptoris *gan to synge*
> *So loude that al the place gan to rynge.*

Not until his tongue was cut out could he cease the anthem and give up the ghost.[265]

Other songs in Chaucer are so far unidentified. There is Absolom singing to the carpenter's wife in *The Miller's Tale:*

> *He singeth in his vois gentil and smal,*
> *'Now, dere lady, if thy wille be,*
> *I preye yow that ye wol rewe on me'.*

Arcite, in *The Knighte's Tale:*

> *And loude he song ageyn the sonne shene:*
> *'May, with all thy floures and thy grene,*
> *Wel-come be thou, faire fresshe May,*
> *I hope that I som grene get may'.*

In *Legend of Good Women*, we meet more 'smale foules':

> *That songen: 'Blissed be Seynt Valentyn!*
> *For on his day I chees yow to be myn,*
> *With-oute repenting, myn herte swete!'*

The Pardoner sings to an improvised Tenor from the Summoner:

> *Ful lowde he sang: 'Come hider, love, to me',*
> *This Sompnour bare to him a stif burdoun,*
> *Was never trompe of half so gret a soun.*

There is the line in 'An amorous Complaint':

> *I may wel singe: 'In sory tyme I spende*
> *My lyf'; that song may have confusion!*

Perhaps the first three of these, at least, are inventions of the moment rather than genuine songs of the day. Particularly interesting, however, for the evidence it gives of the currency of contemporary French song in England and the constant cross-channel influence, is a French line noted twice in Chaucer in different contexts. In *The Parson's Tale* we read:

> Wel may that man that no good werk ne dooth synge thilke newe Frenshe song: 'J'ay tout perdu mon temps et mon labour'.

Near the opening of the group of Ballades on the theme of Fortune, the poet says, if Fortune does not show favour:

> *Ne may not don me singen, thogh I dye.*
> *'J'ay perdu mon temps et mon labour'.*
> *For fynally, Fortune, I thee defye!*

The proverbial line 'Qui bien aime a tard oublie', used to identify a melody to which 'Now welcom Somer, with thy sonne softe', the exquisite Roundel of the birds, is sung at the close of *The Parlement of Fowles*, similarly presents problems.[266] Although Machaut, to whom Chaucer owed so much, did set these words, it was at the opening of his *Lay de Plour*, which can in no way be made to fit Chaucer's Roundel text. Yet Chaucer specifically tells us that French music is in his mind:

> *But first were chosen foules for to singe,*
> *As yeere by yeere was alwey hir usaunce*
> *To sing a roundel at hir departinge,*
> *To do Nature honour and plesaunce.*
> *The note, I trow, maked was in France.*

It is this indication, together with the obvious modelling on French Ballade and Rondeau forms, including his translation of some Ballades by the minor Savoyard knight-poet Oton de Granson, which encourages one to experiment with the combination of Chaucer lyric texts and appropriate contemporary French music, thus restoring to his songs possibly an original but long-forgotten effect.

Arcite's song in *The Knighte's Tale* is described as a *roundel*; in *The Frankeleyn's Tale* the Squire Aurelius sings of despair in love:

> *Of swich matere made he many layes,*
> *Songes, compleintes, roundels, virelayes.*

In the *Prologue* to *The Legend of Good Women*, Chaucer tells us that among his works he has composed:

> *. . . many an ympne for your holy dayes,*
> *That highten Balades, Roundels, Virelayes.*

A three-stanza Ballade is given in *The Legend of Good Women*, a lyric interpolation entirely in the manner of Machaut. Occasionally terms such as *lay* and *song* are used loosely though, and on at least one occasion it is specified that there is no music. The Black Knight, in *The Book of the Duchess*:

> *. . . sayde a lay, a maner song,*
> *Without note, without song.*

A kind of background history to British song comes at the opening of *The Frankeleyn's Tale*, where we are told:

> *Thise olde gentil Britons in hir dayes*
> *Of diverse aventures maden layes,*
> *Rymeyed in hir firste Briton tonge;*
> *Which layes with hir instruments thay songe,*
> *Or elles redden hem for hir plesaunce*

In *Troilus and Criseyde*, Troilus's song, of three stanzas of seven decasyllabic lines each, and Antigone's song, of seven stanzas, are not described formally, though they can be assimilated into Machaut's Chant Royal and Compleinte forms. Antigone's song, incidentally, in which 'an heven was hire vois to here', is said to have been composed by:

> *. . . the goodlieste mayde*
> *Of gret estat in al the town of Troye.*

Singing, of course, comes at all turns, but not always in the same way or for the same effect. Many of the heroes and heroines of Chaucer's tales are paragons of the vocal art. Phebus, for instance, in *The Maunciple's Tale*:

> *Pleyen he coude on every minstralcye,*
> *And singen, that it was a melodye,*
> *To heren of his clere vois the soun.*
> *Certes, the king of Thebes, Amphioun,*
> *That with his singing walled that citee,*
> *Could never singen half so wel as he.*

The Wife of Bath's self-description lowers the tone somewhat:

> *How koude I daunce to an harpe smale,*
> *And synge, ywis, as any nyghtingale,*
> *When I had dronke a draughte of sweet wyn!*

Similarly unsophisticated, no doubt, is the sound produced by Alison, the carpenter's wife in *The Miller's Tale*:

> *But of her song, it was as loude and yerne*
> *As any swalwe sittynge on a berne.*

The Prioress, too, 'madame Eglentyne', produced an individual tone:

> *Ful wel she song the service divine,*
> *Entuned in hir nose ful semely.*

Chaucer clearly has no overawed respect for church music or its celebrants, as we may see in particular from his juxtapositon of the bells and chaunting of Lauds with the euphemistic harmonizing of Alison and Nicholas in *The Miller's Tale*:

> *There was the revel and the melodye;*
> *And thus lyth Alison and Nicholas,*
> *In bisinesse of mirthe and of solas,*
> *Til that the bell of laudes gan to ringe,*
> *And freres in the chauncel gonne singe.*

Chaucer has more fun with singing when he describes the crabbed old January in *The Merchant's Tale*:

> *The slakke skin aboute his nekke shaketh,*
> *Whyl that he sang; so chaunteth he and craketh.*

An odd singing comparison, too, comes into the story of Chauntecleer:

> *Agayn the sonne; and Chauntecleer so free*
> *Sang merier than the mermayde in the see;*
> *For Phisiologus seith sikerly,*
> *How that they singen wel and merily.*

When the Fox flatters Chauntecleer's voice, we are reminded of Chaucer's interest in Boethius:

> *Therwith ye han in musyk moore feelynge*
> *Than hadde Boece, or any that kan synge.*

It is the singing of birds in *The Parlement of Fowles*, a wonderful elaboration of a traditional element stemming from the garden setting of the *Roman de la Rose*, which inspires Chaucer to some of his most ecstatic lines:

> *On every bough the briddes here I singe,*
> *With voys of aungel in hir armonye.*
> *. . .*
> *Ful blisful was the accordaunce*
> *Of swete and pitous songe they made,*
> *For al this worlds it oughte glade.*

Striking is the constant reminder of the medieval association of song with dance, the fact that many song forms derive from the patterns of movement they first accompanied. The birds:

> *. . . songen, thrugh hir mery throtes,*
> *Daunces of love, and mery notes.*

In *The Legend of Good Women*, there is a particularly delightful passage where we meet nineteen ladies who were:

> *Daunsinge aboute this flour an esy pas,*
> *And songen, as it were in carole-wise,*
> *This balade, which that I shal yow devyse.*

As we have seen, the musical interest in Chaucer and his immediate background is considerable. The examination of his surviving works confirms the impression that he was nevertheless not a practising musician, together with the fact that no known contemporary setting of his lyrics has come down to us. Much seems to have been lost, though, and the singing of his songs was clearly an impressive aspect of his art. As John Lydgate wrote of him in the Prologue to his translation from Boccaccio, *The Fall of Princes:*

> *This saide poete, my master in his dayes,*
> *Made and compiled many a fresshe ditee,*
> *Complayntes, ballades, roundels, virelaies,*
> *Full delitable to here and see,*
> *For which men shulde of right and equyte*
> *Sith he in englisshe in makynge was the best.*
> *Pray unto god to yeve his soule good rest.*

5. Minstrels

Se il vous fault menestreus ou aprentis,
alés en la rue aus jougleurs, vous en trouverés de bons
(*Statutes of the Paris Corporation des Menetriers, 1321*)

Minstrelsy in the Middle Ages in general, as in the fourteenth century in particular, was a vital and colourful ingredient in life at all levels, and on all kinds of occasion. The mere fact of singing or performing on an instrument did not necessarily make one a minstrel, of course, and we have immediately to exclude those noble ladies and gentlemen who, as in the descriptions by Boccaccio and Giovanni da Prato, found pleasure in domestic music-making of their own. In the Middle Ages, as later, musical accomplishment was a desirable quality in those of gentle birth, especially in ladies; Jacopone da Todi, in his *Lauda* XXI, depicts women and boys singing and playing instruments as an entirely acceptable spectacle:

> Se vedea assembianto – de donne e de donzelli
> Andava con strumento – con soi canti novelli.[267]

There are some notable instances of noble ladies performing in particular on the harp: Isabeau de Bavière, wife of Charles VI, for instance, who purchased cases and strings in 1394 and 1416,[268] or Valentina Visconti, wife of Louis d'Orléans, who had one of her harps repaired in 1397 and in 1401–2 had as a maidservant 'Marion la harperesse',[269] or Isabelle de France, daughter of Charles VI, married to Richard II in 1396, and who had one of her harps repaired in 1405.[270]

We should also normally exclude Chapel singers and choristers,[271] important members of any noble or ecclesiastical household, but who did on occasion double as secular entertainers. Similarly, 'secretary-composers', the outstanding example of which is Machaut, are a category apart. Broadly speaking, on the professional plane, the distinction is between composers, many of whom we have seen named in the manuscript sources, and performers, though occasionally the two are combined, as for example in Senleches who both composed and played the harp especially in Aragon and in Castile, or J. de Noyon who also served in Milan, or Gaston Febus's 'troubadour' Peyre de Rius.[272]

In descriptions and account-books of the time, a number of words are used to refer to minstrels, indicative of their varied backgrounds and functions: apart from the antique *Goliard* and *Histrio*, who were more actors, we find above all *jugleour* (Lat. *joculator*; Fr. *juglëeur, jongleur*; Sp. & Prov. *juglar*), *Mynstral* (Lat. *minister, ministellus, ministrellus*; Fr.

menestrel, menetrier; It. *menestrerio;* Sp. *ministrile), wait* (Lat. *vigilator;* Fr. *Guet, gaitte*), *heralds* and *trumpeters,* not to mention *waferers, falconers* and *huntsmen.*[273]

In the fourteenth century there were still freelance minstrels of the wandering sort, but this was above all a time of consolidation for the profession, of the formation of guilds, of tighter organization, and most performers were attached to royal or influential households, or to a town as their employer, received regular income and wore a distinctive livery.

Jugglers by tradition had not only to play several instruments but be master of many tricks; as a thirteenth-century poem by the Provençal troubadour Giraud de Calanson tells us, a *jongleur* worthy of the name should be able to speak and rhyme well, be witty, know the story of Troy, balance apples on the points of knives, juggle, jump through four hoops, play the citole, mandora, harp, fiddle, psaltery . . . .[274] A similar picture is given by Langland in *Piers Plowman:*

> *I can nat tabre, ne trompe, ne telle faire gestes,*
> *Ne fithelyn at festes, ne harpen,*
> *Japen ne jagelyn, ne gentilliche pipe,*
> *Nother sailen, ne sautrien, ne singe with the giterne.*

The Savoy Princes of Achaia, in their castle at Pinerlo, near Turin, employed two *goliardis* in 1295, a *menestrerio* with a performing monkey in 1379, and in 1395 in Milan saw minstrels dancing, leaping and playing with swords, performing with a dog, and also heard funny stories and two women *menestrerie* singing.[275] Very occasionally, though far less commonly than in the past, a *jongleur* still chanted or recited the ancient epics or *chansons de geste;* at Beauvais, for instance, it was still the tradition in 1377 for the holder of the fief of the *jonglerie* to sing *gestes* 'in the accustomed place' at Christmas, Easter and Pentecost, and also in the cloister of the church of St. Pierre on Christmas Day before Mass. He could engage outsiders to perform in his place and levy twelve deniers from them. If they refused, he was entitled to confiscate their book of words or their fiddle – *il puet prendre leur livre on leur viele se ils l'ont* – a clear indication of a musical element in such recitations.[276]

Heralds, although sometimes classed with minstrels in account books and descriptions, form a distinct group, playing trumpets of various sizes, essential to add to the brilliance of ceremonial occasions, jousts and battle scenes. In Bologna from 1313 silver trumpets sounded in all religious and state occasions; in 1356 there were nine players, which we may compare with the twenty-four Burgundian trumpeters who performed in 1428 when Philippe le Bon returned from Portugal.[227] In Froissart we read of many such moments: an expedition of the Duc de Bourbon, for instance:

> It was most beautiful and pleasurable to see the manner of their departure, how the banners and pennons richly adorned with noble arms, floated in the wind and shone in the sun, and to hear the trumpets and clarions sound out and proclaim, and other minstrels busy playing pipes and shawms and nakers, so much that the whole sea resounded with it.[278]

Or a reception for the Duc de Bourgogne and his Duchess after the siege of Tournai in 1385:

> The trumpeters, clarions and minstrels on all manner of instruments began to play and sound all together, a pleasing and melodious thing to hear.

No military scene would be complete without the clarion call, and we should remember that, until comparatively recently, this was the method of conveying signals and instructions to an army necessarily deployed over some distance. A scene of manoeuvres in

Jehan Maillart's *Roman du Comte d'Anjou* (1316) seems to show just such a use of instruments:

> *Trompes, nacaires retentissent,*
> *Bondissent cors, chevaus henissent.*[279]

Even in the very heat of battle music still served to spur the soldiers on, or to frighten the enemy, as we see in the fourteenth-century *Orfeo and Heurodis*:

> *Wele attourned ten hundred knightes,*
> *Ich y-armed to his rightes,*
> *. . .*
> *Tabours and trimpes yede him bi,*
> *And al maner menestraci.*[280]

At jousts, too, no important competitor would think of arriving without his train of heralds, minstrels, many-coloured banners and loud music. An account entry for July 1383 tells how the Duc de Bourgogne paid £150 to a number of heralds and minstrels from England who performed at a contest between his chamberlain, Guy de la Tremouille, and Pierre de Courtenay.[281] A little later Christine de Pisan, in her *Livre du duc des vrais amans*,[282] gives an extended description of a tournament with preliminary fanfares, dances at dinner, outbursts of music from the heralds and minstrels next day during the contest, especially when any participant received a heavy blow from his challenger, more music and dancing in the evening at dinner and prize-giving.[283] Heralds were often called upon to be messengers, and in Wales a particular Order of Bard-Heralds, *Arwyddveirdd*, grew up, with the function of registering arms and pedigrees as well as of undertaking embassies of state.[284]

Welsh Bards constitute an important branch of composer-performer in their own right, probably accompanying themselves on the harp in traditional fashion. It is hard to establish the extent of their musicianship, since none of their medieval music has survived; their verses are often impressive and many fourteenth-century examples, by Rhys Goch ab Rhiccert or Davydd ab Gwilym, for instance, bear striking similarity in theme and imagery to contemporary French poetry and song.[285] The bardic songs contain frequent indications of their musical context:

> *Strike the strings with the sound of the streams and the summit of the nine hills.*
> (Rhys Goch)[286]

> *The goodness of Gwen and her intelligence,*
> *Her serious conversation, inspired by the moon,*
> *The sweetness of her voice when she sings,*
> *Her notes more tuneful than the nightingale's,*
> *Have completely carried me away . . .*
> (Davydd ab Gwilym)[287]

> *If I were to compose a song in the five fine metres,*
> *I could not sing her beauty's worthy praise . . .*
> (Davydd ab Gwilym)[288]

Waits, whether employed by a town or by a noble household, were specifically watchmen, with the important function of warning from the castle turrets or the town walls of the approach of strangers, or of invaders in time of war. They were thus necessarily equipped with loud instruments, trumpets or shawms chiefly. An instrument which came itself to be known as a *wayt* (Fr. *gayte*) was probably a small but piercing shawm.[289]

In 1364 we read how the Burgundian Duke Philippe le Hardi, nervous of invasion, purchased horns and brass trumpets for the watchmen of his castles:

> . . . a brass trumpet for the castle turret at Grignon, to be blown when the watchman sees men-at-arms . . .[290]

Six field-horns:

> to be sounded, three for the Château at Cuisery and one at Sagy . . .[291]

Payment to a *waite* is recorded at Amiens in 1387.[292] The signatories to the statutes of the Minstrels' Guild in Paris in 1321 include three *guetes*, one from the Louvre.[293] Waits, naturally, were used in other and more interesting ways than the simple sounding of warnings. They sounded hours of the day,[294] or curfews, for example, and performed for visitors, probably in fanfare style. In 1377 a *gaite* played before the Duc de Berry at Lézignan;[295] in 1389 what must be the waits of Pavia (*menesteriis communitatis Papie*) played a Mayday fanfare for the Prince of Achaia, while four trumpets and two shawms (*parva bombarda*) from Milan (*communis Mediolani*) helped give him an *aubade* in September 1395.[296] Huntsmen, falconers and wayts often prove to be the same men – Ralph Wayt, for instance, appears under both headings in the account books of Edward III.[297]

In the advice on kingship drawn up for Charles VI in 1389 by Philippe de Mézières in *Le Songe du vieil pelerin*,[298] the royal tutor adopts his most moralising tone in recommending above all 'grosses trompes', long trumpets to be sounded in church to mark the elevation of the Holy Sacrament, or at important royal ceremonies, or to assemble nobles around the King to hear his orders on the battlefield. Nevertheless, albeit grudgingly, allowance is made for minstrels playing more intimate instruments (*menestreux a bas instrumens*) for relaxation and to aid the royal digestion – provided that it always be borne in mind that temporal pleasures are shallow and that true melody awaits in Paradise alone:

> . . . et aucune fois te doit souvenir de la vraie melodie des menestreux de paradis . . .[299]

Similar sentiments may be felt in a decree of King James II of Majorca in 1337, whereby *mimi* and *joculatores* may be permitted in the house of a Prince so long as they create happiness and behave decently (*cum honestate servare*), thus encouraging the monarch to be more gracious towards his subjects.[300]

Despite admonitions, Charles VI is known to have indulged excessively in secular luxuries including minstrelsy on all possible occasions. It is, indeed, above all at feasts and banquets that the minstrel proper, playing softer stringed and wind instruments and maybe singing too, comes into his own. The slightly later *Household Book of Edward IV* (1461–83) outlines this part of *mynstrelles'* normal duties:

> . . . whereof one is veriger that directeth them all in festivall dayes to theyre stacions, to blowinges and pipinges, to such offices as must be warned to prepare us for the king and his household at metes and soupers, to be the more redy in all services, and all thies sitting in the hall togyder, whereof sume use trumpettes, some shalmuse and small pipes.

Almost as on the battlefield, instruments mark the various stages of the meal, beginning with the bringing of water, washing of hands and sitting at table:

> *L'en corna l'iaue et laverent*
> *Et puis vont aus tablez seoir.*
> (Roman du Comte d'Anjou)[301]

The Marriage Feast at Cana

After the meal tables are cleared, the minstrels come forward with their various instruments, playing or singing, or dancing begins:[302]

> *Quant les tables ostées furent,*
> *Cil jugleor en piez s'esturent,*
> *S'ont vielles et harpes prises.*
> > (Huon de Mery, Le Tornoiement Antecriz)[303]

> *Erraument les napes osterent.*
> *IIII menestreil de viele*
> *Ont une estampie nouvele*
> *Devant la dame vielée.*
> > (Jean de Condé, Messe des Oiseaux)[304]

> *Chascun maine joie et leesche;*
> *Sonnent cors, trompes et arainez,*
> *Vielles, musez et douçainez,*
> *Psalterions, fresteaus, leüst;*
> *N'i ot nul qui mestier seüst*
> *Qui ne face menestrandie;*
> *Molt y avoit grant melodie*
> *Si con chascun a ce entendi.*
> > (Roman du Comte d'Anjou)[305]

> *In the castel the steward sat atte mete,*
> *And mani lording was bi him sete.*

> *Ther were trompour and tabourers,*
> *Harpours fele and crouders,*
> *Miche melody thei maked alle . . .*
> *And Orfeo sat stille in the halle*
> *And herkneth . . .*
> (Orfeo and Heurodis)[306]

The *Roman du Comte d'Anjou*, which probably originated in the Parisian circle which produced *Fauvel*, provides us with further scenes of minstrelsy, as the players gather from far and near for the rich pickings at a wedding feast:

> And in the evening the minstrels and heralds had their rewards, for no-one was absent from here to Châtellerault who knew anything about playing, and they all had a coat or cloak or some garment at the feast, I tell no lie.[307]

and in procession on the way with the bride to Mass:

> The minstrels make merry; all the houses shake; horns blare, trumpets sound: one would not have heard the thunder of God's voice, they were having such a jolly time.[308]

At the opening of the romance Jehan Maillart suggests that many types of musical entertainment are put on in order to revive the spirits of those who are ill:

> Some sing pastourelles, others perform on the fiddle songs, rondeaux, estampies, instrumental dances and dance tunes, and also on the lute or psaltery, each according to his taste, lais of love, descorts and ballades to cheer up ill persons.[309]

Fairs were another inevitable gathering-ground for minstrels. At Termonde, for instance, there was an annual carnival procession or *ommegang*, for which many minstrels from outside were especially employed by the town; in 1395 players of trumpets, nakers, pipes, lutes and harps took part, with pennons of the town colours hanging from their instruments.[310] A variant of this is the mummers' pageant such as that provided in 1377 by the citizens of London for the amusement of the Black Prince's young son Richard:

> On the Sunday before Candlemas in the night, 130 citizens disguised and wel horsed in a mummerie with sound of trumpets, shackbuts, cornets, shalmes and other minstrels, and

Bagpipes, Tabor, Cymbals, Bells, Imaginary double Trumpet, Fiddle, Organ, Psaltery, Citole

innumerable torch lights of waxe, rode from Newgate through Cheape over the bridge through Southwarke, and so to Kensington . . . After which they were feasted, and the musick sounded, the prince and lords daunced on the one part with the mummers, which did also daunce . . .[311]

Sometimes a minstrel might be sent on a mission which involved no music at all. If we take the accounts of the King of Navarra, for example, we find that in 1400 his singer Johan Huguet was sent to buy a song book for the Chapel, while in 1396 the *chantre* Gourlay was sent to Barcelona simply 'por negocios del rey', and again in 1397 to Barcelona and Saragossa to buy some clothing material for the King.[312] In 1390 Peroto and Felizoto, minstrels of the Prince of Achaia, were sent to Savigliano as an escort for a prisoner captured in Monteuil.[313]

It is often asserted that minstrels were instrumentalists rather than singers, thus:

When in 1324 in Cornhill a dealer in skins named Thomas de Lenne was so angered at the music of a minstrel named Thomas Somer that he struck him with a door-bar and pursued him to kill him, only to be stabbed himself by the said Somer, it was playing and not singing that moved him to such violent criticism.[314]

Froissart records a musical incident when King Edward III was on board ship before the Battle of Winchilsea. Sir John Chandos had brought back from Germany a piece called a 'dance'. The King had his minstrels play the accompaniment, but Chandos himself did the singing.[315]

Masked Mummers (Roman de Fauvel)

There was, however, a type of performer who sang or recited to his own accompaniment specifically described as a vocalist or *menestrel de bouche*. In 1378–79 Adenarde, *menestrerio de boche* of the Count of Flanders, performed for the Prince of Achaia;[316] the Navarra accounts mention as *juglar de boca* Sancho de Bolea in 1366, Jacme Fluvia in 1382 (also called *trobador* in 1360 and *trobador de dances* in 1373) and Pero Guillén de Narbona in 1391.[317] In France we find Hennequin Callemadin *menesterel, lequel a dit diz de bouche* before Charles VI in 1380, Nycholas le Viellart *menesterel de bouche* of the Duc d'Anjou in 1387, Quiquin, a German *menestrel de bouche* in 1393.[318] A French royal edict of 1395 aimed at the suppression of satirical songs critical of the monarchy or of the papacy specifically forbade the performance of such pieces in public places by *tous dicteurs, faiseurs de dits et de chançons, et a tous autres menestriers de bouches et recordeurs de ditz.*[319]

Shawm, Trumpet, Organ, Fiddle, Citole, Psaltery

The rôle of women minstrels also is more important than is often supposed. That their presence and costume were familiar enough to gain them admission to Court is nowhere better illustrated than in the story of how, when Edward II sat in the Great Hall of Westminster at Pentecost in 1316, a certain woman 'in the habit of a Minstrel, riding on a great horse, trapped in the Minstrel fashion', circled the tables several times before mounting the royal dais to deliver a petition. When the doorkeepers were admonished, they replied that 'it was never the custom of the King's palace to deny admission to Minstrels, especially on such high solemnities and feast days'.[320] Among the minstrels of the household of Thomas and Edmund, brothers of Edward II, we find a lady with the delightful name of Matilda Makejoye, *saltatrix*.[321] When the Paris minstrels gathered together in 1321 to draw up statutes for their guild, there were eight women signatories[322] and provision made for both *menestreurs* and *menestrelles, jongleurs* and *jongleresses*.[323] In 1319 at Christmas a woman sang before Mahaut, comtesse d'Artois, and at All Saints in 1320 she heard Jehanne *qui joue des orgues.* Her grand-daughter Marguerite de France paid three *chanteresses* in 1338. In 1347 a Jehanne de Crotot was accused of bewitching the clerk of the Bailly of Amiens, partly on the superstitious grounds that she was a *menestrelle de vielle* or *vileresse.* Three women minstrels sang and danced for the duc de Berry in Paris in 1374. In Burgundy Philippe le Hardi heard *deux chanteresses de Paris* in 1375, and twice again in 1378. When he visited Chenonceaux in 1377 he again heard singing from a *menestriere.* At Cambrai in October 1378 we find him paying *pluseurs chanteurs et chanteresses.*[324] Much appreciated in the Aragon Court was Catarina, *jutglaressa de casa nostra,*[325] also named as Catalina de Inglatera, *juglaresa* c.1350;[326] she may well be identified with the Cateline *la chanteresse* who sang for the duc de Berry in 1377.[327] In Aragon, too, we find la Sancha, wife of a Portuguese *juglar* Pedro, and Isabel *la cantadera* who, with her husband Jaquet de Portabert, received forty florins from the King of Navarra in 1385 for their performance as *juglares del rey de Aragon.* In a letter of February 1385 Peter IV of Aragon recommended the couple to the Kings of Navarra, Castile and France.[328] Nor were children excluded: in 1381 a boy of four sang for Charles VI and similar amusements had been provided for his son by the duc de Berry in 1376 and 1377.[329]

Minstrels attached to households generally received regular payments, which are recorded in many surviving account books. These same records also reveal that minstrels could expect additional bonuses during the year, as they played for their own lord or travelled to other Courts near or far. Food and clothing were usually provided, horses too, and on special occasions noble bounty could be generous. In 1290 Queen Eleanor bequeathed 39 shillings for a cup to be purchased as a gift for a minstrel from Champagne, while Edward II even granted houses to his minstrel William de Morlee, otherwise known as *Roy de North.*[330] The Earl of Lancaster, for his part, paid handsomely for special liveries for his minstrels.[331] Of the Burgundian Duke Philippe le Hardi, we read that the least he would give, even to the most humble of wandering minstrels, was worth a pair of high felt boots.[332] In 1365 he gave money to Berholt, a minstrel from Créancy, 'since on St. John's Night just passed, he played his cornamuse', and more to Symon Guiteaul, a sergeant of the Duke, for 'accompanying him softly on the cornett, since he is not an officer and on account of his great poverty'.[333] On Christmas Day 1371 Philippe gave gifts to a number of minstrels who played for him at Dijon,[334] while in 1373 he gave money to help cure his trumpeter, Berthelemi, who had fallen ill.[335] When Froissart was visiting Gaston Febus at Orthez at Christmas 1388, there were enacted great scenes of largesse:

> The same day th'Erle of Foix gave to Heraudes and Minstrelles the somme of fyve hundred frankes; and gave to the Duke of Tourayn's Minstrelles gowns of Cloth of Gold, furred with Ermyns, valued at two hundred frankes . . .
>
> (Froissart, *Chroniques* Book III)

When the Duke of Touraine's minstrels (that is Louis d'Orléans) and those of the duc de Bourbon performed before Gaston Febus and Charles VI in Toulouse in 1390, the comte de Foix gave them two hundred golden crowns, while the Sire d'Albret, to celebrate the permission he had just been granted to quarter his arms with the royal *fleurs-de-lis,* distributed two hundred francs. In Navarra in 1396 the King purchased clothing material for his *chantres de capilla* Huguet and Johaninet, and in 1397 medicines for the sick *capellan* Johan, a fox-skin to compensate his *chantre* Huguet for an injured arm, twenty measures of wheat for the same beneficiary, cloth (*medio paño de Bristol*) for the *chantre* Johan Robert, and two hundred florins to Nicholas Porchin, his organist, on his marriage to the daughter of Pierre du Bar, his harpist – a traditional gift from an overlord. In 1399 more cloth was provided for the *chantre* Enequot de Sangüesa.[336] The French King Jean II gave a silver crown to his *roy des menestrels.*[337]

Particularly important for a minstrel, naturally, was assistance in the purchase and upkeep of instruments. This too was forthcoming. For example, the Prince of Achaia in 1341 purchased for Maltaglato, his minstrel, a red and white cornemuse case bearing the Prince's arms; the minstrels Peroto and Anthonio in 1380 received help to pay for their instruments; in 1390 Peroto and Felizoto had instruments purchased (*certis instrumentis eorum artis*).[338] In Burgundy we find payments in 1368 to Henri Baudet, the Duke's drummer, to buy a new kettledrum; in 1369 to Gillet de Toul to buy a citole; in 1372 to Berthelmi Lyon for a horse and a new trumpet; while in 1384 Nicholas de la Marche was given money to buy a gold trumpet.[339] Charles V gave eight francs to his minstrel Watrequin to buy a fiddle in 1377.[340] An inventory of 1373, including instruments which belonged to Charles V himself, lists: a gittern with lion's head, in leather case; a gittern with lady's head; a gittern with ivory lamb's head; an ivory gittern.[341] Certain centres became important for the manufacture of musical instruments. Many makers settled in Paris, of course: in 1297 three trumpet-makers (*feseeurs de trompes*) petitioned for affiliation to the Paris Guild of metal workers (*forcetiers*), affirming that they were the only practitioners of their trade in the whole town;[342] in tax records from the 1290s we find a fiddle-maker, Henri aus vieles, dwelling in the rue aus Jugleeurs;[343] around 1400 there were two Parisian *luthiers* who mended harps, Lorens du Hest and Jehan du Lige.[344] The minstrels of Jean II de Châtillon travelled from Holland to Malines in 1361, 1365, 1366 and 1374 to buy instruments (*om instrumente te halen*) including flutes and nakers; his minstrel Ansken was sent in 1370 to Courtrai to buy *pipen*.[345] Later in the century organs and early clavichords (*echaquiers*) were in demand. In 1371 Jehan de Tornay was paid £100 for providing, setting-up and tuning an organ for the duc de Berry.[346] A letter written in 1379 by John I of Aragon, which incidentally refers to eight excellent singers from Avignon who sang Mass each day in his Chapel, urgently requests the provision of an organ and of an *xiquier*,[347] while in 1388 the same monarch wrote to the duc de Bourgogne to request not only an *exaquier*, but also someone who could play it.[348]

Each year in the time of Lent, when minstrelsy and merry-making were not allowed at Court, the entertainers journeyed sometimes great distances to annual Schools in order to renew their repertoire – *pro cantilenis novis addiscendis* as a 1402 record from Beauvais describes it.[349] There was a need to seek new pieces, learn new techniques, recruit new assistants, find new outlets, all in an informal way, no doubt, quite unlike the academic University or Cathedral instruction in the sacred and theoretical side of the art. Beauvais was the principal gathering-place in France for the *scolae ministorum*. Town records show that the minstrels 'of the great Lords of the Kingdom of France and of other lands' held their *escoles* there in 1384 and 1385 'as they are accustomed to do each year'. The *assemblée* of *menestrieux et corneurs* in 1399 shows the tradition to be long-lived, and minstrels were still travelling to *apprendre a l'escole de Beauvais* in 1402.[350] Lyon, Geneva and Cambrai were also popular resorts.[351] Often, a King of minstrels would summon a School to meet at a great fair in a town of his choice, as did Maître Symoen at Ypres in 1313, or many of the minstrels might be engaged by town Magistrates for special occasions if local talent was insufficient, in processions at Ascension Tide, for instance. The town records of Bruges record just such a payment to *de menestreulen die hier scole hielden*.[352] Often the host town, which benefited in extra trade and entertainment, felt an obligation to contribute towards the minstrels' expenses in any case, as we find at Mons in 1406,[353] or at Beauvais, *des graces de le ville*, in 1398. In Beauvais even the local Chapter contributed *mimis scolas artis*, and sometimes one town found funds to send its minstrels away for the refresher-course, as Abbeville to Beauvais in 1398.[354] In 1366, when Froissart was twenty-nine, he travelled to Brussels and describes a great assembly of minstrels including some from Denmark, Navarra, Aragon, Lancaster, Bavaria and Brunswick.[355] That Brussels was an important meeting-place for minstrel Schools is confirmed by a further reference in 1370, when two minstrels of Jean II de Châtillon were sent there *mede ter scolen te riden*.[356] In March 1378 Philippe le Hardi paid 100 francs for his minstrels to travel from Ghent to Germany *aux escoles*;[357] the previous year they had journeyed to an unspecified destination.[358] Germany was equally the goal of the Prince of Achaia's minstrel Prior in 1380, while the same Prince sent Hugonino, Anthonio and Peroto *ad scolas* in 1378 and the latter two again in 1379.[359] The Counts of Savoy sent their minstrels particularly to Bourg-en-Bresse; in

1377 and 1378 the châtelain there footed the bill for fodder for the horses of Savoy minstrels who were present during Lent *tenir leur escole,* and in 1387 and 1388 the same châtelain lent money to the minstrel Petreman so that he, together with other minstrels of the Count of Savoy, might hold their School in Bourg.[360] In Aragon, during the reigns of Peter IV and John I especially, it was customary to send minstrels to *las escuelas* in Flanders, Germany and France;[361] in 1378 Jacomi Sentluch (Senleches), Jaquet de Noyon, Johannes Estrumant and another were sent, and in 1379 Jacomi 'lo Bègue' (presumably also Senleches)[362] and J. de Noyon were sent again.[363] In January 1372 John I, as Infante, had provided a safe-conduct for Jacobinus de Bar, Thomas de Xaumont, Tibaut de Barrenes and Lupi *tiberalius* to travel *ad partes Francie et aliarum terrarum* and in the same month Tomasi and companions went with them to *las escuelas de Alemania.*[364] Particularly interesting are letters written by John I in 1378 suggesting that the new repertory (*mester novel*) was eagerly awaited on the return of the minstrels from abroad,[365] and in 1388 when he enquired anxiously as to the reception accorded by Charles VI to his minstrel Everli and companions, who had been instructed not only to attend the Schools, but also to bring back the latest type of instruments, of *novella guisa.*[366] In February 1381 a German minstrel Erman Hans i Henequinus, possibly the fiddler Hannequin employed by Gaston Febus, was sent with a Jacomi to the *scolas eorum artis* by the Count Pere d'Urgell.[367] *Las escuelas de Alemania* was the destination of Jacquemin Baynon and Guillemin, *ministriles,* sent from Pamplona in 1363, and they had 300 gold florins for their journey.[368] Juan and Perrinet de Acx, sent to *las escuelas* in 1375, presumably had less far to go, since they received only 200 gold florins.[369]

It appears that sometimes 'specialist Schools', for a particular type of player, were held. In Malines, for instance, we read of Schools for fiddlers in 1328 – *Dat man den vedeleren gaf te hulpe te haere scole, doen hi de vedel scole was* – and in 1368 – *Allen den vedeleren, in horescheiden, doe si te Mechelen hore schole quamen koude.*[370] Paris, inevitably, was a constant attraction, but it is unclear as to whether the type of gathering under discussion was organized by the composer Johannes Vaillant, who was there in 1369 and *tenoit a Paris escolle de musique,* as the *Règles de la seconde rhétorique* have it.[371] Certainly, it appears that the holding of Schools there grew to such an extent as to become a public nuisance, for in 1407 a Statute of Charles VI specifically forbids any minstrel without prior permission to *commencer escolle pour montrer et apprendre menestrandise,* though this may have been more a regulation to ensure the fair sharing-out of apprenticeships.[372]

Quite apart from the travelling involved in attending the annual Schools, minstrels frequently undertook extensive journeys in the employment or in the train of their patrons. When Charles de Blois was transferred from Brest to England in 1348 he had in his company seven players of the gittern, to whom he himself made an eighth in a 'musical farewell' before leaving Brest castle.[373] Machaut, as secretary-poet to Jean de Bohème, travelled extensively in Eastern Europe, but is also recorded as having received a horse in recompense for one he had lost while undertaking a journey in 1361 in the service of the Queen of Navarra.[374] When Valentina Visconti journeyed from Milan to Paris after her marriage to Louis d'Orléans in 1389, she was accompanied by three minstrels and six trumpeters.[375] Edward I took with him on an expedition to Flanders many instrumentalists and dancers, while in 1363 a *giternario* from Bruges, André Destrer, played for Edward III.[376] In 1397 Charles III of Navarra went to Paris to visit the French King, paying his *capellan y chantre de la capilla* Guillem Doladilla, together with the *chantres de la capilla* Colinet le Forestier and Guiot, to equip themselves with horses for the journey.[377] English minstrels often made their way to the Continent. Walter the Englishman (Vauthier l'Englès) played his harp to Philippe le Hardi in 1375, but came to a bad end when in 1385, at the instigation of the Bad King of Navarra, he was caught in the French royal kitchens with a bagful of poison;[378] in Olite in 1384 the same Bad King Charles heard Robert Vourdetron and his companions, English minstrels on their way to Santiago de

Compostela.[379] Some journeys were long: Guillem and Llorens, *trompeteros* of the King of Navarra, went to Normandy in 1357; two German minstrels (*dos ministriles alemanes*) passed to Navarra via Foix in 1378;[380] when the ex-King of Armenia, Leon de Lusignan, visited Navarra in 1383 he brought his own *juglar*, and in 1384 Navarra welcomed both *ciertos juglares de Borgogne*[381] and a blind entertainer (*juglar ciego*) of the duc de Brabant,[382] possibly a harper, for blind harpers appear fairly frequently in records from about this time.[383] Other journeys were local, in particular between Navarra, Aragon, Castile, Foix and Avignon,[384] or from town to town across N. Italy: for instance, in 1362 the King of Navarra paid Guillot Bertran and Guyon, *minestriles de Bayona*,[385] in 1382 a *juglar de la viola y de la rota* from Milan,[386] in 1386 Arnauton from Aragon.[387] Frequent journeyings took place between Turin, Pinerolo, Monferrato, Saluzzo, Milan, Florence, Rome, Asti, Pavia, Ferrara, Mantua, Ravenna, Genova, Montecarlo, Villefranche, Vienne, Bourg-en-Bresse, Chambery . . . .[388] Among the well-known names we may cite the harpist and composer Senleches, known to have come from the N. of France and to have been in service in Aragon, Castile and Avignon, to which town he was given expenses by the King of Navarra in 1383 to return to his employer of the moment, Pedro de Luna, cardinal of Aragon;[389] or J. Simon de Haspre, who also served in Avignon, in the Chapel of Benedict XIII in 1394, though he had earlier been employed by the King of Portugal in 1378, Charles VI in Paris in 1380, and visited Aragon in his capacity as minstrel of the King of France in 1388.[390]

Minstrel in Costume, Church Singers

Minstrels played a further important rôle by providing music for vernacular drama, both secular and sacred. In the fourteenth century little secular drama survives in anticipation of the great flowering of *farces, sotties* and *moralités* in the fifteenth century, very many of which depend upon songs or song-structures. In religious drama, on the other hand, in France especially, we have several embryonic Passion plays and above all the forty *Miracles de Nostre Dame* of the Paris Goldsmiths' Guild, in which there is clearly heavy dependence on musical effects and interludes of several kinds, quite apart from the angelic Rondeaux which characterize the genre. In this series of plays minstrels, referred to in the text as *menestrez* and *jugleors,* first appear in *Miracle 3* in 1341, with slightly disreputable acting parts as they arrive in town having heard about celebrations for the consecration of a Bishop. They fetch their instruments to play an *estampie,* heads full of thoughts of the drink they will later be able to afford. In *Miracle 7,* 1345, they provide a musical interlude in a banquet scene. These instances seem to have been early experiments, perhaps dictated by the availability of suitable performers. From 1371 to 1382, however, there seems to have been a more established troupe, or minstrel interludes were more in favour, in the climate of increased length and greater spectacular effects in the plays, and the minstrels were involved nearly every year. Formalized promises of gold, money, jewels and clothes are usually proferred with the preremptory summons to play:

> *Alez! Les menesterez vois dire*
> *Qu'ilz y viengnent sanz detriance:*
> *Seigneurs, chascun de vous s'avance*
> *De venir aux noces royaux*
> *Pour gangnier robes et joyaux –*
> *Delivrez vous!*
> (*Miracle 31,* 11. 142–147)

A rare stage direction, in *Miracle 34* of 1376, directs the minstrels to lead a King to his throne and then to bring the Queen while playing:

> Ci viennent les menesterez, et amainnent le roy en son siege; et puis vont querre la royne en jouant.

The occasional use of minstrels to provide the closing music, accompanying the cast in final procession from the stage, finds its echo in later English and Cornish plays. The last four *Miracles 37–40,* 1379–82, further 'promote' minstrels by giving them a few spoken lines either individually or in chorus, though merely to assent to the summons to perform. *Miracle 40* has a particularly charming scene which shows guests dancing to minstrels' music at wedding celebrations.[391]

The place of performance of the Goldsmiths' *Miracles* in Paris was very probably a hall attached to the church of Saint-Josse, in the very parish which was bordered on one side by the *rue aus jugleeurs,* later renamed *rue des ménétriers* and still later replaced by the *rue Rambuteau.* By the end of the thirteenth century minstrels of various kinds tended to gather in this street. The tax records of 1292 list sixty-three inhabitants, at least nineteen of whom are clearly described as *jugleeur, trompeeur* or *jugleresse.* There can be little doubt that the necessary forces for musical interludes in the *Miracle* plays were recruited here. It must have been the very concentration in one place of members of a single profession which led them to draw up statutes of a Minstrels' Guild in 1321 and to register them officially with the Provost's Office in 1341.[392] The original signatories were as follows:

> Pariset, menesterel le roy, pour lui et pour ses enfans; Gervais ot la guete; Renaut le Chastignier; Jehan la guete du Louvre; Jehan de Biaumont; Jehan Guerin; Thibaut le Paage; Vuynant Jehanot de Chaumont; Jehan de Biauvès; Thibaut de Chaumont; Jehanot l'Anglois; Huet le Lorrain; Jehan Baleavaine; Guillot le Bourguegnon; Perrot l'Estuveur; Jehan des Champs; Alixandre de Biauvès; Jaucon, filz le Moine; Jehan Coquelot; Jehan Petit; Michiel de Douay; Raoul de Berele; Thomassin Roussiau; Gieffroy la guete; Vynot le Bourguegnon; Guillaume de Laudas; Raoulin Lanchard; Olivier le Bourguegnon; Isabelet la Rousselle; Marcel la Chartraine; Liegart, fame Bienviegnant; Marguerite, la fame au Moine; Jehan la Ferpiere; Alipson, fame Guillot Guerin; Adeline, fame G. l'Anglois; Ysabiau la Lorraine; Jaque le Jougleur.

This seems to be the first firm grouping of minstrels as a Trade Guild. There had been antecedents, but none so formal or professional. The celebrated thirteenth-century

Confrerie des jongleurs et des bourgeois d'Arras was probably merely a benefit society, and the *Confrerie de Notre Dame des Ardents* in Arras, although founded by *jongleurs* to whom Notre Dame was reputed to have given a miraculous healing candle c.1105, was really a religious Guild.[393] Injunctions were issued to minstrels in Ypres in 1295 to reduce the cost of weddings, but were imposed by Magistrates rather than drawn up by the profession itself: minstrels wishing to play at a wedding feast were to pay a tax; when playing their instruments they should not approach guests within the courtyard where the ceremony was taking place; the bride and groom should pay only two *sous* to minstrels arriving on horseback from elsewhere, and 12 *deniers* if they were on foot; only two minstrels from Ypres, either men or women, could attend the wedding breakfast; there were fines for offenders.[394] There was, however, a regular Guild in Antwerp by the mid fourteenth century.

In Paris the statutes of 1321[395] were essentially framed for the self-protection of the profession, with the aim of excluding external and internal competition as much as possible. In summary, the Articles, several of which highlight contemporary abuses, were as follows:

1. No minstrel shall hire out any other performers than himself and companion, this to overcome the exploitation of inferior and outside players at extra low rates.

2. *Trompeurs* or *autres menestreurs* who have been engaged for a function must wait until it has ended before they move on elsewhere.

3. They may not send a deputy, except in the case of illness, imprisonment, or other emergency.

4. No *menestreurs* or *menestrelles* or *aprentiz* may tout for custom at feasts or weddings in Paris, or else be fined.

5. In taverns no apprentice minstrel should recommend any player, or discuss his profession, and direct any enquiries to headquarters with the words 'Sir, the laws of my profession forbid me to engage anyone but myself, but if you seek minstrels or apprentices, go to the *rue aus jougleurs,* and there you will find good ones'.

6. When a prospective customer appears in Minstrel Street, he is to be allowed to approach whatsoever performer he chooses without interference from rivals.

7. Apprentices must observe the same rules.

8. All minstrels, whether from Paris or without, must swear to obey the Statutes.

9. Any outside minstrel arriving in Paris must be required to swear to the Provost of St. Julian or to a royal appointee in charge of the Guild that he will obey the Statutes, or else be banished for a year and a day.

10. Two or three worthy representatives of the profession shall be chosen to impose fines on any offenders, half of such income to go to the Guild, and half to the Crown.

New Statutes were drawn up in 1407 and confirmed by the royal seal of Charles VI. This time there were fifteen articles which confirm the earlier dispositions while adding others concerning professional standards and making adjustments due to changed circumstances: any new member of the Guild must have been *vu, visité et passé pour suffisant par le roi des menestrels ou ses deputés,* tested and approved; no-one below standard should be permitted to play *aux noces et assemblées honorables;* apprenticeship is six years long and any master minstrel who cuts this period without express permission is to be banned from playing for a year and a day – this is to limit the number of aspirants to the profession, no doubt, and reduce competition; no minstrel may hold an *escolle* without prior permission. Particularly to be noted is the authority now accorded to the *roy des menestriers,* a title not given but implied in 1321 when the signatories were headed by the King's minstrel Pariset. Although this is the first instance of the title specifically being applied to the Head of a Minstrels' Guild, *rex* and *roy* had long been used by outstanding artists, whether elected or self-elected; in French literature Adenet le Roi and Huon le Roi are famous examples. In 1290 at the wedding of Joan of England, King Grey of England and King

Caupenny of Scotland[396] were present, while present at Westminster in 1306 were Le Roy de Champaigne, Le Roy Capenny (who also appears as a regular member of Edward I's household),[397] Le Roy Baisescue, Le Roy Marchis and Le Roy Robert. *Rex Robertus* appears again, together with *Rex Pagius de Hollandia*, in Edward II's account books.[398] There was a *coninc van der speellieden van Vlaenderen en van Artois* and a *roy des menestreulx de Hainaut*.[399] In Paris minstrel Kings included Robert Caveron c.1338–c.1349, Copin de Brequin c.1357–c.1367, Jean Portevin c.1392.[400] After popular uprisings and the 'Révolte des Maillotins' in 1382 Charles VI abolished Trade Guild Kingships, but by 1392 they were re-established. A further notable feature of the 1407 Statutes, strengthened by true royal authority and in line with other contemporary attempts at national unification, is the intention to extend the jurisdiction of the King of the Paris Minstrels' Guild far and wide *par tout nostre royaume*.[401]

The mention of a Provost of St. Julian must have been added into the early Paris Statutes after their original formulation, but refers to a further important circumstance and feature which helped to establish and maintain the Minstrels' Guild there, namely the foundation of a special minstrels' hospital and Chapel, Saint-Julien des Menetriers. In 1328, so the story goes,[402] a minstrel called Jaques Grave de Pistoye *alias* Lappe from Lombardy and Huet, a royal wait and who came from Lorraine, were moved by pity at the sight of a crippled beggar-woman over the road from Lappe's house, where they sat chatting. They found out who owned the land and purchased it in order to build a small

Chapelle de S. Julien des Menetriers, Paris

hospital. They also bought a neighbouring house, erected a cloister and fitted a room up with beds. An alms-box hung at the door, a porter and nurse were soon found. They even had an official seal, the image of which included St. Julian and his wife, Christ as Leper, and St. Genois playing the fiddle. The founder minstrels belonged to the Paris Guild, which increasingly became involved in the running and maintenance of the hospital. Next door a Chapel was built, the façade of which was adorned with angel musicians and larger statues of the two patron Saints on each side of the entry, St. Julian and St. Genois still with his fiddle.

Part of the Guild's funds and income from fines was diverted into this good cause, and this was confirmed in the Statutes of 1407.

One further document of particular interest for the story of fourteenth-century Parisian minstrelsy survives, and this reaffirms the need to control abuses committed by less worthy members of the profession. It is a police order of 1372[403] which requires tavern-keepers not to serve drinks after hours, and minstrels similarly to stop playing, apart from indoors or at weddings, since a number of robberies had been committed using minstrelsy as a cover – *sous umbre de ce que plusieurs menestriers vont jouer et corner de nuit.*

In England the only known example of a fourteenth-century Minstrels' Guild is that of Tutbury, where John of Gaunt, Duke of Lancaster, had a castle. He appointed a King of minstrels there and required all minstrels within his jurisdiction to perform there on set occasions, or else be arrested. Here is the original French charter of 1380, followed by an English translation, both from seventeenth-century sources:

> Johan par la grace de Dieu Roy de Castille et de Leon, Duke de Lancastre, a touts ceux qui cestes nos letres vorront ou orront, saluz. Sachés nous avoir ordenoz, constitut et assignez nostre bien amé le Roy des ministraulx deins nostre Honour de Tuttebury qu'ore est, ou qui pur le temps serra, pur prendre et arrester touts les ministraulx deins meisme nostre Honour et franchise queux refusent de faire lour services et ministralcie as eux appurtenans a faire de ancient temps a Tuttebury suisdit annualment les jours del assumption de nostre dame. Donants et grantants au dit Roy des ministralx pur le temps esteant plein poiar et mandement de les faire resonable-ment justifier et constrener de faire lour services et ministralcies en maner come il appeint et come illonques ad esté usé et de ancient temps accustomé. En testimoigniance de quel chose nous avons facit faire cestes noz letres patents, don souz nostre privie seal a nostre Castell de Tuttebury le .xxij. jour de August le an de regne nostre tresdulces le roy *Richard* second quart.[404]

> JOHN By the Grace of God King of Castile and Leon, Duke of Lancaster, to all them who shall see or hear these our Letters greeting. Know ye we have ordained constituted and assigned to our wellbeloved the King of the Minstrells in our Honor of Tutbury, who is, or for the time shall be, to apprehend and arrest all the Minstrells in our said Honor and Franchise, that refuse to doe the Services and Minstrelsy as appertain to them to doe from ancient times at Tutbury aforesaid, yearly on the days of the Assumption of our Lady: giving and granting to the said King of the Minstrells for the time being, full power and commandement to make them reasonably to justify, and to constrain them to doe their Services, and Minstrelsies, in manner as belongeth to them, and as it hath been there, and of ancient times accustomed. In witness of which thing, we have caused these our Letters to be made Patents. Given under our privy Seal at our Castle of Tutbury the 22 day of Aug. in the 4th year of the raigne of the most sweet King Richard the second.[405]

Beverley in Yorkshire was an important meeting-place from early times for minstrels between the rivers Trent and Tweed; the superb collection of fourteenth-century stone carvings of minstrels playing many different instruments in the Minster, and others in St. Mary's Church, prove the importance of this assembly, although renewed Statutes for a Guild date only from 1555:

Whereas it has and hath bene a very auncient custome oute of the memories of dyvers aiges of men heretofore contynually frequented from the tyme of kyng Athelstone of famous memorie somtyme a notable kyng of Englande as may appeare by olde bookes of antiquitie that all or the more part of the mynstralls playing of any musicall instruments and thereby occupying there honest lyvinge inhabiting dwelling or serving any man or woman of honoure or worshipe or citie or towne corporate or otherwise between the rivers of Trent and Twede have accustomed yerely to resorte unto this towne and borough of Beverley at the rogation days and then and there to chose yearly one alderman of the mynstralls with stewards and deputies authorized to take names and to receyve customable dueties of the bretherin of the sade mynstralle fraternytie. And the alderman to correcte amende execute and contynue all such laudable ordynances and statutes as the have heretofore ever used for the honestie and profit of there science and art musicall to be only exercised to the honour of God and the conforthe of man . . .[406]

There are some signs of fourteenth-century religious Guilds with mainly or even entirely minstrel membership, however. Among the Guilds submitting certificates as to their history and status, by royal edict of 1398, we find one for Minstrels and Actors in Lincoln, and another for Minstrels alone, founded in 1350, at St. Giles in Cripplegate, London – 14d a week was provided for any minstrel unable to exercise his profession by reason of poverty or old age.[407] Possibly of later date, but curious nonetheless, is the appointment of a minstrel together with other officials and a cook, at a salary of 1s 4d per year, in the Guild of St. Peter at Bardwell, Suffolk.[408]

Minstrels were attached to households great and small. The surviving evidence alone for their great activity in the fourteenth century is overwhelming and it would be tedious here to catalogue all the names that have come down to us. We find them employed by military leaders such as Bertrand du Guesclin[409] or a Captain of Piedmont.[410] Important churchmen employed them, such as the Cardinal of Aragon[411] or the Prior of Durham.[412] The Lord of Mantua, Marquises of Ferrara and Monferrato, Counts of Savoy and Flanders, Princes of Achaia,[413] Dukes of Milan and Brabant,[414] as we have seen, all had their minstrels, as did all members of the English[415] and French[416] royal families.

As we have observed, minstrelsy was a necessary adjunct to all kinds of festivity in the fourteenth century; no important occasion, no wedding, no celebration could take place, at whatever level of society, without music being there. But it is, of course, royal celebrations which most impress, with vigour, colour and often quite amazing numbers of entertainers. A glance across the century's history reminds us of the lavish scale of such events and reveals how it was that so many minstrels could continue to exist, even throughout the Hundred Years War. In April and July 1290, for instance, there were splendid ceremonies at Westminster, first for the marriage of Edward I's daughter, Joan of Acre, to the Earl of Gloucester, then of the fifth daughter, Margaret, to John, the son of the duc de Brabant.[417] King Grey and King Caupenny were there, and no less than 426 minstrels attended the second celebration. The bridegroom gave £100 which the King's harper, Walter de Storton, distributed among the players. More celebrated is the assembly at Whitsuntide 1306 in Westminster,[418] which Edward I held preparatory to his punitive expedition to Scotland. An enormous number of entertainers arrived at this *magnum convivium,* as the *Annales Londoniensis* put it:[419] apart from the minstrel Kings and the tantalising listing of Maistre Adam le Boscu,[420] there were players on harps, lutes, psalteries, tabors, fiddles, organs, trumpets, nakers, gitterns, bells, citoles, crowds and flutes; there were minstrels from the service of the Count of Warwick, the Bishop of Durham, the Patriarch, the Prince, the Count and Countess of Hereford, Lord Percy, The Count and Countess of Lancaster, the Count of Arundel and of several lesser households; minstrels came from all directions, including from across the channel – Champagne, Boulogne, Brabant, Quitacre, Leylonde, Blida, Duffelde, Swylingtone, Normanville, Colecestria, Salopia, Trenham, Brayles, Clorleye, Scardeburghe etc.; some had delightful 'professional' names such as Matilda Makejoye, 'Perle in the Eghe', or Reginald 'le Menteur'.[421]

In 1377 the Emperor Charles V visited the French King Charles V in Paris, and again music was provided, as Christine de Pisan tells us:

> After supper the King retired, and with him the Emperor's son and as many barons as could enter, into the Parliament Chamber, and there, as is their wont, minstrels played on soft instruments as sweetly as it is possible to play; and there the two Kings sat on two high thrones, each canopied with a ceiling embroidered in golden fleurs-de-lis.
>
> (*Livre des fais et bonnes moeurs du sage roy Charles Quint*)

At the coronation of Charles VI in 1380 in Reims, Froissart tells us that 'more than thirty trumpets rang out so clearly that it was amazing'. When his Queen, Isabeau de Bavière, made her entry into Paris in 1389 there were entertainments and tableaux-vivants the length of her route. Froissart was again present to see:

> The procession then passed on the second Gate of Saint-Denis, where a castle had been set up, as at the first Gate, and a heaven full of stars with a representation of God the Father, the Son and the Holy Spirit, sitting there in majesty. In this heaven young choir-boys dressed as angels were singing very sweetly. As the Queen passed beneath it in her litter, the Gates of Paradise opened and two angels came out and began to descend. They held in their hands a magnificent crown of gold set with precious stones, and this then set gently on the Queen's head, at the same time singing these lines:

> > *Lady with the lilied gown,*
> > *Queen you are of Paris town,*
> > *Of France and all this fair countrie:*
> > *Now back to Paradise go we.*

> After this, the lords and ladies saw on the right-hand side of their route, in front of the Chapel of Saint-Jaques, another platform covered with finely woven cloth and curtained like a private room. In it were men playing an organ very melodiously . . .[422]

The most celebrated 'party' of Charles VI's reign must surely be the wedding in the hôtel St. Pol in Paris, attended by the King and five companions dressed up as 'wild men' in canvas and flax costumes; this *mommerie* turned into a *Bal des Ardents* with fatal consequences for four of the participants due to Louis d'Orléans's carelessness with a torch. Before this tragic turn of events, however, music and dance prevailed:

> Puis saillirent avant trompettes, menestreux, flutes, tamburins et chalemies quy jouerent melodieusement . . .
>
> (*Le Livre des Trahisons de France envers la Maison de Bourgogne*)[423]

Attitudes towards minstrels varied considerably. For the noble patrons of most of Europe, they were no more than household servants. A notable exception is found in the case of the Irish Kings, considered elsewhere as barbaric, who were accustomed to have minstrels share their meals with them at the same board as equals:

> When they had sat down and were served with the first course, they would get their minstrels and the principal servants to sit with them and eat off their plates and drink from their goblets.
>
> (*Froissart*)[424]

The excessive numbers of minstrels at large, with consequent lowering of standards and accompanying abuses were the subject of a number of legislative measures, mostly aimed at reducing the nuisance element caused by so many noisy people peddling for trade. As far back as 1181 Philippe Auguste had excluded such minstrels from his Court.[425] Edward I issued decrees which had the effect of suppressing nomadic musicians, *clerwr,* in Wales, as opposed to traditional bards, though both categories were harshly treated by Henry IV in 1402, who had been irritated by the part played by bards in the revolt of Owen Glendwr.[426] The decree issued in 1315 by Edward II shows very clearly how seriously disruptive the uncontrolled spread of minstrelsy could become:

> . . . Forasmuch as . . . many idle persons, under colour of Mynstrelsie, and going in messages, and other faigned business have been and yet be receaved in other mens houses to meate and drynke, and be not therwith contented yf they be not largely consydered with gyftes of the Lordes of the houses . . . We wylling to restrain suche outrageous enterprises and idleness . . . have ordeyned . . . that to the houses of prelates, earles, and barons, none resorte to meate and drynke, unlesse he be a Mynstrel, and of those Minstrels that come none except it be three or four Minstrels of honour at the most in one day, unless he be desired of the lorde of the house. And to the houses of meaner men that none come unlesse he be desired, and that such as shall come so, holde themselves contented with meate and drynke, and with such curtesie as the maister of the house wyl shewe unto them of his owne good wyll, without their askyng of any thyng. And yf any one do agaynst this ordinaunce, at the first tyme he to lose his *Minstrelsie,* and at the second time to forsweare his craft, and never to be receaved for a Minstrel in any house . . .[427]

In France, the edicts of 1372, to prevent minstrelsy being used as a cover for burglary by night, and in 1395, to stop the spread of satirical songs about King or Pope,[428] represent further moves by authority to curb the excesses of minstrelsy.

Traditional Church attitudes against secular and worldly entertainment, and against minstrels in particular, continued to be heard from the pulpit. Such hostile preaching produced a particularly witty riposte from the poet Jean de Condé, in his *Dis des Jacopins et des Fremeneurs.* The lesser Orders of mendicant friars, like the minstrels, depended for their existence on a welcome at the castle gate and the two groups came to be implacable rivals. Their sermons suggested that minstrels were servants of the devil, and that anyone making gifts to them was aiding the devil's work:

> *Jacobin et frere meneur*
> *Veulent conquerre grant honneur*
> *Quant sus les menestrez sermonnent,*
> *Et dient que ceulx qui leur donnent*
> *Font au deable sacfrifice;*
> *Tout menestrel de tel servisce*
> *Oeuvrent ou deables oeit part,*
> *Sages est qui d'eulz se depart.*

Jean de Condé's reply is to remind the friars that King David played his harp before Saul and recommended in his Psalms the use of instruments to praise the Lord; furthermore, certain mental defectives said to be possessed by the devil nevertheless react violently against having the fiddle played to them; nor would the Virgin have appeared to minstrels in Arras to present them with the Holy Candle if they had been unworthy![429]

A further priest, the Franciscan Jehan de Neufchâteau, had a less vested interest in opposing the minstrels, but is at such pains, in his 1389 adaptation of Henry Suso's *Horologium sapientiae,* to extol the pleasures of Paradise that he enumerates at greater length than was perhaps seemly the effects of earthly music said to be surpassed in the skies; in so doing, he displays more than a passing acquaintance with and weakness for the sounds of flute, cornemuse, harp, fiddle, psaltery, shawms, hurdy-gurdy, lute, crowd, organ, trumpets, cymbals, nakers and singing![430] Clearly, pleasure in music and minstrelsy was not to be denied, even by such as the poet Eustache Deschamps in his most cynical mood, in a Ballade 'Contre la danse au son du chalumeau': dancing to the sound of the shawm, and instruments played by *bestial* men who put a spell on people and make them lose their senses, of all the arts this alone is the one with no sensible reason for its existence!

> *. . . Prince, l'en puet en tout cause trouver*
> *Des ars mondains, excepté du dancer*
> *Aux instruments des hommes bestiaulx,*
> *Qui par leur son font les gens enchanter*
> *Et hors du sens maintefois ressembler:*
> C'est de dancier au son des chalemiaulx.[431]

6. Instruments

Puis soulaçoient mes oreilles,
Mon cuer, mon pis et mes entreilles,
Les notes de voix armonique
Et les instruments de musique
Que souvent faisoie sonner
Pour moy esbatement donner.
(*Jehan le Fèvre, La Vieille*)

We have already encountered a large number of different musical instruments both in Chaucer and in other descriptions and accounts. Although the use of any particular instrument is never prescribed in the music of the age, there can be no doubt as to their importance and presence in most kinds of performance. Broadly, they were divided into *haut* and *bas,* that is loud instruments such as those played by heralds and waits – trumpet, shawm, nakers – and soft, more intimate instruments more suitable for indoor entertainment – lute, gittern, fiddle, harp, psaltery, flute.[432]

Some instruments were already old-fashioned in the fourteenth century: the rote (quadrangular harp), for instance, or the crowd or *crwyth,* a bowed rote or lyre favoured by the Welsh.[433] Certain other instruments were favoured more on the popular level: pipe and tabor, bagpipes, hurdy-gurdy, citole.

More varieties of instruments were available in the Middle Ages than we find in the modern symphony orchestra, though many of them, such as Chaucer's 'pypes made of greene corne' or Machaut's 'flaiot de saus', are rustic or ephemeral. Nevertheless, the difficulty of equating literary descriptions abounding in inexact or mis-spelt terminology with representations of instruments in painting, stone or glass, which may vary enormously in detail and embrace the fanciful as well as the inaccurate, is considerable. Extra caution is necessary at every turn when assigning a name to an object and although very recent research has done much to make matters clearer, much of it has served to point the great complexity of the subject, which is far from exhausted yet. For detailed accounts of medieval instruments, often copiously illustrated, the reader should consult articles in journals, especially *Early Music, The Galpin Society Journal* and *The Consort* (Dolmetsch Foundation), together with such excellent books as: D. Munrow, *Instruments of the Middle Ages and Renaissance,* O.U.P., 1976 (with accompanying records SAN 391 and 392); *The New Oxford History of Music,* Vol. II, 466–502; articles under specific headings in the 6th edition of *The New Grove Dictionary of Music and Musicians;* M. Remnant, *Musical Instruments of the West,* London, 1978; A. Baines, *Woodwind instruments and their History,* London, 1957; C. Sachs, *History of Musical Instruments,* London, 1940.

The present chapter merely lists the most important instruments in use in Chaucer's Age, with brief descriptions and illustrations, as a companion to what has gone before.

In medieval art, instruments are often grouped together for aesthetic or symbolic reasons, and their association in pictures does not necessarily imply their combination in the practical music-making of the time. Nevertheless, such assemblies of instruments constitute pleasing visual catalogues of contemporary instrumental resources.

In the illustration of the story of Pygmalion from the *Roman de la Rose,* we see on the wall of his workshop, where he is dancing and holding a positive organ in an effort to amuse the statue he has created, from left to right and bottom to top: psaltery, cymbals, bagpipes, trumpet, pan-pipes, small drum and stick, flute or recorder, hurdy-gurdy, bow and rebec, harp, flute, two shawms, clock with bell, gittern, lute.

The Stem of Jesse (Grande Bible historique)

In the musical depiction of the Tree of Jesse we see: S-shaped trumpet, rebec, lute, psaltery, harp, fiddle, nakers, shawm, bass-shawm or bombard, gittern, flute or recorder.

The Story of Pygmalion (Roman de la Rose)

Stringed Instruments

a) Plucked

1. Harp

Orpheus plays the Harp

The fourteenth-century harp was small enough to be held on the knee or suspended from the neck or waist. It normally had less than twenty strings, made of gut. The harp dominated its ancient rival the lyre, and harpers were the most common and possibly the most welcome type of minstrel. As Adam Davy wrote c.1312 in his *Life of Alexander*:

> *Mery it is in halle to here the harpe,*
> *The mynstrall synge, the jugelour carpe.*[434]

2. Psaltery

David plays the Psaltery

Normally trapezoid but with many variants in shape, the psaltery is played on the knees or else downwards across the chest. The strings are of metal and often a plectrum was used, rather than the fingers, to pluck them. The *micanon*, a diminutive of *canon* from Arabic *qānun*, is to be understood as a smaller type.

3. Lute

The lute is well illustrated in the Tree of Jesse illumination. One of the principal instruments inherited from the Arab world through moorish Spain, in the fourteenth century the lute still played mostly single-line melodies; it had fewer strings and had not yet developed the chordal style of Renaissance playing. The rounded back, short neck, bent-back peg-box and use of frets on the fingerboard are important characteristics.

Medieval lutes were normally carved from the solid, as opposed to the lighter Renaissance construction from separate ribs glued together. Strings were of gut and a plectrum was normally used.

4. Gittern

The gittern is represented here in a line of instruments, from left to right: portative organ, harp, gittern, fiddle, psaltery, bagpipes. There has been some controversy and confusion of the nature and nomenclature especially of the gittern and of the citole,[435] but it seems to be established that the gittern was basically a small version of the lute,

Style of Orcagna: Coronation of the Virgin

particularly characterized by its sickle-shaped peg-box. The back was slim and pear-shaped, like that of the rebec, but might on occasion be flattened off, as in the later mandora. Machaut distinguishes between *guiterne* and *morache / moresche,* by which presumably is meant *guiterne latine* or the normal type we have described, and *guiterne moresche,* an unusual moorish or Turkish type probably with no frets and more strings, which Machaut may have encountered in Bohemia.

5. Citole

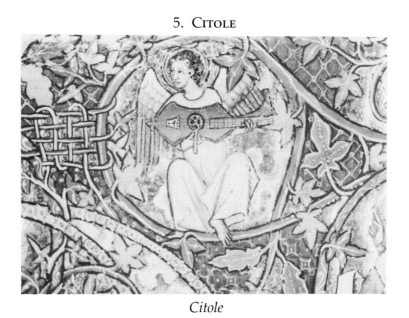

Citole

The citole, usually referred to as a gittern in musicological literature prior to 1977, is a plucked instrument of guitar type and roughly of guitar dimensions. It is often formed in a characteristic 'holly-leaf' shape, has frets and metal strings, and is played with a quill plectrum.

b) Bowed

1. Fiddle

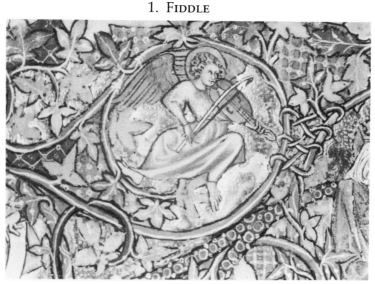

Fiddle

The popular fiddle was about the size of a large modern viola. The strings were of gut, four or five in number, usually with the top two tuned to a unison and the bottom two to a drone fifth, essential for consonance, since the flattish bridge caused all strings to be sounded simultaneously. Medieval bows were convex, sometimes large and unwieldy, but usually affording the possibility of changing pressure due to the direct contact of the player's fingers with the hair. Frets were often used and sometimes the instrument was played on the knees, viol-fashion.

2. REBEC

Rebec (left-handed)

The slim, pear-shaped rebec was normally carved from the solid. It has three or four strings of clear, nasal quality.[436]

Keyboard Instruments

1. ORGAN

In the fourteenth century large organs with cumbersome systems of hydraulics or bellows and slides for keys had fallen from favour. Small portative organs to be played on a table or even suspended from the player's neck, or perched upon his knee, were now the preferred types – the sort of instrument used so brilliantly by Landini. The right hand performed upon a keyboard, while the left pumped a hand-bellows up and down. By the late fourteenth century such instruments had a chromatic compass of over one octave.

Fiddle, Organ

2. Clavichord

Described by John I of Aragon as 'an instrument similar to the organ but sounded by strings'. Very little is known about the early clavichord,[437] but it seems that it was a practical adaptation of the monochord (more useful for theoretical demonstrations of proportion in pitch), and used keys to stop a single string with a movable bridge, which sounded the string very softly as it came into contact with it.

3. Hurdy-Gurdy

This traditional beggar's instrument is most suited to popular and street music. One hand turns a handle which rotates a resined wheel against all three or four strings simultaneously, necessitating a drone tuning. The other hand operates a system of tabs or keys which stop the top, melody string.

Hurdy-Gurdy

Wind Instruments

1. SHAWM

Shawms

The shawm, always in evidence in 'loud' and out-door occasions, is a double-reed instrument of oriental origin. Its sound is clear and piercing. The range of early wind-instruments is usually limited to just over one octave, and this in turn led to the development of groups in different sizes. In the fourteenth century a larger shawm appeared, known as the bombard.

2. Douçaine, Dolzaine

This is an instrument hitherto unidentified, though frequently described in literature as soft or sweet. It may have been a type of muted shawm of the reed-cap variety so common in the late fifteenth and sixteenth centuries.

3. Flutes and Pipes

Identification of these instruments is usually difficult, since they are normally depicted in the process of being played and it is thus impossible to tell if they are reed or fipple pipes. Vertically-held flutes (recorders), and pipes made of substances from reed to horn were certainly common, though normally they are to be rated as folk-instruments.

Tabor, Bells, Flute

The transverse flute was already in use, however, and presents no such problems of identification, even though the depiction may sometimes leave much to be desired.

Panpipes, although again folk-instruments, were known, and are capable of being played with virtuosity.

Flageolets or double pipes are frequently referred to and are also instruments to be found on the village green rather than in sophisticated music-making. The pipe played by one hand along with a tabor is sometimes depicted as double.

4. Trumpets and Horns

The typical herald's trumpet was about six feet long. Sometimes this was made more manageable by being bent into an S-shape. Shorter types of higher pitch were called clarions. Sometimes the bell was flared, sometimes not. Occasionally, for special instruments, silver was used, and materials such as ivory for the cup-shaped mouthpiece. Apart from *trompe / trompette* and *buse / buisine*, other French terms for instruments of similar type are: *cor, cor sarrazinois, graisle, moinel, araine*. The *cor*, like *buisine*, probably implies a large cattle horn, either straight or curved. A short bull's horn is described as *bugul* in Middle English:

> *The kynge his bugul con blau, opon the bent tides.*
> (*The Anturs of Arthur*)[438]

Trumpets, Fiddle, Citole, Harp, Psaltery

5. BAGPIPES

Bagpipes

This instrument surpasses even the harp in its widespread use from Scotland to Czechoslovakia, Ireland to Egypt. It is, of course, a folk-instrument not normally suitable for taking part in sophisticated polyphony. The bag was of an animal skin, with air supplied through a mouth-piece tube. Melodies are fingered on the chanter. Not all early bagpipes possessed a drone pipe, and normally there was only one of these, tuned two octaves below the fundamental note of the chanter.

Percussion

A large variety of percussion instruments were available in the Middle Ages especially for popular use in the dance repertory.[439] Drums of various sizes, tambourines, rattles, clappers, cymbals were all well known.

Nakers

Particularly important for 'loud' music were the nakers (French *nacaires* from the Arabic *naqqāra*), a pair of hemispherical unequal-sized small drums played with a pair of sticks. They were either suspended from a belt at the player's waist, or fastened onto a companion's back, or simply placed upon the ground.

Suspended Bells

Sets of suspended bells of different size and pitch are often depicted, especially in church books. They were beaten with a pair of small hammers and had their place in theoretical instruction as well as in liturgical use.

Select Bibliography

Detailed references to critical works and editions of poetry and music are given in the text and Notes. The list of books below is limited to general and reference works.

Apel, W., *The Notation of polyphonic Music, 900–1600*, Cambridge, Mass., 5th ed. 1953.

Bent, M. & Wathey, A., *Fauvel Studies: allegory, chronicle, music and image in Paris*, Oxford, 1998.

Brewer, D., *Chaucer and his World*, London, 1978.

Caldwell, J., *Medieval Music*, London, 1978.

Certaldo – Centro di Studi – *L'Ars Nova italiana del Trecento*, Certaldo, 1962 & 1968.

Dobson, E. & Harrison, F., eds., *Medieval English Songs*, London, 1979.

Earp, L., *A Guide to Machaut*, New York, 1995.

Fischer, K. von, *Studien zur italienischen Musik des Trecento*, Bern, 1956.

Gagnepain, B., *Histoire de la musique au Moyem Age. 2. XIIIe–XIVe siècle*, Paris, 1996.

Gallo, A., *Music of the Middle Ages II*, Cambridge, 1985.

Gomez, M. Carmen, *La música en la casa real Catalano-Aragonesa, 1336–1442*, 2 vols., Barcelona, 1977.

Grove's Dictionary of Music and Musicians, 6th ed. (*New Grove*), London, 1979.

Guide de la Musique du Moyen Age, Paris (Fayard), 1999.

Hagopian, V., *Italian Ars Nova Music: a Bibliographic Guide to modern Editions and related literature*, Berkeley, 2nd ed., 1973.

Harrison F., *Music in medieval Britain*, Oxford, 1958.

Hoppin, R., *Medieval Music*, 2 vols., New York, 1978.

Hughes, A., *Medieval Music: the sixth Liberal Art*, Toronto, 1974.

Le Vot, G., *Vocabulaire de la Musique médiévale* (Minerve), 1993.

New Oxford History of Music, vol. III, 'Ars Nova and the Renaissance', Oxford, 1960.

Reese, G., *Music in the Middle Ages*, London, 1940.

RISM: Répertoire Internationale des Sources musicales
    Vol. IV[1], ed. G. Reaney, *MSS of Polyphonic Music C11th – early C14th*, 1966.
    Vol. IV[2], ed. G. Reaney, *MSS of Polyphonic Music c.1320–1400*, 1969.
    Vol. IV[3] & Vol. IV[4], ed. K. von Fischer, *Handschriften mit mehrstimmiger Musik des 14., 15. und 16. Jahrhunders*, 1972.
    Vol. IV *Supplement*, 1993.

Seay, A., *Music in the Medieval World*, New Jersey, 1965.

Strohm, R., *The Rise of European Music, 1380–1500*, Cambridge, 1993.

Tomasello, A., *Music and Ritual at Papal Avignon, 1309–1403*, Ann Arbor, 1983.

Wégimont – Les Colloques de Wégimont – *II L'Ars Nova*, Paris, 1959.

Wilkins, N., *The Lyric Art of Medieval France*, Cambridge, 1988.

Wright, C., *Music at the Court of Burgundy, 1364–1419: a documentary History*, Henryville, 1979.

Notes

1. Ed. K. de Lettenhove, Louvain, 1882, I, 88–89.
2. See S. Clercx & R. Hoppin, 'Notes biographiques sur quelques musiciens français du XIVe siècle', in *Colloques de Wégimont – II L'Ars Nova*, Paris, 1959, 63–92.
3. (*Pic*) B.N., coll. de. Picardie, vol.67, f.67.
4. Ed. F. Harrison, *Motets of French Provenance*, Vol. V of *Polyphonic Music of the C14th*, Monaco, 1968; *and* M. Bent, *Two C14th Motets in Praise of Music*, Antico Ed., 1977.
5. *Ch* f. 67v/68r, ed. U. Günther, *The Motets of the MSS Ch and* Mod, CMM 39, 1965, 40–45, plus Notes XLIII–XLVII.
6. See below, pp. 87–88; there are musical and textual links between all four of the 'Musician Motet' series.
7. Ed. K. de Lettenhove, Louvain, 1882, I, 8.
8. Ed. A. Fourrier, Paris, 1963, 47.
9. *Li Maintiens des Béghines*, ed. K. de Lettenhove, Louvain, 1882, I, 240.
10. *Li Complainte, ibid.,* 260.
11. Ed. R. Carey, Chapel Hill, 1972.
12. *The Lyric Works of Adam de la Hale,* ed. N. Wilkins, CMM 44, 1967.
13. See below, p. 141.
14. See F. Gégou, 'Adam le Bossu était-il mort en 1288?', in *Romania* LXXXVI (1965), 111–117; *and* N. Cartier, 'La mort d'Adam le Bossu', in *Romania* LXXXIX (1968), 116–124.
15. *Ed. cit.,* 56.
16. See articles BALLADE, VIRELAI, RONDEAU, in *The New Grove Dictionary of Music and Musicians,* 1979.
17. *The Works of Jehan de Lescurel,* ed. N. Wilkins, CMM 30, 1966.
18. See N. Wilkins, *One Hundred Ballades, Rondeaux & Virelais ..*, Cambridge, 1969.
19. Text ed. A. Långfors, Paris, 1914; polyphonic music ed. L. Schrade, in *Polyphonic Music of the C14th,* Vol.I, Monaco, 1956; monodic music ed. A. Gennrich, *Rondeaux, Virelais und Balladen ..*, Dresden & Göttingen, 1921–27; *and* G. A. Harrison, *The monophonic Music in the 'Roman de Fauvel'*, Columbia University Diss., 1963.
20. Ed. L. Schrade, *op. cit.,* I.
21. Transl. after Schrade.
22. Coussemaker, *Scriptores,* IV, 257a; III 336b & 337a.
23. For a complete description of medieval notation systems, see W. Apel, *The Notation of polyphonic Music 900–1600,* Cambridge, Mass., 1953.
24. For a fuller biographical account of Machaut, see: A Machabey, *Guillaume de Machaut, 130?–1377,* 2 vols., Paris, 1955; V. Chichmareff, *Guillaume de Machaut: Poésies lyriques,* 2 vols., Paris, 1909; N. Wilkins, *Guillaume de Machaut: La Louange des Dames,* Edinburgh, 1972.
25. See: W. Calin, *A Poet at the Fountain: Essays on the narrative Verse of Guillaume de Machaut,* Lexington, 1974; E. Hoepffner, *Oeuvres de Guillaume de Machaut,* 3 vols., Paris, 1908–21; P. Paris, *Le Livre du Voir Dit de Guillaume de Machaut,* Paris, 1875 (reprint 1969); M. L. de Mas

Latrie, *Guillaume de Machaut: La Prise d'Alexandrie*, Geneva, 1877; N. Wilkins, 'Guillaume de Machaut, 1300–1377', in *The Consort* 33 (1977), 213–221.

26. See e.g. J. Wimsatt, *Chaucer and the French Love Poets*, Chapel Hill, 1968.

27. See G. Reaney, *Machaut*, London, 1971.

28. Principal music editions: F. Ludwig, *Guillaume de Machaut: Musikalische Werke*, 4 vols., Leipzig, 1926–43; L. Schrade, *Polyphonic Music of the C14th*, Vols. II & III, Monaco, 1956 (reprint 1977); S. Leguy, *Guillaume de Machaut: Oeuvres complètes*, 7 vols., Paris, 1977– .

29. See G. Anderson, 'Responsory Chants in the Tenors of some fourteenth-century Continental Motets', in *Journal of the American Musicological Society* XXIX (1976), 119–127. Also N.B. F. Harrison, in *Motets of French Provenance*, Vol.V of *Polyphonic Music of the C14th*, Monaco, 1968, xvii: '. . . motets were produced in the C14th for a relatively small group of the upper ecclesiastical and lay society of the time. They were performed by singers trained in written part-music, probably on a few special kinds of occasion. Motets originally written to mark a specific event or for a particular time and place might be copied and sung in other places and on occasions with less direct bearing on their subjects. Motets with amorous texts in one or more upper voices were not sung in sacred precincts (which do not include the common hall of a cathedral or collegiate church, nor the dwelling of a monastic abbot or prior); there was, however, no restriction on the subjects of motets sung in non-consecrated buildings of a religious community or in the hall of a palace or great house. The fact that a motet, whether devotional, admonitory, laudatory, moral, didactic, courtly-amorous or rustic-amorous, could be composed on either a sacred or secular tenor cannot have influenced its context of performance, since the tenor was not normally sung to a text, but was usually identified by an incipit – often incomplete – and sometimes left unidentified.'

30. Ed. N. Wilkins, *Armes, Amours, Dames, Chevalerie*, London, 1980, No. 5.

31. See e.g. S. Cape, 'The Machaut Mass and its performance', in *Score* 25 (1959), 38–57 & *Score* 26 (1960), 20–29; A. Parrott, 'Performing Machaut's Mass on Record', in *Early Music* 5 (1977), 492–495.

32. Ed. N. Wilkins, Edinburgh, 1972.

33. *Ibid.*, Appendix, 121–170.

34. See e.g. E. Hoepffner, *op. cit.*, I, xliv ff.; F. Ludwig, *op. cit.*, II; G. Reaney, 'A Chronology of the Ballades, Rondeaux and Virelais set to Music by Guillaume de Machaut', in *Musica Disciplina* VI (1952), 33 ff.; U. Günther, 'Chronologie und Stil der Kompositionen G. de Machauts', in *Acta Musicologica* XXXV (1963), 96 ff.; G. Reaney, 'Towards a Chronology of Machaut's Musical Works', in *Musica Disciplina* XX (1966), 87–96; A. Swartz, 'A new Chronology of the Ballades of Machaut', in *Acta Musicologica* XLVI (1974), 192–207; E. Keitel, *A Chronology of the Compositions of Guillaume de Machaut based on a Study of Fascicle-Manuscript Structure in the larger Manuscripts*, Cornell University Diss., 1976; U. Günther, 'Contribution de la musicologie à la biographie et à la chronologie de Guillaume de Machaut', paper delivered at the Machaut Conference in Reims, 1978.

35. See N. Wilkins, *One Hundred Ballades, Rondeaux & Virelais*, Cambridge, 1969, 17–20.

36. *Ibid.*, 21–22 & 159–161, *passim* for detailed discussion and examples of the late medieval short lyric forms; for general background see D. Poirion, *Le Poète et le Prince; l'évolution du lyrisme courtois de Guillaume de Machaut à Charles d'Orléans*, Paris, 1965.

37. C.f. N. Wilkins, 'The Structure of Ballades, Rondeaux & Virelais in Froissart and in Christine de Pisan', in *French Studies* XXIII (1968), 337–348.

38. Ed. N. Wilkins, *Armes, Amours, Dames, Chevalerie*, London, 1980, No.9.

39. See below, p. 30.

40. See J. Maillard, *Evolution et esthétique du lai lyrique des origines à la fin du XIVe siècle*, Paris, 1963; D. Fallows, 'Guillaume de Machaut and the Lai', in *Early Music* 5 (1977), 477–483.

41. See T. Walker & M. Hasselman, in *Musica Disciplina* XXIV (1970), 7 ff; R. Hoppin, in *Musica Disciplina* XII (1958), 96 ff.

42. Ed. L. Schrade No.18 – a fault in transcription had obscured the polyphonic possibility.

43. See T. Marrocco, *Fourteenth-Century Italian Cacce*, Cambridge, Mass., 1961.

44. Ed. W. Apel, *French Secular Music of the late C14th*, Cambridge, Mass., 1950; W. Apel, *French Secular Compositions of the C14th*, 3 vols., CMM 53, 1970–72.

45. See: G. Reaney, 'The MS Chantilly, Musée Condé, 1047', in *Musica Disciplina* VIII (1954), 59–113; K. v. Fischer, 'The MS Paris, B.N., nouv.acq. fr. 6771 (Cod. Reina: PR)', in *Musica*

Disciplina XI (1957), 38–78; N. Wilkins, 'The Codex Reina: a revised description', in *Musica Disciplina* XVII (1963), 57–73; U. Günther, 'Das Manuskript Modena, Biblioteca Estense, ∝.M.5.24 (*olim* lat.568 Mod)', in *Musica Disciplina* XXIV (1970), 17–67; also see below, p. 55.

46. For biographical sketches of many of the principal figures, see: S. Clercx & R. Hoppin, 'Notes biographiques sur quelques musiciens français', in *Les Colloques de Wégimont – II L'Ars Nova*, Paris, 1959, 63–92; R. Hoppin, 'Some Remarks à propos of *Pic*', in *Revue Belge de Musicologie* X (1956), 105–111; N. Wilkins, 'The Post-Machaut Generation of Poet-Musicians', in *Nottingham Medieval Studies* XII (1968), 40–84; U. Günther, 'Zur Biographie einiger Komponisten der Ars Subtilior', in *Archiv für Musikwissenschaft* XXI (1964), 172–199; U. Günther, 'Die Musiker des Herzogs von Berry', in *Musica Disciplina* XVII (1963), 79–95.

47. Ed. N. Wilkins, *Armes, Amours, Dames, Chevalerie*, London, 1980, No. 18.

48. See above, p. 2 & below, p. 34; ed. U. Günther, *The Motets of the MSS Ch and Mod*, CMM 39, 1965, 40–45.

49. See below, p. 87.

50. *Iv*, Ivrea, Bibl. capitolare, Cod.115; see G. Borghezio, in *Archivium Romanum* V (1921), 173–186.

51. Ed. U. Günther, *op. cit., and* F. Harrison, *Motets of French Provenance*, Vol.V of *Polyphonic Music of the C14th*, Monaco, 1968; see also U. Günther, 'The C14th Motet and its Development', in *Musica Disciplina* XII (1958), 27–58; U. Günther, 'Das Wort-Ton Problem bei Motetten des späten 14. Jahrhunderts', in *Festschrift Heinrich Besseler*, Leipzig, 1962, 163–178.

52. C.f. above, p. 7.

53. See H. Anglès, 'El Músic Jacomí al servei de Joan i Marti I durant els anys 1372–1404', in *Homenatge a Antoní Rubió i Lluch*, Barcelona, 1936, 10–11.

54. Froissart, *Voyage en Béarn* (*Chronicles*, Book III), ed. A. Diverres, Manchester, 1953, 68.

55. Ed. F. Harrison, *op. cit.*, Nos.29, 2, 3; N.B. the particularly useful *Supplement* to this edition, which contains synopses and translations of the texts by A. Rigg and E. Rutson.

56. F. Pedrell, 'Jean I d'Aragon, compositeur de musique', in *Riemann-Festschrift*, Leipzig, 1909, 229–240.

57. See A. Pagès, *La poésie française en Catalogne du XIIIe siècle à la fin du XVe*, Paris, 1936.

58. See especially H. Anglès, *op. cit.*

59. Ed. N. Wilkins, *Armes, Amours, Dames, Chevalerie*, London, 1980, No.11.

60. Ed. N. Wilkins, *The C14th Repertory from the Codex Reina*, CMM 36, 1966, No.21.

61. See below, p. 70.

62. Ed. N. Wilkins, *Three French Songs from the C14th*, Antico Ed., 1974.

63. See W. Apel, *French Secular Music of the late C14th*, 9–15.

64. Facsimile and music example are given below, pp. 108–109.

65. See *Denkmäler der Tonkunst in Oesterreich* IX, i, 179.

66. Strasbourg, Bibl. de la Ville, M.222.c.22. Destroyed by fire in 1870. See C. van den Borren, *Le MS musical M.222.c.22 . . .* , Antwerp, 1924.

67. Munich, Staatsbibliothek, mus.3232a; see K. Dezès, in *Zeitschrift für Musik-Wissenschaft* X, 65 ff.

68. Prague, Univ. Lib., XI.E.9; ed. F. Kammerer, *Die Musikstücke des Prager Codex*, Brno, 1931.

69. See e.g. G. Reaney, 'New Sources of Ars Nova Music', in *Musica Disciplina* XIX (1965), 53–67; J. Sučžková, 'Les Traces de Guillaume de Machaut dans les sources musicales à Prague' & L. Vachulka, 'Problème d'interprétation de la musique de Guillaume de Machaut', papers delivered at the Machaut Conference in Reims, 1978.

70. Ed. R. Hoppin, *The Cypriot-French Repertory*, CMM 21, 4 vols., & 'The Cypriot-French Repertory', in *Musica Disciplina* XI (1957), 79–125.

71. See above, p. 2.

72. See below, p. 82.

73. See H. Stäblein-Harder, ed., *C14th Mass Music in France*, CMM 29, 1962, & MSD 7; L. Schrade, ed., *Polyphonic Music of the C14th*, Vol.I, Monaco, 1956.

74. See above, p. 14.

75. See F. Ludwig, in *Archiv für Musikwissenschaft* V (1923), 284 ff.; H. Besseler, in *Archiv für Musikwissenschaft* VII (1925), 197 ff.

76. See L. Schrade, 'A C14th Parody Mass', in *Acta Musicologica* XXVII (1955), 13 ff.; R. Jackson,

'Musical interrelations between C14th Mass Movements', in *Acta Musicologica* XXIX (1957), 54 ff.

77. See N. Wilkins, 'Music in the C14th *Miracles de Nostre Dame*', in *Musica Disciplina* XXVIII (1974), 39–75.

78. Ed. G. Paris & U. Robert, *Les Miracles de Nostre Dame*, 8 vols., Paris, 1876–83; G. Runnalls, ed., *Le Miracle de l'enfant ressuscité* (No.15), Geneva/Paris, 1972; N. Wilkins, ed., *Two Miracles* (Nos.7 & 25), Edinburgh, 1972.

79. See H. Cocheris, *La Vieille, ou les dernières amours d'Ovide*, Paris, 1861.

80. C.f. Ex.65 below, p. 107.

81. See p. 89.

82. See D. Plamenac, 'Keyboard Music of the C14th in Codex Faenza 117', in *Journal of the American Musicological Society* IV (1951), 179–201.

83. The main editions of Trecento music are: N. Pirrotta, *The Music of C14th Italy*, CMM 8, vols.1–5, 1954–64; *Polyphonic Music of the C14th*, Vol.IV (Landini), ed. L. Schrade, 1958, *and* vols. VI–VIII, ed. W. Marrocco, 1967–72. Many pieces still unpublished are transcribed in Part I of N. Wilkins, *A critical Edition of the French & Italian Texts & Music contained in the Codex Reina*, Nottingham University Diss., 1964.

84. See N. Pirrotta, '*Dulcedo* e *Subtilitas* nella pratica polifonica franco-italiana al principio del '400', in *Revue Belge de Musicologie* II (1948), 125 ff.

85. See S. Clercx, ed., *Johannes Ciconia (c.1335–1411): un musicien liégeois et son temps*, Bruxelles, 1960.

86. Called by Sacchetti *Magister Guiglielmus pariginus – frater romitanus*, in *Il Libro delle rime*, 122.

87. See N. Pirrotta, CMM 8, Vol.5, II–III; also G. Corsi, *Poesie musicali del Trecento*, Bologna, 1970, XLII, where the observation is made that the opening line of Guglielmo's Ballata 'Piacesse a Dio ch'io non fussi mai nata' is quoted in Ball. V of the *Pecorone* of Ser Giovanni Fiorentino, dated 1378.

88. See C. Fauriel, *La Poésie provençale en Italie*, in *Bibl. de l'Ecole des Chartes* IV (1842–43), 23–41, 93–110, 189–207.

89. See G. Corsi, *Rimatori del Trecento*, Turin, 1969.

90. See G. Corsi, *Poesie musicali del Trecento*, Bologna, 1970; N. Sapegno, *Poeti minori del Trecento*, vol.10 of *La Letteratura italiana* Milan & Naples, 2nd ed. 1964; M. Carducci, 'Musica e poesia nel mondo elegante italiane del sec. XIV', in *Opere*, vol. VIII, Bologna, 1893; E. Li Gotti, *La poesia musicale italiana del sec. XIV*, Palermo, 1944.

91. Transl. W. Anderson, Penguin Classics, 1964.

92. Transl. A. Howell, London, 1890.

93. Transl. D. L. Sayers, Penguin Classics, 1955.

94. See below, p. 96; also L. Jeffery, *The earliest English Lyric & Franciscan Spirituality*, Lincoln, Nebraska, Ch.II; F. Liuzzi, *La Lauda ed i primordi della melodia italiana*, 1935; *New Oxford History of Music*, vol.II, 266–269; E. Levi, ed., *Lirica italiana antica*, Florence, 1905; E. Underhill, *Jacoponi da Todi, Poet & Mystic, 1228–1306*, London, 1929; *Laudi spirituali del Bianco da Siena, povero Gesuato del sec, XIV*, Lucca, 1851; J. Handschin, in *Acta Musicologica* X, 14.

95. K. von Fischer, in *Les Colloques de Wégimont*, 223.

96. *Il Libro delle rime*, ed. A. Chiari, Bari, 1936, 139.

97. See A. Ghislanzoni, 'Les formes littéraires et musicales italiennes au commencement du XIVe siècle', in *Les Colloques de Wégimont*, 149–163.

98. *Boccaccio: The Decameron*, transl. G. McWilliam, Penguin Classics, 1972, 67.

99. *Ibid.*, 112–113.

100. *Ibid.*, 230.

101. *Ibid.*, 321.

102. *Ibid.*, 520.

103. *Ibid.*, 584.

104. *Ibid.*, 681.

105. *Ibid.*, 731.

106. See N. Pirrotta, 'Cronologia e Denominazione dell'Ars Nova italiana', in *Les Colloques de Wégimont*, 93–109.

107. G. Fiamma, *Opusculum*, 35.

108. G. Corsi, *op.cit.*, xxxiv.

109. See N. Pirrotta, 'Marchettus de Padua & the Italian Ars Nova', in *Musica Disciplina* IX (1955), 57–71.
110. See e.g. J. Wimsatt, *The Marguerite Poetry of Guillaume de Machaut,* Chapel Hill, 1970, & a review of this in *French Studies* XXVI (1972), 441–443.
111. N. Pirrotta, *op.cit.,* 68; c.f. also the anon. two-voice *canzona* 'Pyançe la bella Yguana', in MS Rossi 215, f.6r.
112. See O. Strunk, 'Intorno a Marchetto da Padova', in *La Rassegna musicale* XX (1950), 312.
113. G. Corsi, *op.cit.,* xxviii.
114. See N. Wilkins, 'A Madrigal in Praise of the Della Scala Family', in *Revue Belge de Musicologie* XIX (1965), 82–88; also G. Corsi, *op.cit.,* 365.
115. *Il Libro delle rime,* 93.
116. *Ibid.,* 18, 24, 29, 78, 104, 109.
117. See K. von Fischer, *Studien zur italienischen Musik des Trecento und frühen Quattrocento,* Bern, 1956, 77–78.
118. Ed. A. Lanza, Rome, 1975.
119. *Paradiso, ed.cit.,* 165; see also 166.
120. *Ibid.,* 170; see also 173–174.
121. *Ibid.,* 176; it is interesting to note that in the musical source *Sq,* f.142r, the name **Petra** is substituted for **Cosa,** showing that the piece had been adapted subsequently in another lady's favour.
122. *Ibid.,* 236–7; see also 275 ff., in which Francesco relates the final *novella.*
123. See L. Ellinwood, *The Works of Francesco Landini,* Cambridge, Mass., 1939.
124. See H. Noltenhuis, 'Een autobiographisch madrigal van F. Landino', in *Tijdschrift voor Muziekwetenschap* XVII (1955), 237–41.
125. Ed. S. Debenedetti, Supplemento No.15 of *Giornale storico della letteratura italiana,* Turin, 1913.
126. *Saporetto,* 106.
127. *Ibid.,* 109.
128. *Ibid.,* 110.
129. *Ibid.,* 104; see also 107–110, 116–117.
130. Ed. N. Wilkins, in *Three Madrigals by Jacopo da Bologna,* Antico Ed., 1973.
131. See pp.31–32 above.
132. p. 107 below.
133. Ed. N. Wilkins, in *Bartolino da Padova: Three Madrigals,* Antico Edition, 1976.
134. *Ibid.*
135. G. Corsi, *op.cit.,* xliv–xlv; the text does not lend itself to N. Goldine's interpretation of it as a deploration on the capture of Padua by Gian Galleazo Visconti in 1388, in 'Fra Bartolino da Padova, Musicien de Cour', in *Acta Musicologica* XXXIV (1962), 142–155.
136. See below, p. 86.
137. See U. Günther, 'Zur Datierung des Madrigals *Godi, Firenze . . .*', in *Archiv für Musikwissenschaft* XXIV (1967), 99–119, with facsimile and transcription.
138. See K. von Fischer, in *Musica Disciplina* XI (1957), 38–78; N. Wilkins, in *Musica Disciplina* XVII (1963), 57–73.
139. Ed. N. Wilkins, *A C14th Repertory from the Codex Reina,* CMM 36, 1966.
140. Ed. N. Wilkins, *A C15th Repertory from the Codex Reina,* CMM 37, 1966.
141. See U. Günther, in *Musica Disciplina* XXIV (1970), 17–67.
142. See G. Reaney, in *Musica Disciplina* XIV (1960), 33–63; U. Günther, in *Archiv für Musikwissenschaft* XXIII (1966), 73–92.
143. See G. Reaney, in *Musica Disciplina* XII (1958), 67–91.
144. See F. Ludwig, in *Sammelbände der Internationalen Musikgesellschaft* IV (1902–03), 12 ff., & VI (1904–05), 614 ff.
145. Ed. erratically by J. Wolf, *Der Squarcialupi-Codex . . . ,* Lippstadt, 1955.
146. See F. Ghisi, in *Musica Disciplina* I (1946), 173–191; A. Bonaccorsi, 'Un nuovo codice dell' 'Ars Nova', Il codice lucchese', in *Atti della accademia nazionale dei Lincei, Memorie* (Serie VII, vol.I, fasc.12, 606 ff.), Rome, 1948; N. Pirrotta, in *Musica Disciplina* III (1949), 119 ff.
147. See D. Plamenac, 'Another Paduan Fragment of Trecento Music', in *Journal of the American Musicological Society* VIII (1955), 165 ff; S. Clercx, in *Revue Belge de Musicologie* X (1956), 158 ff.

148. See above, p. 16 ff.
149. See W. Marrocco, in *Speculum* XXVI (1951), 449 ff.
150. See W. Marrocco, *Fourteenth-Century Italian Cacce*, Cambridge, Mass., 1961.
151. See N. Pirrotta, 'Per l'origine e la storia della caccia e del madrigale trecentesco', in *Rivista Musicale Italiana* XLVIII (1964), 305–323.
152. Sercambi, *Il Novelliere*, ed. L. Rossi, Rome, 1974, I, 185.
153. See U. Günther, *The Motets of the MSS Ch & Mod*, CMM 39, 1965; also p. 24 above.
154. See B. Layton, *Italian Music for the Ordinary of the Mass 1300–1450*, Harvard University Diss., 1960.
155. See above, p. 35.
156. *Liber de civitatis Florentiae famosi civibus*, ed., Florence, 1847.
157. Ed. S. Boorman, *Bartolino da Padova: Three Madrigals* (for Keyboard), Antico Ed., 1976.
158. See L. Dittmer, ed., *The Worcester Fragments*, MSD 2, 1957.
159. Ed. F. Hammond, CM 14, 1970.
160. The MS is today at Wolfenbüttel, Herzogl. Bibl. 677. Facsimile ed., J. Baxter, St. Andrews University Publications, 1931.
161. See M. Bukofzer, 'Two C14th Motets on St. Edmund', in *Studies in medieval and Renaissance Music*, London, 1950.
162. *See New Oxford History of Music*, vol.III, 94–95.
163. *Ibid.*, vol.III,83.
164. M. Bukofzer, *op.cit.*, 24.
165. Y. Rokseth, *Polyphonies du XIIIe siècle*, Paris, 1939, vol.IV, 140.
166. *New Oxford History of Music*, vol. III, 89–93.
167. Ed. M. Bent, *Five Sequences for the Virgin Mary*, O.U.P. Early Music Series No.7, London, 1973.
168. See A. Hughes & M. Bent, *The Old Hall Manuscript*, ed., CMM 46, 1969; M. Bukofzer, *Studies in medieval & Renaissance Music*, London, 1950, 34–85; *New Oxford History of Music*, vol.III, 101–106 & 167–181.
169. See N. Wilkins, *Armes, Amours, Dames, Chevalerie*, London, 1980, Notes to No.21.
170. A. Hughes & M. Bent, *op.cit.*, 423.
171. Ed. N. Wilkins, *op.cit.*, No.21.
172. The MS provides an alternative *Contratenor*.
173. See *New Oxford History of Music*, vol.III, 143.
174. M. Bukofzer, *op.cit.*, 54.
175. See *New Oxford History of Music* III, 168–169.
176. Ed. A. R. Myers, Manchester, 1959.
177. See B. Trowell, *Music under the later Plantagenets*, Cambridge University Diss., 1960.
178. See B. Trowell, 'A C14th ceremonial motet and its composer', in *Acta Musicologica* 29 (1957), 65–75; the Motet is ed. by U. Günther, *The Motets of the MSS Ch & Mod*, CMM 39, 49–52 plus Notes L–LV; also ed. F. Harrison, No.31 in Vol.V of *Polyphonic Music of the C14th*, Monaco, 1968, *and* ed. M. Bent, *Two C14th Motets in Praise of Music*, Antico Ed., 1977.
179. See P. Tucoo-Chala, *Gaston Fébus et la vicomté de Béarn*, Bordeaux, 1960, 93–100. Further details of minstrels in the service of the Black Prince may be found in R. Barber, *Edward, Prince of Wales and Aquitaine*, London, 1978, 22, 30, 37, 40, 43, 93, 155, 227.
180. U. Günther, *op.cit.*, LI, after Trowell, *op.cit.*
181. *New Oxford History of Music*, Vol.II, 337.
182. Ed. P. Aubry, *Cent Motets du XIIIe siècle*, Paris, 1907.
183. *New Oxford History of Music*, vol.III, 410–411.
184. *Ibid.*, vol.II, 338.
185. J. Wolf, 'Die Tänze des Mittelalters', in *Archiv für Musikwissenschaft* I (1918–19), 10–42.
186. See above, p. 71.
187. See W. Apel, *The Notation of Polyphonic Music 900–1600*, Cambridge, Mass., 1953, 22.
188. Ed. W. Apel, *Early Keyboard Music*, CEKM I, vol.I, 1–9; also partly ed. J. Handschin, in *Zeitschrift für Musikwissenschaft* XII (1929), 14–18.
189. See p. 39 above.
190. Ed. W. Apel, *op.cit.*; also ed. J. Wolf, in *Kirchenmusikalisches Jahrbuch* XIV (1890), 19–28.
191. Ed. L. Schrade, *Polyphonic Music of the C14th*, IV, 60–63.

192. *Ibid.*, Notes, 33.
193. *Ibid.*, 45–56.
194. *Ibid.*, Notes, 94.
195. *Ibid.*, Notes, 92.
196. Ed. W. Apel, *op.cit.*; also ed. J. Wolf, in *Geschichte der Mensuralnotation*, Leipzig, 1904, III, 191–199.
197. See P. Dronke, *Medieval Latin and the Rise of the European Love Lyric*, 2 vols., Oxford, 1966.
198. See C. Brown, *Religious Lyrics of the C14th*, Oxford, 1924, 15–29.
199. *Ibid.*, 251–3.
200. N. Bozon, *Contes moralisés*, ed. L. T. Smith & P. Meyer, Paris, 1889.
201. R. Greene, *The Early English Carols*, 2nd. ed., Oxford, 1977, cliii.
202. Ed. R. Greene, *The Lyrics of the Red Book of Ossory*, Medium Aevum Monographs, New Series V, Oxford, 1974.
203. Full text, ed. R. Davies, *Medieval English Lyrics*, London, 1963, 102.
204. Full text, ed. R. Greene, *op.cit.*, 15–17.
205. S. Wenzel, 'The Moor-Maiden – a contemporary View', in *Speculum* XLIX (1974), 69–74.
206. Ed, F. Furnivall, EETS, Or. Ser., Nos.119, 123, 1901–03, 11.9039–51.
207. E.g. The Mosburg Gradual, Munich University MS 57; H. Spanke, 'Das Mosburger Graduale', in *Zeitschrift für romanische Philologie* L (1930), 582–595; flagellant songs recorded by Hugo von Reuttingen c.1349, ed. Runge, Leipzig, 1900.
208. See E. Underhill, *Jacoponi da Todi, Poet and Mystic, 1228–1306*, London, 1919; L. Jeffery, *The earliest English Lyric and Franciscan Spirituality*, Lincoln, Nebraska, 1975.
209. See Dom G. Suñol, in *Analecta Montserratensia* I (1918), 100–192.
210. R. Greene, *The Lyrics of the Red Book of Ossory*, xxx.
211. A Watkin, *Dean Cosyn and Wells Cathedral Miscellanea*, Somerset Record Society LVI (1941), 23.
212. *Registrum Radulphi Baldock*, Canterbury and York Society VII (1911), 73–74.
213. See C. Brown & R. Robbins, *The Index of Middle English Verse*, The Index Society II, New York, 1943; R. Robbins, *Secular Lyrics of the C14th and C15th*, Oxford, 1952; R. Davies, *Medieval English Lyrics*, London, 1963; J. Speirs, *Medieval English Poetry*, London, 1971.
214. See p. 121; also see C. Olson, 'Chaucer and the Music of the Fourteenth Century', in *Speculum* XVI (1941), 64–92; J. Wimsatt, 'Chaucer and French Poetry', in *Geoffrey Chaucer*, ed. D. Brewer, London, 1974, 109–136.
215. See below, p. 107.
216. Ed. M. Bukofzer, in *Music & Letters* 17 (1936), 232–3.
217. Ed. G. Brook, *The Harley Lyrics*, Manchester, 1964.
218. See R. Robbins, *Historical Poems of the C14th & C15th*, New York, 1959.
219. *The Early English Carols*, No.440.
220. *Ibid.*, 483.
221. Ed. R. Davies, *op.cit.*, 99.
222. Ed. J. Speirs, *op. cit.*, 61.
223. See K. Bartsch, *Altfranzösische Romanzen und Pastourellen*, Leipzig, 1870.
224. A unique collection of examples bearing this title is in the MS Bodleian Library, Douce 308, text ed. G. Steffens, in *Archiv für das Studium der neueren Sprachen* XC (1900), 339–388.
225. See F. Gennrich, *Rondeaux, Virelais und Balladen . . .* , Dresden & Göttingen, 2 vols., 1921–27; N. Wilkins, *One Hundred Ballades, Rondeaux & Virelais . . .* , Cambridge, 1969; articles under the headings BALLADE, RONDEAU, VIRELAI, in *The New Grove Dictionary of Music & Musicians*, London, 1979.
226. Ed. Real Academia Española, 3 vols., Madrid, 1889–1922.
227. See J. Stevens, in *Report of the Tenth Congress of the International Musicological Society, Ljubljana 1967*, Basel, 1970, 207–9.
228. See Chapter 2.
229. 2nd. ed., Oxford, 1977.
230. Ed. F. Lecoy, Paris, 1963, l. 507 ff.
231. Ed. L. Buffum, Paris, 1928, l. 92 ff.
232. Ed. E. Langlois, Paris, 1914–24, l. 734 ff.
233. Ed. R. Morris, EETS, Or. Ser., Nos 57 etc., 1874–93, Fairfax Text, ll. 7599–7602.
234. Ed. G. Macaulay, EETS, Ex. ser., Nos.81–82, 1900–01.

235. Ed. J. Stevens, *Medieval Carols*, Musica Britannica, Vol.IV, London, 2nd ed., 1958.
236. R. Greene, *The Early English Carols*, 126.
237. *Ibid.*, 125–6.
238. *Ibid.*, 6.
239. *Ibid.*, 30.
240. *Ibid.*, 274.
241. *Ibid.*, 106–7.
242. *Ibid.*, 170.
243. *Ibid.*, 92–95.
244. *Ibid.*, 103–4.
245. See C. Brown, *Religious Lyrics of the C14th*, xvi–xix.
246. R. Greene, *op.cit.*, 92–95; J. Stevens, *op.cit.*, 110.
247. R. Greene, *op.cit.*, 87; J. Stevens, *op.cit.*, 1; F. Harrison describes this carol as C14th in his ed. *Now make we merthe*, Book II, Oxford, 1968, 2–9.
248. *Confessio Amantis*, Book I, 2708–9.
249. *Ibid.*, Book I, 2726–34.
250. C.f. the discussion of the Ballade contest in the *Parfait du Paon*, p. 2 above.
251. *French Metrical History of Richard II,* transl. Webb, in *Archeologia* XX.
252. Ed. E. Arnould, Oxford, 1940.
253. *Ibid.*, 22.
254. *Ibid.*, 10.
255. Ed. R. Steele, *The English Poems of Charles of Orleans*, EETS, Series 215, 1941.
256. Facs. & ed. in J. Stainer, *Early Bodleian Music: Sacred & Secular Songs*, 2 vols., London, 1901.
257. Ed. L. S. Myers, *Music, Cantilenas, Songs etc. from an early C15th MS.*, Cambridge, 1906; R. Rastall, *Four French Songs from an English Song Book*, Antico Ed., 1976; also facsimile ed., *A Fifteenth-Century Song Book*, Leeds, 1973; R. Rastall & A.-M. Seaman, *Six C15th English Songs*, Antico Ed., 1979.
258. Ed. N. Wilkins, *Three French Songs from the late C14th*, Antico Ed., 1974, 4–5.
259. Ed. Federhofer, in *Acta Musicologica* XXII (1950), 1 ff.
260. See N. Wilkins, 'The Post-Machaut Generation of Poet-Musicians', in *Nottingham Medieval Studies* XII (1968), 41–42.
261. Ed. N. Wilkins, *A C14th Repertory from the Codex Reina*, CMM 36, 1966, No. 18.
262. Ed. S. Kenney, CMM 19.
263. Ed. D. Fallows, Oxford University Press Early Music Series 28, 1977; also 'Words and music in two English songs of the mid-C15th: Charles d'Orléans and John Lydgate', in *Early Music* 5 (1977), 38–43.
264. C.f. p. 94.
265. C.f. p. 92.
266. See. N. Wilkins, 'Guillaume de Machaut 1300–1377', in *The Consort* 33 (1977), 219; also J. Wimsatt, 'G. de Machaut and Chaucer's Love Lyrics', in *Medium Aevum* 47 (1978), 66–87; D. Chambers, in *Chaucer Review* V (1970–71).
267. Ed. G. Ferri, Rome, 1910, 28.
268. A. Pirro, *La Musique à Paris sous le règne de Charles VI*, Paris, 1930, 2nd ed. 1958, 27.
269. *Ibid.*, 12, 26; B. Bernhard, in *Bibl. de l'Ecole des Chartes* IV (1842–43), 530.
270. A. Pirro, *op.cit.*, 26.
271. See e.g. M. Brenet, *Les musiciens de la Sainte- Chapelle du Palais*, Paris, 1910 (reprint 1973).
272. M. de Riquer, 'Le troubadour Peyre de Rius et Gaston Febus, comte de Foix', in *Annales du Midi* 66 (1954), 269–73.
273. See E. Chambers, *The Medieval Stage*, Oxford, 1903, II, 230–233; R. Rastall, 'The Minstrels of the English Royal Household', in *Royal Musical Association Research Chronicle* IV (1967), 1–27.
274. Quoted by E. vander Straeten, *La Musique au Pays-Bas avant le XIXe siècle*, Brussels, 1875 (reprint 1969), IV, 236–7.
275. Sarceno, *Regesto dei principi di casa d'Acaja*, 1881, 258, 261, 264.
276. B. Bernhard, in *Bibl. de l'Ecole des Chartes* III (1841–42), 398–9.
277. Straeten, *op.cit.*, 101.
278. Froissart, *Chroniques*, after K. de Lettenhove, Froissart: *Etude littéraire*, Paris, 1875, II, 180.
279. Ed. M. Roques, Paris, 1931, ll. 7041–2.

280. See H. Farmer, *Music in medieval Scotland*, London, 1930, 13.
281. E. Petit, *Itinéraires des ducs de Bourgogne* (Documents inédits sur l'histoire de France), Paris, 1888, 516.
282. Ed. E. Roy, *Oeuvres*, Paris, 1886–96, III, 79–94.
283. See E. Bowles, 'Instruments at the Court of Burgundy', in *The Galpin Society Journal* VI (1953), 41–51.
284. W. Chappell, *Old English Popular Music*, London, 1893, I, 17, n.2.
285. See E. David, *Etudes historiques sur la poésie et la musique dans la Cambrie*, Paris, 1884.
286. *Ibid.*, 242.
287. *Ibid.*, 249.
288. *Ibid.*, 252.
289. See R. Rastall, *op.cit.*, 5.
290. M. Brenet, *Musique et musiciens de la vieille France*, Paris, 1911, 6.
291. B. Prost, *Inventaires mobiliers et extraits des comptes des ducs de Bourgogne*, Paris, 1902–04, I, 24.
292. M. Delpit, 'Etudes sur l'ancienne administration des villes de France', in *Bibl. de l'Ecole des Chartes* IV (1842–43), 162.
293. B. Bernhard, *op.cit.*, III, 402.
294. A town wait sounds the hours to this day in Cracow, and his playing precedes the mid-day Radio News.
295. A. Pirro, *op.cit.*, 5.
296. Sarceno, *op.cit.*, 262, 264.
297. R. Rastall, *op. cit.*, 19–20.
298. Ed. G. Coopland, Cambridge, 1969, 2 vols.
299. C.f. A. Pirro, *op.cit.*, 14–15.
300. B. Bernhard, *op.cit.*, III, 380.
301. *Ed.cit.*, ll. 2364–5.
302. For samples of earlier such descriptions, see A. Dinaux, *Les trouvères cambrésiens*, Paris, 1837, 18–20.
303. Ed. G. Wimmer, Marburg, 1888, ll. 481–483.
304. Ed. J. Ribrard, Geneva, 1970, ll. 640–643.
305. *Ed.cit.*, ll. 2376–83; c.f. ll. 2852–56.
306. H. Farmer, *op.cit.*, 13.
307. *Ed.cit.*, ll. 2860–66.
308. *Ed.cit.*, ll. 3007–11.
309. *Ed.cit.*, ll. 11–18.
310. Straeten, *op.cit.*, 197–8.
311. J. Stow, *A Survay of London*, 1598, 71–72.
312. H. Anglès, *Historia de la musica medieval en Navarra*, Pamplona, 1970 (posth.), 265, 254, 260–1.
313. Sarceno, *op.cit.*, 263.
314. E. Rickert, *Chaucer's World*, New York, 1948, 17–18.
315. C. Olson, 'The Minstrels at the Court of Edward III', in *Proceedings of the Modern Language Association* LVI (1941), 611–612.
316. Sarceno, *op.cit.*, 261.
317. H. Anglès, *op.cit.*, 214–215.
318. B. Bernhard, 'Recherches sur l'histoire de la corporation des ménétriers ou joueurs d'instruments de la Ville de Paris', in *Bibl. de l'Ecole des Chartes* III (1841–42), 377–404; IV (1842–43), 525–548; V (1843–44), 254 ff., 339 ff.; VI, 398.
319. B. Bernhard, *op.cit.*, III, 404.
320. W. Chappell, *op.cit.*, I, 18–19.
321. R. Rastall, *op.cit.*, 14.
322. See below, p. 137.
323. B. Bernhard, *op.cit.*, III, 382–383.
324. See Y. Rokseth, 'Les femmes musiciennes du XIIe au XIVe siècles', in *Romania* 61 (1935), 464–480; also A. Pirro, *op.cit.*, 5.
325. U. Günther, 'Die Musiker des Herzogs von Berry', in *Musica Disciplina* XVII (1963), 88, n.62.
326. H. Anglès, *op.cit.*, 218.
327. U. Günther, *op.cit.*, 81.

328. H. Anglès, *op.cit.*, 218, 228.
329. A. Pirro, *op.cit.*, 5.
330. W. Chappell, *op.cit.*, I, 15–16.
331. *Ibid.*, 8.
332. M. Brenet, *Musique et musiciens de la vieille France*, Paris, 1911, 14, 7.
333. B. Prost, *op.cit.*, I, 82.
334. *Ibid.*, I, 270.
335. E. Petit, *op.cit.*, 493.
336. H. Anglès, *op.cit.*, 251, 258, 261, 265.
337. B. Bernhard, *op.cit.*, III, 396.
338. Sarceno, *op.cit.*, 260, 261, 263.
339. M. Brenet, *op.cit.*, 7; B. Prost, *op.cit.*, I, 226 & II, 171.
340. A. Pirro, *op.cit.*, 2.
341. L. Wright, 'The medieval Gittern and Citole . . .', in *The Galpin Society Journal* XXI (1977), 14.
342. Ed. Depping, *Livre des Métiers de Paris*, 360–361.
343. B. Bernhard, *op.cit.*, 379, n.1.
344. B. Bernhard, *op.cit.*, IV, 530.
345. Straeten, *op.cit.*, 251, 137.
346. U. Günther, *op.cit.*, 81.
347. H. Anglès, *op.cit.*, 176.
348. F. Pedrell, 'Jean I d'Aragon, compositeur de musique', in *Riemann-Festschrift*, 1909, 229.
349. L. Gautier, *Les Epopées*, Paris, 1892, II, 176; Gautier, p.175, describes the assembly in the following picturesque terms: 'Quel charmant tableau de genre on ferait avec une de ces assemblées de jongleurs à la mi-carême, avec tous ces costumes bizarres, avec toutes ces têtes de cabotins, et les allures tapageuses des jongleresses qui ne devaient certes pas manquer à pareille fête!'
350. L. Gautier, *op.cit.*, 176–7.
351. *Ibid.*
352. Straeten, *op.cit.*, 78, 95, 122, 133.
353. *Ibid*, 246.
354. L. Gautier, *op.cit.*, 177.
355. C.f. K. de Lettenhove, *Froissart: Etude littéraire*, Paris, 1857, I, 74.
356. Straeten, *op.cit.*, 154.
357. *Ibid.*, 122.
358. L. Gautier, *op.cit.*, 177.
359. Sarceno, *op.cit.*, 260–261.
360. L. Gautier, *op.cit.*, 177–178.
361. H. Anglès, *op.cit.*, 209–210.
362. C.f. N. Wilkins, 'The Post-Machaut Generation of Poet-Musicians', in *Nottingham medieval Studies* XII (1968), 59–60.
363. *Ibid.*
364. H. Anglès, *op.cit.*, 223.
365. N. Wilkins, *op.cit.*, 46.
366. A. Pirro, *op.cit.*, 14.
367. N. Wilkins, *op.cit.*, 45.
368. H. Anglès, *op.cit.*, 210.
369. *Ibid.*, 217.
370. Straeten, *op.cit.*, 251.
371. Ed. E. Langlois, *Recueil d'arts de seconde rhétorique*, Paris, 1902, 13.
372. B. Bernhard, *op.cit.*, IV, 529.
373. *Les Grandes Chroniques*, ed. P. Paris, Paris, 1836–38, IV, 478.
374. H. Anglès, *op.cit.*, 196–197.
375. A. Pirro, *op.cit.*, 11.
376. Straeten, *op.cit.*, 95–96.
377. H. Anglès, *op.cit.*, 259–260.
378. A. Pirro, *op.cit.*, 9.
379. H. Anglès, *op.cit.*, 226.

380. *Ibid.*, 197–8, 220.
381. *Ibid.*, 225.
382. *Ibid.*, 226.
383. C.f. William Dodmore, blind harper, who served Richard II: R. Rastall, *op.cit.*, 23.
384. For journeys to Avignon from Aragon in 1396, 1397 & 1399, see H. Anglès, *op.cit.*, 180–181, 253–254, 259.
385. H. Anglès, *op.cit.*, 198.
386. *Ibid.*, 225.
387. *Ibid.*, 229.
388. Sarceno, *op.cit.*, 258–265.
389. H. Anglès, *op.cit.*, 178, 224; N. Wilkins, *op.cit.*, 59–60.
390. H. Anglès, *op.cit.*, 181.
391. See N. Wilkins, 'Music in the C14th *Miracles de Nostre Dame*', in *Musica Disciplina* XXVIII (1974), 39–75.
392. B. Bernhard, *op.cit.*, *passim*.
393. C.f. F. Warne, ed., *Jean Bodel: Le Jeu de Saint Nicolas*, Oxford, 1958, xvi; A. Dinaux, *Les trouvères artésiens*, Paris, 1843, 9–10.
394. Straeten, *op.cit.*, 130.
395. Printed in B. Bernhard, *op.cit.*, III, 400–403.
396. A number of Scottish minstrels are listed in the Account Books of Durham Priory; see E. Chambers, *op.cit.*, II, 240–244.
397. R. Rastall, *op.cit.*, 7.
398. E. Chambers, *op.cit.*, II, 238–9.
399. Straeten, *op.cit.*, 78; A. Dinaux, *Les trouvères Brabançons, Hainuyers, Liégeois et Namurois*, Paris, 1863, 570–573.
400. B. Bernhard, *op.cit.*, III, 395–6.
401. *Ibid.*, IV, 532.
402. Quoted from Breul's *Théâtre des antiquités de Paris* by B. Bernhard, *op.cit.*, III, 388–394.
403. Printed in B. Bernhard, *op.cit.*, 403–4.
404. G. Dugdale & R. Dodsworth, *Monasticon Anglicanum*, London, 1682, 355.
405. R. Plot, *The Natural History of Staffordshire*, Oxford, 1686.
406. Reproduced in the Church Magazine of St. Mary's, Beverley, 1976; see also G. & J. Montagu, 'Beverley Minster reconsidered', in *Early Music* 6 (1978), 401–415.
407. H. Westlake, *The Parish Guilds of Medieval England*, London, 1919, 173, 237.
408. *Ibid.*, 62–63.
409. U. Günther, *op.cit.*, 80; N. Wilkins, in *Nottingham Medieval Studies* XII (1968), 51.
410. Sarceno, *op.cit.*, 260.
411. H. Anglès, *op.cit.*, 178.
412. E. Chambers, *op.cit.*, II, 240–244.
413. Sarceno, *op.cit.*
414. Straeten, *op.cit.*
415. R. Rastall, *op.cit.*
416. C.f. J. Viard, 'L'Hôtel de Philippe VI de Valois', in *Bibl. de l'Ecole des Chartes* LV (1894), 602, 614, 615, 620; N. Wilkins, *op.cit.*; U. Günther, *op.cit.*; A. Pirro, *op.cit.*; H. Anglès, *op.cit.*; E. Bowles, *op.cit.*
417. Public Record Office, *Chancery Miscellanea* C47/4/5, f.45v & f.48r.
418. Public Record Office, *Exchequer Roll* E101/369/6; see C. Bullock-Davies, *Menestrellorum Multitudo: Minstrels at a Royal Feast*, University of Wales Press, 1978.
419. Ed. W. Stubbs, 1882.
420. See above, p. 3.
421. See E. Chambers, *op.cit.*, II, 234; W. Chappell, *op.cit.*, I, 15–16.
422. Froissart, *Chronicles*, transl. G. Brereton, Penguin Classics, 1968, 353–4.
423. Ed. K. de Lettenhove, 1873, 5.
424. Transl. G. Brereton, *op.cit.*, 414.
425. A. Dinaux, *Les trouvères de la Flandre et du Tournaisis*, Paris, 1839, 56–57.
426. E. David, *op.cit.*, 237–9, 258–9.
427. W. Chappell, *op.cit.*, I, 17–18.

428. See B. Bernhard, *op.cit.*, III, 403–4.
429. A. Dinaux, *Trouvères Brabaçons, Hainuyers, Liégeois, Namurois*, Paris, 1863, 226–228.
430. A. Pirro, *op.cit.*, 17.
431. *Oeuvres*, ed. G. Raynaud, Paris, 1878–1904, vol.V, 127–128.
432. See E. Bowles, 'Haut and bas: the grouping of musical instruments in the Middle Ages', in *Musica Disciplina* VIII (1954), 115–140.
433. See E. David, *op.cit.*, 158–161.
434. W. Chappell, *op.cit.*, I, 20.
435. See L. Wright, 'The medieval Gittern and Citole: a case of mistaken identity', in *The Galpin Society Journal* XXX (1977), 8–42.
436. See M. Remnant, 'Rebec, Fiddle and Crowd in England', in *Proceedings of the Royal Musical Association* 96 (1970).
437. See E. Ripin, 'Towards an identification of the chekker', in *The Galpin Society Journal* XXVIII (1975), 11–25.
438. *New Oxford History of Music* IV, 476.
439. See J. Blades, *Percussion Instruments and their History*, London, 1970.

Index of Composers

Chaucer Songs

The note, I trow, maked was in France (*Chaucer*)

CONTENTS

INTRODUCTION

The connection between French song and Chaucer is evident from the use the poet makes of the fourteenth-century Ballade and Rondeau forms, the fact that he translated some Ballades by Oton de Granson, the inclusion of French lines or titles in several of his lyrics, and the extensive use he has been shown to have made particularly of lyrics by Guillaume de Machaut in many of his longer narrative works.

Finding contemporary French music to fit Chaucer's texts is straightforward especially in the case of Ballades with stanzas of seven lines of ten syllables each. All of these can be found in Machaut, though the French musician preferred to have a shorter fifth line of seven syllables. For Ballade stanzas of eight or nine lines of decasyllables it is necessary to look a little beyond Machaut, to his late fourteenth-century successors of the 'Ars Subtilior', poet-musicians such as Senleches and Solage. The exchanges between the poet and Fortune in the first two Ballades of the Group of three entitled *Balades de visage sanz Peinture*, each using stanzas of eight lines and decasyllables, can be accommodated in the Andrieu setting of Deschamps's Double Ballade on the death of Machaut. Triple Ballades are relatively rare, but the grouping of poems in threes is most likely to derive from the polytextual tradition first applied to the Ballade by Machaut on the model of the traditional Motet.

Of Chaucer's several poems in an amalgam of Complainte and Chant Royal forms, although neither of Machaut's single examples of these (set to music in his *Remède de Fortune*) will match structurally, the rhyme scheme used by Chaucer, together with his favourite stanzas of seven lines and ten syllables, allows the use of further music from Machaut Ballades.

In musical settings, as opposed to independent poems, in the fourteenth century the thirteen-line Rondeau was rare in France. Machaut happily provides a single example, thus enabling a performance of the roundel from the *Parlement of Foules* to be attempted; no other suitable settings are available to fit the Triple Roundel 'Merciles Beaute', which seems nevertheless to be in the musical polytextual tradition. Several polytextual Rondeau settings of different metrical structure are known from the late fourteenth century, while a small number of settings of thirteen-line types is known from the thirteenth and from the early fifteenth centuries (Adam de la Hale and Baude Cordier respectively).

Although there is generally no attempt at word setting in the Schubertian sense in music as early as this, and a serious Ballade text or love song will fit any number of serious Ballade settings, certain special connections may be contrived: for instance, Chaucer's Ballade 'Madame, for your newe-fangelnesse', with its refrain 'In stede of blew, thus may ye were al grene', fits in striking fashion Machaut's parallel Ballade 'Se pour ce muir qu'Amours ay bien servi', with its refrain 'Qu'en lieu de bleu, dame, vous vestés vert'; it may be appropriate to choose from the important Cypriot-French repertory a setting for Chaucer's translation from Oton de Granson, in view of the latter's visit to the island of Cyprus in 1393 in the company of Henry Bolingbroke and his possible influence on poetry writing there.

Performance Note

The vocal lines may be doubled, at the discretion of the performers, by an unobtrusive instrument such as recorder, rebec, fiddle or lute. Instrumental lines should be taken by recorder, rebec, fiddle, lute, viol, harp etc. according to the convenience of pitch and the availability of performers. One or two parts may sometimes be taken by a portative organ; citole or gittern would be welcome, though modern reconstructions of these are rare. This type of sophisticated polyphony is not suitable for the 'loud' or the 'rustic' instruments; nor is percussion any advantage here, apart from the occasional discreet use of bell chimes to heighten a melodic line.

Speeds must be determined by the nature of the words and music; if there is obviously florid passagework, the speed must be sufficient for brilliance to be achieved. Dynamic variation is not really characteristic of the period or of the capabilities of contemporary instruments.

The text used in the following settings is from the standard edition of Chaucer by W.Skeat.

1. Hyd, Absolon, thy gilte tresses clere (*The Legend of Good Women*) [Machaut: Nes qu'on porroit]

your wyf- -hod no com-pa- ri-soun; 6. Hyde ye your beau- -tes, I-

-soude and E- -leyne,

7. My la- dy cometh that al this may dis-

-teyne.

Hyd, Absolon, thy gilte tresses clere;
Ester, ley thou thy meknesse al a-doun;
Hyd, Jonathas, al thy frendly manere;
Penalopee, and Marcia Catoun,
Mak of your wyfhod no comparisoun;
Hyde ye your beautes, Isoude and Eleyne,
My lady cometh, that al this may disteyne.

Thy faire body, lat hit nat appere,
Lavyne; and thou, Lucresse of Rome toun,
And Polixene, that boghten love so dere,
And Cleopatre, with al thy passioun,
Hyde ye your trouthe of love and your
        renoun,
And thou, Tisbe, that hast of love swich
        peyne;
My lady cometh, that al this may disteyne.

Herro, Dido, Laudomia, alle y-fere,
And Phyllis, hanging for thy Demophoun,
And Canace, espyed by thy chere,
Ysiphile, betraysed with Jasoun,
Maketh of your trouthe neyther boost ne
        soun;
Nor Ypermistre of Adriane, ye tweyne;
My lady cometh, that al this may disteyne.

can not love ful half yeer in a place; 6. To ne-we thing

your lust is e-ver kene; 7.In stede of blew,

thus may ye were al grene.

Madame, for your newe-fanglenesse,
Many a servaunt have ye put out of grace,
I take my leve of your unstedfastnesse,
For wel I wot, whyl ye have lyves space,
Ye can not love ful half yeer in a place;
To newe thing your lust is ever kene;
In stede of blew, thus may ye were al grene.

Right as a mirour nothing may enpresse,
But, lightly as it cometh, so mot it pace,
So fareth your love, your werkes bereth
      witnesse.
Ther is no feith that may your herte en-
      brace;
But, as a wedercok, that turneth his face
With every wind, ye fare, and that is sene;
In stede of blew, thus may ye were al grene.

Ye might be shryned, for your brotelnesse,
Bet than Dalyda, Creseide or Candace;
For ever in chaunging stant your sikernesse,
That tache may no wight fro your herte
      arace;
If ye lese oon, ye can wel tweyn purchace;
Al light for somer, ye woot wel what I mene,
In stede of blew, thus may ye were al grene.

3. To you, my purse, and to non other wight

[Machaut: S'Amours ne fait]

184

To you, my purse, and to non other wight
Compleyne I, for ye be my lady dere!
I am so sory, now that ye be light;
For certes, but ye make me hevy chere,
Me were as leef be leyd up-on my bere;
For whiche un-to your mercy thus I crye:
Beth hevy ageyn, or elles mot I dye!

Now voucheth sauf this day, or hit be night,
That I of you the blisful soun may here,
Or see your colour lyk the sonne bright,
That of yelownesse hadde never pere.
Ye be my lyf, ye be myn hertes stere,
Quene of comfort and of good companye:
Beth hevy ageyn, or elles mot I dye!

Now purs, that be to me my lyves light,
And saveour, as doun in this worlde here,
Out of this toune help me through your
      might,
Sin that ye wole nat been my tresorere;
For I am shave as nye as any frere.
But yit I pray un-to your curtesye:
Beth hevy ageyn, or elles mot I dye!

Lenvoy de Chaucer.

[O conquerour of Brutes Albioun!
Which that by lyne and free eleccioun
Ben verray king, this song to you I sende;
And ye, that mowen al our harm amende,
Have minde up-on my supplicacioun!]

185

The firste stok, fader of gentilesse —
What man that claymeth gentil for to
Must folowe his trace, and alle his wittes
    dresse
Vertu to sewe, and vyces for to flee.
For unto vertu longeth dignitee,
And noght the revers, saufly dar I deme,
Al were he mytre, croune, or diademe.

This firste stok was ful of rightwisnesse,
Trewe of his word, sobre, pitous, and free,
Clene of his goste, and loved besinesse,
Ageinst the vyce of slouthe, in honestee:

And, but his heir love vertu, as dide he,
He is noght gentil, thogh he riche seme,
Al were he mytre, croune, or diademe.

Vyce may wel be heir to old richesse;
But ther may no man, as men may wel see,
Bequethe his heir his vertuous noblesse
That is appropred unto no degree,
But to the firste fader in magestee,
That maketh him his heir, that can him
    queme,
Al were he mytre, croune, or diademe.

187

5. Som tyme this world was so stedfast and stable

[Machaut: Gais et jolis]

188

Som tyme this world was so stedfast and
  stable,
That mannes word was obligacioun,
And now hit is so fals and deceivable,
That word and deed, as in conclusioun,
Ben no-thing lyk, for turned up so doun
Is al this world for mede and wilfulnesse,
That al is lost for lak of stedfastnesse.

What maketh this world to be so variable,
But lust that folk have in dissensioun?
Among us now a man is holde unable,
But-if he can, by som collusioun,
Don his neighbour wrong or oppressioun.
What causeth this, but wilful wrecchednesse,
That al is lost, for lak of stedfastnesse?

Trouthe is put doun, resoun is holden fable;
Vertu hath now no dominacioun,

Pitee exyled, no man is merciable.
Through covetyse is blent discrecioun;
The world hath mad a permutacioun
Fro right to wrong, fro trouthe to fikelnesse,
That al is lost, for lak of stedfastnesse.

Lenvoy to King Richard.

[O prince, desyre to be honourable,
Cherish thy folk and hate extorcioun!
Suffre no thing, that may be reprevable
To thyn estat, don in thy regioun.
Shew forth thy swerd of castigacioun,
Dred God, do law, love trouthe and worthi-
  nesse,
And wed thy folk agein to stedfastnesse.]

189

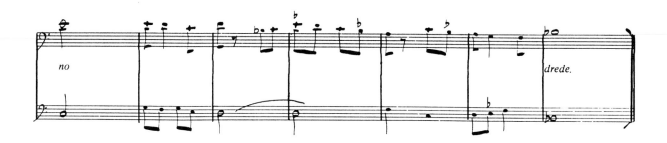

no   *drede.*

Flee fro the prees, and dwelle with sothfast-
    nesse,
Suffyce unto thy good, though hit be smal;
For hord hath hate, and climbing tikelnesse,
Prees hath envye, and wele blent overal;
Savour no more than thee bihove shal;
Werk wel thy-self, that other folk canst rede;
And trouthe shal delivere, hit is no drede.

Tempest thee noght al croked to redresse,
In trust of hir that turneth as a bal:
Gret reste stant in litel besinesse;
And eek be war to sporne ageyn an al;
Stryve noght, as doth the crokke with the
    wal.
Daunte thy-self, that dauntest otheres dede;
And trouthe shal delivere, hit is no drede.

That thee is sent, receyve in buxumnesse,
The wrastling for this worlde axeth a fal.
Her nis non hoom, her nis but wildernesse:
Forth, pilgrim, forth! Forth, beste, out of
    thy stal!
Know thy contree, look up, thank God of al;
Hold the hye wey, and lat thy gost thee lede:
And trouthe shal deliver, hit is no drede.

Envoy

[Therefore, thou vache, leve thyn old
    wrecchednesse
Unto the worlde, leve now to be thral;
Crye him mercy, that of his hy goodnesse
Made thee of noght, and in especial
Draw unto him, and pray in general
For thee, and eek for other, hevenlich mede;
And trouthe shal deliver, hit is no drede.]

7. Madame, ye ben of al beautè shryne (*To Rosemounde*) [Senleches: En attendant esperance]

1. Ma- -da- -me, ye
3. For as cri-

ben of al beau-tè shry- -ne, 2. As fer as cer-
-stal glo-ri- ous ye shy- -ne, 4. And ly- -ke ru-

-cled is the
-by ben your

map- -pe-
che- -kes

-mounde; rounde.

192

Madame, ye ben of al beautè shryne
As fer as cercled is the mappemounde;
For as the cristal glorious ye shyne,
And lyke ruby ben your chekes rounde.
Ther,with ye ben so mery and jocounde,
That at a revel whan that I see you daunce,
It is an oynement unto my wounde,
Thogh ye to me ne do no daliaunce.

For thogh I wepe of teres ful a tyne,
Yet may that wo myn herte nat confounde;
Your seemly voys that ye sò smal out-twyne
Maketh my thoght in joye and blis habounde.

So curteisly I go, with lovë bounde,
That to my-self I sey, in my penaunce,
Suffyseth me to love you, Rosemounde,
Thogh ye to me ne do no daliaunce.

Nas never pyk walwed in galauntyne
As I in love am walwed and y-wounde;
For which ful ofte I of my-self divyne
That I am trewe Tristam the secounde.
My love may not refreyd be nor afounde;
I brenne ay in an amorous plesaunce.
Do what you list, I wil your thral be founde,
Thogh ye to me ne do no daliaunce.

194

woman- -ly con- -te- -naun-

-ce, 6. Your fres- she fe- -tures and your com- -li-

-nesse 7. That, whyl I live, my herte

to his mais- tresse 8. You hath

ful chose, in trew per- -se- -ve-

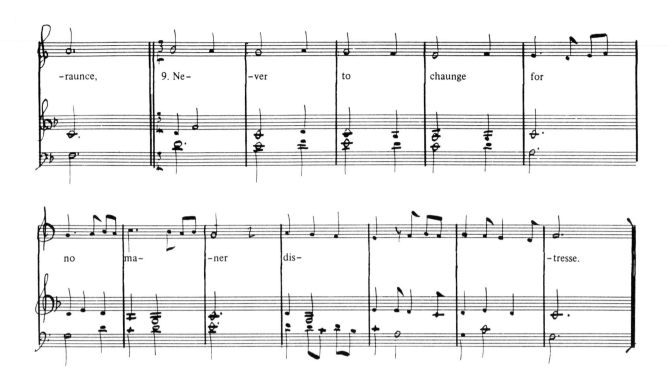

-raunce, 9. Ne- -ver to chaunge for

no ma- -ner dis- -tresse.

So hath my herte caught in rémembraunce
Your beautè hool, and stedfast governaunce,
Your vertues allè, and your hy noblesse,
That you to serve is set al my plesaunce;
So wel me lykth your womanly contenaunce,
Your fresshe fetures and your comlinesse,
That, whyl I live, my herte to his maistresse,
You hath ful chose, in trew perséveraunce,
Never to chaunge, for no maner distresse.

And sith I [you] shal do this observaunce
Al my lyf, withouten displesaunce,
You for to serve with al my besinesse,
[Taketh me, lady, in your obeisaunce]
And have me somwhat in your souvenaunce.
My woful herte suffreth greet duresse;
And [loke] how humbl[el]y, with al simplesse,
My wil I cónforme to your ordenaunce,
As you best list, my peynes to redresse.

Considring eek how I hange in balaunce
In your servycè; swich, lo! is my chaunce,
Abyding grace, whan that your gentilnesse
Of my gret wo list doon allegeaunce,
And with your pitè me som wyse avaunce,
In ful rebating of my hevinesse;
And think resóun, that wommanly noblesse
Shuld nat desyre for to doon outrance
Ther-as she findeth noon unbuxumnesse.

Lenvoye.

[Auctour of norture, lady of plesaunce,
Soveraine of beautè, flour of wommanhede,
Take ye non hede unto myn ignoraunce,
But this receyveth of your goodlihede,
Thinking that I have caught in remembraunce
Your beautè hool, your stedfast governaunce.]

9. This wrecched worldes transmutacion/ [F.Andrieu/E.Deschamps: Armes, amours, dames, chevalerie/
No man is wrecched, but himself it wene (from *Balades de visage sanz peinture*) O flour des flours de toute melodie]

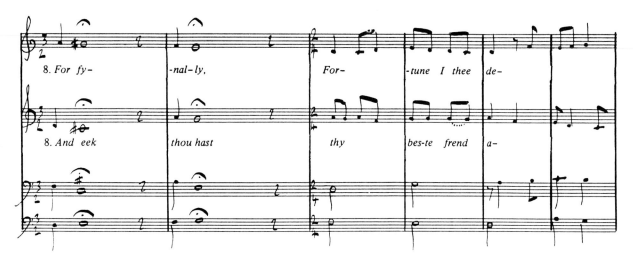

8. For fy- -nal-ly, For- -tune I thee de-

8. And eek thou hast thy bes-te frend a-

-fye!

-lyve!

I. Le Pleintif countre Fortune.

This wrecched worldes transmutacioun,
As wele or wo, now povre and now honour,
With-outen ordre or wys discrecioun
Governed is by Fortunes errour,
But natheles, the lak of hir favour
Ne may nat don me singen, though I dye
'Iay tout perdu mon temps et mon labour:'
For fynally, Fortune, I thee defye!

Yit is me left the light of my resoun,
To knowen frend fo in thy mirour.
So muche hath yit thy whirling up and doun
Y-taught me for to knowen in an hour.
But trewely, no force of thy reddour
To him that over him-self hath the maystrye!
My suffisaunce shal be my socour:
For fynally, Fortune, I thee defye!

O Socrates, thou stedfast champioun,
She never mighte be thy tormentour;
Thou never dreddest hir oppressioun,
Ne in hir chere founde thou no savour.
Thou knewe wel deceit of hir colour,
And that hir moste worshipe is to lye.
I knowe hir eek a fals dissimulour:
For fynally, Fortune, I thee defye!

II. La respounse de Fortune au Pleintif.

No man is wrecched, but him-self hit wene,
And he that hath him-self hath suffisaunce.
Why seystow thanne I am to thee so kene,
That hast thy-self out of my governaunce?
Sey thus: 'Graunt mercy of thyn habound-
aunce
That thou has lent or this.' Why wolt thou
stryve?
What wostow yit, how I thee wol avaunce?
And eek thou hast thy beste frend alyve!

I have thee taught divisioun bi-twene
Frend of effect, and frend of countenaunce;
Thee nedeth nat the galle of noon hyene,
That cureth eyen derke fro hir penaunce;
Now seestow cleer, that were in ignoraunce.
Yit halt thyn ancre, and yit thou mayst
arryve
Ther bountee berth the keye of my sub-
staunce:
And eek thou hast thy beste frend alyve.

How many have I refused to sustene,
Sin I thee fostred have in thy plesaunce!
Woltow than make a statut on thy quene
That I shal been ay at thyn ordinaunce?
Thou born art in my regne of variaunce,
Aboute the wheel with other most thou
dryve.
My lore is bet than wikke is thy grevaunce,
And eek thou hast thy beste frend alyve.

[III. La respounse du Pleintif countre Fortune.

Thy lore I dampne, hit is adversitee.
My frend maystow nat reven, blind goddesse!
That I thy frendes knowe, I thanke hit thee.
Tak hem agayn, lat hem go lye on presse!
The negardye in keping hir richesse
Prenostik is thou wolt hir tour assayle;
Wikke appetyt comth ay before seknesse:
In general, this reule may nat fayle.

La respounse de Fortune countre le Pleintif.

Thou pinchest at my mutabilitee,
For I thee lente a drope of my richesse,
And now me lyketh to with-drawe me.
Why sholdestow my realtee oppresse?
The see may ebbe and flowen more or lesse;
The welkne hath might to shyne, reyne, or
hayle:
Right so mot I kythen my brotelnesse.
In general, this reule may nat fayle.

Lo, the' execucion of the magestee
That al purveyeth of his rightwisnesse,
That same thing 'Fortune' clepen ye,
Ye blinde bestes, ful of lewednesse!
The hevene hath propretee of sikernesse,
This world hath ever resteles travayle;
Thy laste day is ende of myn intresse:
In general, this reule may nat fayle.

Lenvoy de Fortune.

Princes, I prey you of your gentilesse,
Lat nat this man on me thus crye and pleyne,
And I shal quyte you your bisinesse
At my requeste, as three of you or tweyne;
And, but you list releve him of his peyne,
Preyeth his beste frend, of his noblesse,
That so som beter estate he may atteyne.]

10. Ther nis so hy comfort to my plesaunce (*The Compleynt of Venus* – Granson)　　　　[French-Cypriot anon.: *Sous un bel arbre*]

1. Ther nis
3. As for

so　hy　com-ley- -fort

to　my　ple-saun- -ce,　2. Whan that
of　re- -mem-braun- ce　4. U- -pon

I　am
the　man-

in　a- -hod　and

-ny　he- -vi- thi- -nesse,
the　wor- thi-

-nesse,
5. U-
7. Ther

-pon
o-

the
-ghte

trouthe, and on the sted- fast- -nesse
bla- -me me no cre- a- -ture,

6. Of him whos I am al whyl I may dure;
8. *For e-* *-very wight* *prei-seth* *his gen-* *-ti-*

-lesse.

Ther nis so hy comfort to my plesaunce,
Whan that I am in any hevinesse,
As for to have leyser of remembraunce
Upon the manhod and the worthinesse,
Upon the trouthe, and on the stedfastnesse
Of him whos I am al, whyl I may dure;
Ther oghte blame me no creature,
For every wight preiseth his gentilesse.

In him is bountee, wisdom, governaunce
Wel more than any mannes wit can gesse;
For grace hath wold so forforth him avaunce
That of knighthode he is parfit richesse.
Honour honoureth him for his noblesse;
Therto so wel hath formed him Nature,
That I am his for ever, I him assure,
For every wight preiseth his gentilesse.

And not-withstanding al his suffisaunce,
His gentil herte is of so greet humblesse
To me in worde, in werke, in contenaunce,
And me to serve is al his besinesse,
That I am set in verrey sikernesse,
Thus oghte I blesse wel myn aventure,
Sith that him list me serven and honoure;
For every wight preiseth his gentilesse.

203

11. If no love is, O god, what fele I so? (*Cantus Troili, Troilus and Criseyde*)   [Machaut: J'aim mieus languir]

Cantus Troili.

'If no love is, O god, what fele I so?
And if love is, what thing and whiche is he?
If love be good, from whennes comth my wo?
If it be wikke, a wonder thinketh me,
When every torment and adversitee
That cometh of him, may to me savory
    thinke;
For ay thurst I, the more that I it drinke.

And if that at myn owene lust I brenne,
Fro whennes cometh my wailing and my
    pleynte?
If harme agree me, wher-to pleyne I thenne?

I noot, ne why unwery that I feynte.
O quike deeth, o swete harm so queynte,
How may of thee in me swich quantitee,
But-if that I consente that it be?

And if that I consente, I wrongfully
Compleyne, y-wis; thus possed to and fro,
Al sterelees with-inne a boot am I
A-mid the see, by-twixen windes two,
That in contrarie stonden ever-mo.
Allas! what is this wonder maladye?
For hete of cold, for cold of hete, I dye.'

And to the god of love thus seyde he
With pitous voys, 'O lord, now youres is

My spirit, which that oughte youres be.
Yow thanke I, lord, that han me brought to
    this;
But whether goddesse or womman, y-wis,
She be, I noot, which that ye do me serve;
But as hir man I wole ay live and sterve.

Ye stonden in hire eyen mightily,
As in a place un-to your vertu digne;
Wherfore, lord, if my servyse or I
May lyke yow, so beth to me benigne;
For myn estat royal here I resigne
In-to hir hond, and with ful humble chere
Bicome hir man, as to my lady dere.'

205

12. O love, to whom I have and shal (Antigone's song, *Troilus and Criseyde*)   [Machaut: De desconfort, de martyre amoureus]

joye and seur-tee, out of

drede.

[She seyde,] 'O love, to whom I have and
 shal
Ben humble subgit, trewe in myn entente,
As I best can, to yow, lord, yeve ich al
For ever-more, myn hertes lust to rente.
For never yet thy grace no wight sente
So blisful cause as me, my lyf to lede
In alle joye and seurtee, out of drede.

Ye, blisful god, han me so wel beset
In love, y-wis, that al that bereth lyf
Imaginen ne cowde how to ben bet;
For, lord, with-outen jalousye or stryf,
I love oon which that is most ententyf
To serven wel, unwery or unfeyned,
That ever was, and leest with harm dis-
 treyned.

As he that is the welle of worthinesse,
Of trouthe ground, mirour of goodliheed,
Of wit Appollo, stoon of sikernesse,
Of vertu rote, of lust findere and heed,
Thurgh which is alle sorwe fro me deed,
Y-wis, I love him best, so doth he me;
Now good thrift have he, wher-so that he be!

Whom sholde I thanke but yow, god of love,
Of al this blisse, in which to bathe I ginne?
And thanked be ye, lord, for that I love:

This is the righte lyf that I am inne,
To flemen alle manere vyce and sinne:
This doth me so to vertu for to entende,
That day by day I in my wil amende.

And who-so seyth that for to love is vyce,
Or thraldom, though he fele in it distresse,
He outher is envyous, or right nyce,
Or is unmighty, for his shrewednesse,
To loven; for swich maner folk, I gesse,
Defamen love, as no-thing of him knowe;
They speken, but they bente never his bowe.

What is the sonne wers, of kinde righte,
Though that a man, for feblesse of his yën,
May nought endure on it to see for brighte?
Or love the wers, though wrecches on it
 cryen?
No wele is worth, that may no sorwe dryen.
And for-thy, who that hath an heed of verre,
Fro cast of stones war him in the werre!

But I with al myn herte and al my might,
As I have seyd, wol love, un-to my laste,
My dere herte, and al myn owene knight,
In which myn herte growen is so faste,
And his in me, that it shal ever laste.
Al dredde I first to love him to biginne,
Now woot I wel, ther is no peril inne.'

13. I, which that am the sorwefulleste man

[Machaut: Riche d'amours et mendians d'amie]

An amorous Compleint, made at Windsor.

I, which that am the sorwefulleste man
That in this world was ever yit livinge,
And leest recoverer of him-selven can,
Beginne thus my deedly compleininge
On hir, that may to lyf and deeth me bringe,
Which hath on me no mercy ne no rewthe
That love hir best, but sleeth me for my
    trewthe.

Can I noght doon ne seye that may yow lyke,
For certes, now, allas! allas! the whyle!
Your plesaunce is to laughen whan I syke,
And thus ye me from al my blisse exyle.
Ye han me cast in thilke spitous yle
Ther never man on lyve mighte asterte;
This have I for I lovë you, swete herte!

Sooth is, that wel I woot, by lyklinesse,
If that it were thing possible to do
T'acompte youre beutee and goodnesse,
I have no wonder thogh ye do me wo;
Sith I, th'unworthiest that may ryde or go,
Durste ever thinken in so hy a place,
What wonder is, thogh ye do me no grace?

Allas! thus is my lyf brought to an ende,
My deeth, I see, is my conclusioun;
I may wel singe, 'in sory tyme I spende
My lyf;' that song may have confusioun!
For mercy, pitee, and deep affeccioun,
I sey for me, for al my deedly chere,
Alle thise diden, in that, me love yow dere.

And in this wyse and in dispayre I live
In lovë; nay, but in dispayre I dye!
But shal I thus [to] yow my deeth for-give,
That causeles doth me this sorow drye?
Ye, certes, I! For she of my folye
Hath nought to done, although she do me
    sterve;
Hit is nat with hir wil that I hir serve!

Than sith I am of my sorowe the cause
And sith that I have this, withoute hir reed,
Than may I seyn, right shortly in a clause,
It is no blame unto hir womanheed
Though swich a wrecche as I be for hir deed;
[And] yet alwey two thinges doon me dyë
That is to seyn, hir beutee and myn yë.

So that, algates, she is the verray rote
Of my disese, and of my dethe also;
For with oon word she mighte be my bote,
If that she vouched sauf for to do so.
But [why] than is hir gladnesse at my wo?

It is hir wone plesaunce for to take,
To seen hir servaunts dyen for hir sake!

But certes, than is al my wonderinge,
Sithen she is the fayrest creature
As to my dome, that ever was livinge,
The benignest and beste eek that nature
Hath wrought or shal, whyl that the world
    may dure,
Why that she lefte pite so behinde?
It was, y-wis, a greet defaute in kinde.

Yit is al this no lak to hir, pardee,
But god or nature sore wolde I blame;
For, though she shewe no pite unto me,
Sithen that she doth othere men the same,
I ne oughte to despyse my ladies game;
It is hir pley to laughen whan men syketh,
And I assente, al that hir list and lyketh!

Yit wolde I, as I dar, with sorweful herte
Biseche un-to your meke womanhede
That I now dorste my sharpe sorwes smerte
Shewe by worde, that ye wolde ones rede
The pleynte of me, the which ful sore drede
That I have seid here, through myn un-
    conninge,
In any worde to your displesinge.

Lothest of anything that ever was loth
Were me, as wisly god my soule save!
To seyn a thing through which ye might be
    wroth;
And, to that day that I be leyd in grave,
A trewer servaunt shulle ye never have;
And, though that I on yow have pleyned here,
Forgiveth it me, myn owne lady dere!

Ever have I been, and shal, how-so I wende,
Outher to live or dye, your humble trewe;
Ye been to me my ginning and myn ende,
Sonne of the sterre bright and clere of hewe,
Alwey in oon to love yow freshly newe,
By god and by my trouthe, is myn entente;
To live or dye, I wol it never repente!

This compleynt on seint Valentynes day,
Whan every foul [ther] chesen shal his make,
To hir, whos I am hool, and shal alwey,
This woful song and this compleynt I make,
That never yit wolde me to mercy take;
And yit wol I [for] evermore her serve
And love hir best, although she do me sterve.

209

14. Now welcom somer, with thy sonne softe

[Machaut: Dame, se vous n'avez aperceü]

'Now welcom somer, with thy sonne softe,
That hast this wintres weders over-shake,
And driven awey the longe nightes blake!
Seynt Valentyn, that art ful hy onlofte;—
Thus singen smale foules for thy sake—
  Now welcom somer, with thy sonne softe,
  That hast this wintres weders over-shake.

Wel han they cause for to gladen ofte,
Sith ech of hem recovered hath his make;
Ful blisful may they singen whan they wake;
  Now welcom somer, with thy sonne softe,
  That hast this wintres weders over-shake,
  And driven awey the longe nightes blake.'

210